MAX BAER AND BARNEY ROSS

MAX BAER AND BARNEY ROSS

Jewish Heroes of Boxing

Jeffrey Sussman

ROWMAN & LITTLEFIELD
Lanham • Boulder • New York • London

Published by Rowman & Littlefield
A wholly owned subsidiary of The Rowman & Littlefield Publishing Group, Inc.
4501 Forbes Boulevard, Suite 200, Lanham, Maryland 20706
www.rowman.com

Unit A, Whitacre Mews, 26-34 Stannary Street, London SE11 4AB

British Library Cataloguing in Publication Information Available

Library of Congress Cataloging-in-Publication Data

Names: Sussman, Jeffrey, author.
Title: Max Baer and Barney Ross : Jewish heroes of boxing / Jeffrey Sussman.
Description: Lanham, [Maryland] : ROWMAN & LITTLEFIELD, [2016] | Includes bibliographical
    references and index.
Identifiers: LCCN 2016017216 (print) | LCCN 2016033013 (ebook) | ISBN 9781442269323 (hard-
    back : alk. paper) | ISBN 9781442269330 (electronic)
Subjects: LCSH: Baer, Max, 1909-1959. | Ross, Barney. | Boxers—United States—Biography. |
    Jewish boxers—United States—Biography. | Racism in sports—History—20th century.
Classification: LCC GV1131 .S86 2016 (print) | LCC GV1131 (ebook) | DDC 796.830922 [B]—
    dc23
LC record available at https://lccn.loc.gov/2016017216

Printed in the United States of America

To my wife, Barbara

CONTENTS

ACKNOWLEDGMENTS

I would like to thank the following people: Steven Spataro, head of Adult Reference at the East Hampton Library, for his indefatigable pursuit of newspaper and magazine articles and photos; Christen Karniski for her interest in my original proposal and for her close reading of the text, which resulted in important and thoughtful suggestions; Peter Wood, author and former Golden Gloves boxer, for inspiring me to write about boxing; Max Baer Jr., the son of a great boxing champion and an actor on *The Beverly Hillbillies*, for his generosity in taking time to speak with me about his father during numerous telephone conversations; and Robert Ecksel, editor in chief of Boxing.com, for publishing my articles and short stories about boxing—a prelude to writing this book.

INTRODUCTION

In the 1920s and 1930s, America's melting pot was a stew contaminated by anti-Semitism. Thousands of hotels, resorts, nightclubs, and golf clubs were "restricted," that is, no Jews allowed. Many companies refused to hire Jewish employees. Those who were hired often had to change their names and disguise their Jewish heritage.

The climate of anti-Semitism in the United States in the 1920s and 1930s was promoted by a series of diverse demagogues. During the 1930s, Father Charles Coughlin, a Roman Catholic priest of the National Shrine of the Little Flower Church in Detroit, ignited the hatred of anti-Semites with fiery harangues, spewing hatred like bombs full of nails. With one of the most popular radio shows in the country, with more than 30 million listeners each week, his messages were quick-burning fuses to powerful powder kegs of prejudice. Coughlin broadcast vicious defamation and slander against President Roosevelt, communists, and Jews. He snidely referred to Roosevelt as President Rosenfeld. He published a newspaper called *Social Justice*, which ran installments of the Czarist-fabricated anti-Semitic screed *The Protocols of the Elders of Zion*. Legendary folk singer Woody Guthrie sang, "Yonder comes Father Coughlin, wearin' the silver chain, Gas on the stomach and Hitler on the brain." Coughlin continued to praise the policies of Hitler and Mussolini, while condemning Roosevelt, until he was forced off the air in 1939. World War II effectively ended his career, but Jews throughout the United States had wished he had never been given a microphone.

Another earlier menace to Jews who regularly turned up the flame under an already boiling pot of anti-Semitism was inventive car maker Henry Ford. He published a newspaper called the *Dearborn Independent*, which was distributed from every Ford dealership throughout the land. It had a circulation of 700,000. As with *Social Justice*, it too published *The Protocols of the Elders of Zion*. Each week for more than two years, the *Dearborn Independent* published a series of front-page articles entitled "The International Jew: The World's Problem"—22 in all. The articles claimed that Jews, unlike gentiles, had an aversion to hard work, had a capacity for exploitation, were shrewd money speculators, were physical cowards, and had an Oriental love of display, among various other negative traits. They warned Jews to reform their behavior. Ford was vague about what the consequences would be if the Jews did not follow his instructions; however, he did add an article entitled "An Address to Gentiles on the Jewish Problem." Should gentiles witness Jewish subversion, Ford advised them to "open their eyes, and stop it peacefully but firmly."

Ford was undeterred when the Federal Council of Churches issued a resolution condemning the "International Jew" articles. In addition, he was unconcerned that both Woodrow Wilson and William Howard Taft expressed their disapproval. In the face of mounting criticism, Ford remained true to his bigoted beliefs, saying to a reporter, "Jews are the scavengers of the world."[1] His crude, nutty anti-Semitic obsession reached its peak when he not only declared that the traitor of the American Revolution, Benedict Arnold, had created a Jewish front for Jewish warmongering financiers, but also that Hitler owed his rise to powerful Jewish financiers. In the documentary *Jews and Baseball*, Ford is quoted as saying, "If fans wish to know the trouble with American baseball they have it in three words—too much Jew."

So popular among Nazis in Germany were Ford's anti-Semitic screeds that they were published in a four-volume set entitled *The International Jew: The World's Foremost Problem*. The books were required reading by the Nazi hierarchy. Indeed, Ford was such a favorite of Hitler and his circle that he is the only American praised in *Mein Kampf*. Hitler kept a photograph of Ford on his desk and told friends that he revered Ford as his inspiration. He said, "I shall do my best to put his theories into practice in Germany." Ford was delighted.

It was not until he was successfully sued by a union organizer named Aaron Sapiro, who brought an action against Ford and the *Dearborn*

Independent for libel and defamation, that Ford had to retract his vitriolic anti-Semitic statements and issue a formal apology. His apology was preceded by much foot dragging and legal maneuvers to delay the inevitable. Although he issued his apology publicly, he continued to rail against the Jews in private, foolishly confessing to a reporter that the Jews had not only brought on World War I, but were also agitating for World War II.

A third demagogue, Charles Lindbergh, repeated Ford's accusation that the Jews were advocating America's entrance into World War II on the side of the British. He roiled the Jewish community with a speech entitled "Who Are the War Agitators?" It was delivered to an audience of thousands of American Firsters. In it, Lindbergh declaimed that there were three groups agitating for war with Germany: "the British, the Jews, and the Roosevelt Administration. Instead of agitating for war, the Jewish groups in the country should be opposing it in every possible way, for they will be among the first to feel its consequences."[2] His comments were printed in newspapers throughout the country and initiated a debate about America's role in the world.

In *War Within and Without*, her diaries and letters, Lindbergh's wife, Anne Morrow Lindbergh, writes that as a result of her husband's speeches, the "anti-Semitic forces will rally to him."[3] She further notes that her husband was being " attacked on all sides—administration, pressure groups, and Jews, as now openly a Nazi following Nazi doctrine."[4] She disapproved of her husband's speeches and comments because she felt that he was "segregating them as a group, setting the ground for anti-Semitism." She went further, comparing his words to a lit match set near a "pile of excelsior." She thought it terrible that he was made a "symbol of anti-Semitism,"[5] but—of course—he brought it upon himself, much like the old joke where the child who has murdered his parents cries that he is now an orphan.

A month before the bombing of Pearl Harbor, Anne recorded that she told her husband that the Jews must be given a land of their own. Her husband replied, "It isn't as simple as all that. Whose land are you going to take? From whom? All the good land is taken."[6] And he was right about that, which is why the Jews were given land that was basically all desert, which—it was felt—they would leave for greener pastures. Instead, they made the desert bloom, but that's another story. It is somewhat pathetic that both Ford and Lindbergh believed that Jews were warmongers and had tricked the United States into declaring war on Germany, when, in fact, Germany declared war on America shortly after the Japanese devastation at Pearl Harbor.

To many, Jew and non-Jew alike, Lindbergh's speeches against Jewish support for war sounded like an implicit threat. In 1940, President Roosevelt had told his secretary of the treasury, "If I should die tomorrow, I want you to know this: I am absolutely convinced Lindbergh is a Nazi." Somewhat later, Roosevelt wrote to his secretary of war,

> When I read Lindbergh's speech I felt that it could not have been better put if it had been written by [Joseph] Goebbels himself. What a pity that this youngster has completely abandoned his belief in our form of government and has accepted Nazi methods because apparently they are efficient.[7]

It is no wonder then that American Jews felt they were the target of virulent prejudice. They needed not only symbols of strength to fight against their enemies, but also gladiators. And they found such heroic tough guys in two outstanding world champions who loudly fought against the heroes and symbols of the anti-Semites. Max Baer and Barney Ross were celebrated in every Jewish neighborhood, and in many non-Jewish neighborhoods, in the United States. When they entered the boxing ring, they were regarded as heirs of King David (thus the Star of David on their boxing shorts) and Maccabees whose fists were hammers of wrath and vengeance.

JEWS IN BOXING

During the 1920s, 1930s, and 1940s, two of the most popular sports in the United States were baseball and boxing. While there were a few Jewish baseball players, there were more Jewish boxers from 1910 to 1940 than at any other time. None was more popular than Max Baer, who was movie-star handsome. A 1942 biography of him by Nat Fleischer is titled *Max Baer: The Glamour Boy of the Ring*. Baer fought the great heavyweight boxing hero of Adolf Hitler and the Third Reich, Max Schmeling, and soundly beat him. In fact, he beat him so badly that the referee had to stop the fight. In addition to being a hero of the Third Reich, Schmeling was lionized by the German American Bund, an obstreperous pro-Nazi group in the 1930s. A bout between an alleged Nazi and a Jew was what fight promoters had dreamed of. The gate would be phenomenal, and the fans didn't disappoint. It was reported that the fight netted $1 million, the largest box office for a heavyweight fight up to that time.

It was 1933, and Hitler had recently come to power. His plans for Jews had been spelled out in *Mein Kampf*. Max Schmeling became a symbol of Nazi designs for the elimination of Jews. He had been signed to fight Max Baer at Yankee Stadium in the Bronx. Baer wore a Star of David on his trunks. It was a call to arms and a symbol of Jewish pugnacity. It was David's shield against his enemies. Jewish fans couldn't wait to see the fight, to see their handsome Jewish hero defeat the champ of the Nazi fatherland.

My father attended that fight, and here's how he described it to me:

> I was district manager for Land O' Lakes at the time, and my boss asked if I would like a pair of tickets to the Baer–Schmeling fight. "Since you're a Jew, you're going to like this," he said. "It'll be a fight between Max Baer and Max Schmeling, a favorite of Hitler. I thought it would have special meaning for you."

"So tell me about the fight," I said.

> Well, first of all, I had reservations about Max Baer. He had killed a guy in the ring, and some people just said he was a mean son of a bitch. But, it was 1933, Hitler had come to power in Germany, and the Nazis wanted to get rid of the Jews. We hated everything the Nazis stood for, especially their propaganda about the Jews. We were look-ing for a Jewish hero, someone who could take on a Nazi strongman and beat him. Schmeling seemed like just such a target. We didn't know he had a Jewish manager. We just knew that he was Hitler's favorite boxer, and he was a champ in Germany. So Jews all over New York rallied to Max Baer, who was only half Jewish. As far as I was concerned, he had Jewish fists that could pummel Schmeling. That was enough for me and for lots of others. Even if he were only pre-tending to be Jewish that would have been enough for me.
>
> When my boss gave me two tickets to go to Yankee Stadium to see the fight, I was excited. I asked your mother if she wanted to go, but she didn't like the fights, so I took a friend, Bob Potash. Like most people, we took the subway up to the Bronx. The stadium was packed. Out of 60,000 attendees, there must have been 30,000 Jews. You

know, it was the Depression, and a lot of people wouldn't pay to go to a fight, but this was special. The Jewish fans yelled their lungs out for Baer, especially after he took off his robe and we saw a Jewish star on his trunks. There were also some German Bund types who cheered for Schmeling, but that was expected. There was a large German community up in Yorkville, and the German Bund had some sort of club up there.

As soon as the fight began, Baer came out punching. He must have landed five punches in round one for every one that Schmeling landed. Baer had this technique, which I never saw in the ring before, of grabbing his opponent by the back of the neck, then punching his head with his other hand. Sometimes he would just grab Schmeling by the neck and push him away. When Baer got hit, he would laugh at Schmeling, as if to say, "You can't hurt me." In the 9th round, Baer was well ahead of Schmeling, but in the 10th Baer came out of his corner like a tiger. He hit Schmeling punch after punch, really pummeling him. Schmeling went down, and the crowd erupted with what sounded like one spontaneous cheer. They roared their approval. I thought it was over, but Schmeling managed to get up. A big mistake, because Baer pummeled him again so hard and so fiercely that the referee had to stop the fight. We cheered again and felt great. Everybody I knew was excited.

Baer was in all the papers, the *News*, the *Mirror*, the *Journal-American*, the *Post*. He was our hero. Afterward, the gossip columnists reported that he had an affair with Greta Garbo. He even starred in a movie, *The Prizefighter and The Lady*, with Myrna Loy. Not a bad picture. His later fights were not very impressive. He beat Primo Carnera, who nobody thought was any good. It turns out Carnera was owned by the mob, and they set him up to fight a bunch of has-beens and palookas who could be paid off to take a dive. He never had to fight anyone as tough as Baer, and he lost that fight badly. I think that Baer knocked him down 11 times in as many rounds. The mob made a fortune from Carnera, and then they just dumped him. He was a poor victim who got badly screwed. He later had a career as a wrestler, and you know those matches are all faked. They're as scripted as Hollywood movies. But it was reported that at least Carnera made some money. He was finally free of the mob's clutches.

Baer went on to fight Jimmy Braddock and lost the title to him. Later, Baer fought Joe Louis and lost again. I heard that Baer's right hand was broken during that fight and so he couldn't land his famous knockout blow. When it healed, Baer wanted a rematch with Louis, but Louis' manager, Mike Jacobs, wouldn't let him fight Baer again. Louis was a great heavyweight, one of the greatest, and he beat my pal Abe Simon in two bouts. But that one fight with Schmeling was the most exciting fight I had ever seen. It made Jews feel good. You know, he was the only Jewish heavyweight champion, but we only needed one at that time. Later, we rooted for Joe Louis against Max Schmeling, and though Louis lost the first fight, he came back like a tiger in the second. After the war was over, I used to think that the Baer and Louis knockouts of Schmeling were the preface to America winning the war.

I should probably digress at this point and explain why a successful PR consultant in the twenty-first century would be drawn to the primitive, brutal sport of boxing, especially the world of Jewish boxers. It began when I was in the eighth grade. I was one of the smaller boys in my class. My father didn't want the bigger boys to pick on me. One day, he came home with a pair of boxing gloves, a punching bag, and a body bag. We went into the basement, and there he taught me how to jab with my left fist, block an opponent's punches, slide the punches off my forearm, and throw right crosses. I also learned to how to duck, weave, and project a fake punch from my right so that I could connect with my left. The lessons went on week after week, and I spent additional time shadowboxing, punching the bag, and skipping rope. I was developing an outsized image of myself.

During the 1950s, boxing was still one of the most popular sports in the United States. On Friday nights, there were televised fights from Sunnyside Gardens, St. Nicholas Arena, and Madison Square Garden. I couldn't wait to watch those fights. I saw Sugar Ray Robinson, no longer in his prime, but still a magnificent athlete, who had the grace of a dancer. In fact, prior to becoming a professional prizefighter, he had been a dancer. It was his poverty and lack of opportunity that drove him, like thousands of others, into the ring. I also saw Carmen Basilio, Jake LaMotta, Rocky Graziano, Kid Gavilan, Gene Fullmer, and many others. I preferred the middleweights, for they were more graceful and, in my mind, more skillful fighters, lighter on their feet, and faster with their jabs and uppercuts than the heavyweights, some of whom reminded me of charging rhinos. For example, I thought Tony Galento was just a fat slob and had no right to be in a boxing ring. He fought like a street thug who corners some guy in a dark alley and knees him in the groin and jabs a thumb into his eye.

But there was one heavyweight who interested me. He was a friend of my father and of my father's brother, Harold. Beginning in his teens, he had a reputation as a tough guy. He played high school football and once broke the leg of a running back. He weighed 260 pounds and was 6-foot-4. His name was Abe Simon, and he got to fight Joe Louis twice for the heavyweight championship in the early 1940s. The high point of Abe's career was knocking out heavyweight contender Jersey Joe Walcott, who, years later, in 1951, became the champ. When Abe knocked out Walcott, he became a heavyweight contender, which led to his bouts in 1941 and 1942 with Joe Louis, both of which he lost.

Growing up, I heard many stories about Abe. He was regarded as a hero in his community, because as a teenager, he knocked out three members of the German Bund who were shouting anti-Semitic curse words outside a Jewish social club. For that, he was briefly known as the "Knight of Woodhaven Boulevard."

After his fighting career ended, he acted in several movies, the most important being *On the Waterfront*. He also appeared in *Requiem for a Heavyweight* and *Never Love a Stranger*. He had a big, rectangular head that had taken some punishment throughout the years, and although a kind man, he looked like a thug who would kill you if you looked at him askance.

My father had a film of Abe's two fights with Joe Louis, which seemed more important than those in which he acted. We watched those flickering black-and-white newsreels, and Abe's mistakes were pointed out to me. Watching boxing films, however, was not quite as beneficial as actually getting in the ring with a skilled professional. And so my father took me to Stillman's Gym, located at 919 Eighth Avenue in Manhattan, a focal point for the world of boxing that A. J. Liebling referred to as the "University of Eighth Avenue." My father knew a young boxer there who would take me aside and give me lessons. For $100, I got 10 lessons. My father also gave Mr. Stillman a few bucks for letting me into a gymnasium of tough, determined men who wanted to have careers as boxers.

Stillman wore a .38-caliber pistol in a shoulder holster and puffed on a fat cigar that smelled like a cross between rotten cabbage and sweat. He was a crude and acerbic character out of a Damon Runyon story. Stillman's real name was Lou Ingber; following his retirement as a New York

City cop, he began his employment at a boxing gym in Harlem known as the Marshall Stillman Athletic Club. Because everyone thought he owned the place, they called him Mr. Stillman. He got tired of correcting them, so he legally changed his name to Lou Stillman, and that is how he is known to boxing historians and was known to bygone generations of boxers. He not only managed the gym but also trained fighters. And when he wasn't doing that, he hired himself out as a private detective.

Many famous boxers trained there, and according to Joseph Page's biography of heavyweight champ Primo Carnera, more Italian Americans crowded into the gym to watch their former countryman go through his paces than any other ethnic group at any other time. In fact, there were so many people on the street who could not squeeze into the gym and who desperately wanted to see the man known as the "Ambling Alp," a true giant of the boxing ring, that the police had to be called to clear the street. Page quotes Stillman as commenting, "When Carpentier was in training, the place was always crowded with Broadway chorus girls, while Carnera trained the gallery was packed with Italian women carrying their babies. I liked them better than the chorus girls, so I always let the babies in for free."[8] I, however, had to pay 25 cents each time I entered for my lessons. When I complained that my father had given him a few dollars during my first visit, Stillman said, "That was then, now you gotta pay." Even so, I eagerly looked forward to each visit. I liked watching the boxers, some of whom were title contenders.

I once saw Rocky Marciano there and was impressed by his enormous biceps. To this day, I can vividly recall the sounds of leather gloves thwack, thwack, thwacking punching bags and soft-soled shoes swiftly skipping rope. I was fascinated and beguiled, not only by the activities of the boxers, but also by the atmosphere of the place. It was filthy; the windows looked as if they had never been cleaned, and the floor was covered with layers of grime. Stillman commented to anyone who asked why the place was never cleaned, "The golden age of prizefighting was the age of bad food, bad air, bad sanitation, and no sunlight. I keep the place like this for the fighters' own good. If I clean it up they'll catch a cold from the cleanliness."

If you watch the movie *Somebody Up There Likes Me*, starring Paul Newman as Rocky Graziano, you can get some idea of the place. The only famous boxer who reportedly refused to train at Stillman's due to the filth was heavyweight champ Gene Tunney. It's a shame that Stillman's

Gym no longer exists; it closed in 1959, and the building was knocked down, as have been many unofficial landmarks in New York City, and replaced by a developer's more profitable edifice. Stillman told a reporter how sad he was that the place was gone; he would have no one to talk with, no one to abuse.

I'll always have fond memories of Stillman's as a place where I learned to defend myself and developed enough confidence not to be intimidated by boys bigger than myself. On the day of my last lesson, I opened my locker, preparing to change into street clothes, and found a gray polo shirt that had the following message on the front: "Stillman's Gym, Training Here Daily." I have no idea who put the shirt in my locker, but I was grateful for it and wore it daily under my regular shirt. I think it eventually fell apart from either too much sweat or too much washing.

It was not until I turned 14 that I actually got to use my newly developed boxing skills. One day, after school, my best friend's sister had been assaulted by a classmate. My friend told the other boy that he would have to fight one of us. Since I was four inches shorter than my friend, I was fingered as the likely pushover. "I'll fight the little guy," the boy said, grinning at me. It was not until he had thrown me into a rose bush, my mouth and lips bleeding from an assortment of thorns, that I became angry enough to fight. My opponent, however, was sitting on my chest, attempting to pin my wriggling arms to the ground.

"So you give up? Huh Jew?" he questioned.

I responded by spitting a mouthful of blood into his face, pushing him off of me, and fighting with a rage I could not control. The last thing I recall was a roundhouse right that I threw at the boy's temple. He screamed and fell to the ground. I was momentarily stunned, then relieved, when a few minutes later he got up, stumbled slightly, and walked away. When that night I told my father what had happened, he said,

> I'm glad you gave it to that shit heel of an anti-Semite. When you have to fight, you have to fight. I wanted you to learn how to fight, so that you could defend yourself. Your friend did you no favor in getting you into that fight. He set you up to take responsibility for what he should have done. It's like hiring a bodyguard, except no one paid you. But still you did all right.

After that, I never got into another fistfight.

By the 1980s, my interest in boxing had been reignited. I had an opportunity to publicize an Olympic gold medal boxer named Howard Davis. He seemed both graceful and gentle. Stillman's gym was long gone, and the new place was the Times Square Gym on West 42nd Street. That's where Howard trained, and it was a pleasure to watch him spar. He knew something that many other fighters did not: how to win without getting hurt. He fought beautifully and won match after match. I'd watch him on ABC's *Wide World of Sports* and was thrilled by his fistic grace. I'd sit in front of the TV and think, "Man can he fight. No wonder he won a gold medal." Within a short period of time, he made enough money and retired. Good for him.

I started writing for the website Boxing.com and began to revisit my past, as well as my father's. Boxing was in our blood. My father had been a tough guy, growing up when anti-Semitism was rampant in the United States and spreading like an unchecked and deadly virus in Europe. It's to honor my father and explore the role of anti-Semitism in the history of Jewish boxing that propelled me to write about two of the greatest Jewish boxers of the twentieth century: Max Baer and Barney Ross. And to write about some of their opponents, who were symbols of bigotry to many anti-Semites.

I

THE PROTOTYPES

Benny Leonard and Abe Attell

Years before Max Baer and Barney Ross had tied on boxing gloves, there were two Jewish boxing champs who won the plaudits of boxing fans throughout the world. They proved that Jews could be heroes in the ring and attract fight fans of various religions and ethnic backgrounds. Baer and Ross would follow their examples and emerge as celebrities under the spotlight in the ring of boxing fame.

First on the scene was the inimitable, meticulous, and dapper Benny Leonard. He was born Benjamin Leiner and given the Hebrew name of Dov Ber ben Araham Gershon. Born in 1896 and raised in a poor Jewish ghetto on New York's Lower East Side, young Benny learned to defend himself on mean slum streets where fighting was necessary for survival. Being short and slight, he was an easy target for bullies, but he used his brain to outwit his opponents, while his fast, flashing fists performed the necessary tactical missions that led to his reputation as a tough kid. The blood on his fists had poured from the battered noses of his presumptuous opponents. Leonard had the ability to see flaws in his opponents' attacks, and he turned those flaws into winning opportunities. He not only thought quickly on his feet, sizing up his opponents, but he also responded with a magician's quick hands. His reputation as an unbeatable pugilist spread among the local young gangs. Better leave Benny alone, unless you sneak up behind him with a club. One would no more challenge skinny Benny to fight than one would hold up one's hand against the wind.

Benny joined a local gym, where he refined his skills, training rigorously every day. The training went on for hours. He worked on the body
bag, the speed bag; he skipped rope. He shadowboxed. He learned the art
of the feint, to duck and weave like a mesmerizing cobra. He was as agile
as a dancer. His punches landed with the precision of arrows hitting the
bull's-eye on a target. His physique was becoming more muscular. He
was no longer the skinny little street kid who looked like a pushover. In
fact, to coaches and promoters who watched him train, he was a promis-
ing young combatant. While sparring with other ambitious young boxers,
Leonard would win round after round, occasionally pulverizing an opponent who had tried to knock him into yesterday.

Looking at the full-grown Benny Leonard, attired in a fine shirt and
suit, one might think he was a haberdasher's model. Some began referring to him as Mr. Benny Leonard. His hair was parted in the middle,
slicked back, and there wasn't a mark on his face. He hardly looked like a
palooka whose face had been a punching bag. How could such a dandy be
such a ferocious fighter in the ring? How could he emerge without the
scars of his trade?

Leonard brought not only ferocity, intensity, and intelligence into the
ring, but also a strong determination not to be hit, not to have his face
misshapen by the pounding of an opponent's gloves. He did not want to
sport a cauliflower ear, a broken nose, or scar tissue around his eyes. His
mother would not have approved, and Benny, a good boy, did what his
mama said. So meticulous were Leonard's ring performances that it was
often said he emerged from his fights with not a single hair out of place.
He left the ring as smartly as he had entered, smiling and waving for the
news photographers.

He was known as a scientific fighter, the first of his kind. He evaluated
the choreography of his opponents, their fistic tactics, and understood
their plans for attacking him. He would rapidly formulate a brilliant
counterattack. His strategic thinking was fast and deep. He knew that he
could control a fight from the center of the ring rather than from the ropes
or the corners. The center permitted him to be an effective defensive or
offensive fighter. If an opponent went on the offense, Leonard's tactics
were those of a fine defensive counterpuncher. When he had an opponent
on the defense, he went on the offense and would not let up.

Leonard's tactics and strategy were unparalleled. His jab was issued
from the best possible angle. It was the longest weapon aimed at the

closest target, and it quickly intimidated an opponent. An opponent could be distracted by Leonard's footwork and feints, and then the jab would erupt like a missile from a hidden silo. Those feints and footwork had never been equaled in the ring. Years later, Sugar Ray Robinson would display similar qualities, enacted with a grace and style that stymied opponents and seduced fans. In our age of technology, one might think of Leonard's performances in the ring as something that had been programmed by a computer. And, indeed, he was such a thoughtful student of boxing that it would not be an exaggeration to say that he programmed himself to win, which is not the same thing as "psyching oneself up." Yet, he was no robot; he was passionate about his craft, a quality no machine can duplicate. Nat Fleischer writes in *Ring Magazine*,

> Leonard had a hair-trigger brain. As he shifted about the ring, the fans could almost read his thoughts as he mapped out his plans of attack. An opponent had to be ever on the alert to avoid a quick knockout. Leonard knew his trade, knew it so thoroughly that almost invariably he could "call his shots," if and when the occasion warranted. [1]

In *The Sun Also Rises*, Ernest Hemingway based a character, Robert Cohn, on Benny Leonard. The character is presented as a scientific pugilist without the heart of a true fighter. The implication, clear to many, was that Cohn, as a Jew, could never be a real fighter. He lacked a passion for blood; he did not have the heart of a lion, did not have a lion's killer instinct. Jews were thought of as people of the book, not fighters. In the minds of some, Jews were even perceived as cowards, hunched-over pencil pushers on high stools in badly lit Victorian offices. Leonard helped to destroy such stereotypes, although not for Hemingway. Hemingway, the writer, ironically attributed Leonard's skills to those learned from a handbook; however, as Arthur Brisbane, a prominent editor and journalist of the time, wrote, "Benny Leonard, by his example, did more to destroy anti-Semitism than any legislation or good government group." [2]

His destruction of stereotypes did not occur overnight, for he lost his first four professional bouts. The three years from 1912 to 1915 were ones during which Benny honed his skills, learning like a laboratory scientist from his numerous mistakes. Having emerged from those years of failure, he went on to win 19 fights and lost only three. From 1915 to 1932, he had 219 fights, won 183 (7 by knockout), and lost 24. He even fought and beat fighters larger and heavier than he was. He beat the formidable Ted "Kid" Lewis and went on to challenge Jack Britton for the welterweight title in 1922. Although Briton was bigger than Leonard, he was not as clever, and Leonard knocked Britton to the canvas in the 13th round. Unfortunately, Leonard was overeager and proceeded to deliver the final knockout blow when Britton was supine on the canvas. For that rash act, he was disqualified on a technicality. Such overeagerness was not typical of the "Wizard of the Ghetto," as he had been dubbed by some sportswriters.

Losses were not in Leonard's repertoire, so when they came late in his a career, he and his fans were surprised and disappointed. Leonard had staged an unwise and desperate comeback when he was well past his fighting prime. As the world lightweight champion during the 1920s, he had become a millionaire. He could retire whenever he wanted. He had enough to live on and to support his mother for the rest of her days. No one was surprised, then, when, at his mother's urging, he retired in 1925, thinking that he would live on his investments. The cushion and comfort of affluence did not last. Four years later, the stock market crashed to earth, shattering investments and leaving shards of broken dreams wrapped in bankruptcy. And Leonard, like many others, went down for the count. He suffered a knockout that drained his optimism and left him with visions of a darkness closing in on him.

With few opportunities to recover his losses, he decided to embark on a comeback. It was pure desperation. He was willing to take a daring risk that he might regain some of what he had lost. He was like a gambler betting on one more spin of the roulette wheel. In 1931, he was no longer the picture of the elegant young dandy of a pugilist. He was not as leanly muscular and as hard as he had been; much of his finely tonsured hair had left for parts unknown. A bald spot could be seen on the crown of his head. His fast, flashing fists had slowed. In the ring, his stance seemed stiff-legged, rather than agile and flexible. When he entered the ring to take on Jimmy McLarnin, one of the best fighters of the 1930s, Leonard's fans were surprised to see their once-brilliant hero looking older, more like a bookkeeper in shorts than a boxer.

To prepare for his fight with McLarnin, Leonard had worked diligently to beef up his reputation and body by fighting one undistinguished palooka after another. Each afforded Leonard an easy win and much-needed cash. Then, almost believing (at age 36, which is old for a fighter) that he had recovered his skills, Benny foolishly signed to fight devastating puncher Baby Face Jimmy McLarnin (age 26), whose powerful right fist caused opponents to nearly shudder with fear. He had an impressive record, having already beaten such notables as Abie Gordon, Jackie Fields, Joe Glick, Louis "Kid" Kaplan, Sid Terris, Ruby Goldstein, and Al Singer, a stable of formidable Jewish opponents. McLarnin had become known as the "Jew Killer," and Leonard thought he could put an end to such talk. But it would be the brilliant heir of Leonard's style and moxie, Barney Ross, who would put an end to McLarnin's reputation as the "Hebrew Scourge," following a trilogy of some of the most celebrated and brutal fights of the 1930s. Those fights thrilled sportswriters and attracted hundreds of thousands of fight fans. That trilogy of bouts is still ardently watched on YouTube by fight fans and historians of the sport.

Leonard emerged after the bell in the first round sizing up his opponent, testing and probing with a series of left jabs. McLarnin was more aggressive and worked hard to dominate the older man, to put him on the defensive, to force him to counterpunch. In that first round, Leonard's fans gasped as he was nearly knocked out. He seemed stunned by what had happened. In the second round, McLarnin was clearly dominating Leonard, seemingly unconcerned by Leonard's left jabs, and he swarmed all over Leonard, connecting often with devastating left hooks. He knocked Leonard down; sitting on the canvas, shaking his head, trying to clear his thoughts, Leonard took a full count before rising. Fans could now see that Leonard was overmatched by the younger man, a fast-moving slugger who seemed unharmed by the former champion's stiff-armed left jabs. His fans sensed that he could not win. He was slowing down. He didn't have the energy or the stamina of the younger man. It came in spurts, almost as if he were trying to rally hidden forces within himself.

In round four, Leonard briefly seemed to get in touch with his younger self and began demonstrating his old footwork, dancing out of range of McLarnin's swift punches. Yet, his punches were too few and no longer targeted missiles. Leonard's defenses, try as he did, would not be sufficient to stop McLarnin's brutal attack. McLarnin's punches were coming fast and furious, and never missing their targets. It all came to a sad end in round 6, when McLarnin unleashed a swift barrage of powerful punches—a machine gun of assaults. Each punch pounded Leonard's head. The former champ stumbled around the ring as McLarnin continued to throw punch after punch. When it was apparent that Leonard could not withstand any more blows and was unable to defend himself, referee Arthur Donovan separated the two fighters, declaring McLarnin the winner. It was a tragic end to a magnificent career. And yet, it is the way many boxing careers end. A once young and brilliant pugilist fights well past his prime, either for money or glory, and is relieved of his crown by a younger, tougher opponent who will one day face the same end, if he too doesn't retire in his prime.

After Leonard suffered that sixth-round technical knockout, the course of his life changed. He was the former champ, the ex-champ, but still regarded as one of the greatest lightweight fighters of all time. Some of his fans had wept when he was defeated; others simply wished he had never returned to the ring. McLarnin continued to be known as the "Hebrew Scourge" and the "Jew Killer," much to the frustration of Jewish boxing fans.

Now that his boxing career had crashed like his investment portfolio, Leonard had to choose a new path. What was the quickest, easiest way to replenish his depleted bank balances? An offer came from a man named Bill O'Dwyer, who wanted Leonard to front as owner of the National Hockey League's New York Americans. The team was an embarrassment of losses. As if assuming their errors would be less obvious in another city, the team was moved to Philadelphia; however, their reputation as losers not only followed then, but it was also extended, and hockey fans in the "City of Brotherly Love" gleefully booed themselves silly. A sports tout wondered if the team should take off their ice skates and try roller skates. It was as if the ice had melted under the team's feet, and the Americans sank into oblivion, never to be mourned.

Where would Leonard go now? The only home he had known was in the boxing ring. Too old and too tired to fight, he turned down offers from some fast-buck promoters who didn't care if he got killed in the ring. Leonard had had enough. But his brain still operated beyond the speed limit. Who better to referee fights than the man who had packed fans into arenas? His name still had a dollar value, and fans would want to see him separating the new guys. It was the profession of over-the-hill boxers. Leonard accepted it with grace and a sense of fatalism, and the knowledge that it always came with a paycheck.

My grandfather, who was of Benny Leonard's generation, provided me with an eyewitness account of Leonard, an assessment of his rise and fall:

I lived in Benny's old neighborhood, and we trained at the same gym. I had arrived in America a couple of years earlier. I was glad to be out of Russia, where there were all those terrible pogroms. The czar, we hated the son of a bitch; and he hated the Jews. He couldn't have cared less what happened to the Jews. And the Cossacks knew it. The czar only would have been happy to draft us into his army for 30 years. Who would want that? Fight for a country that spit on us? Here in New York, I felt free, like a prisoner who had escaped. The streets weren't paved with gold, but what the hell, you could earn a living and there were no political parties that wanted to hurt the Jews. By comparison with Russia, this was paradise.

When I settled in the neighborhood, I rented an apartment next-door to where the Leiner's lived. That was Benny's last name. A few weeks later, I joined the Fondon Athletic Club, where I decided to take boxing lessons. It made me feel good, that I could take care of myself. In Russia, Jews didn't take boxing lessons. It was unheard of. I saw Benny the first day I was in that gym. You could tell right away he was something special. He knew how to do everything that I wanted to learn. I used to watch him and try to copy what he did. I learned, but I knew I would never be like him. You know, I think he was the greatest fighter of his time. There was nobody as good as him.

The Fondon Athletic Club was just a few blocks from where I lived, and so I would go there whenever I had some free time. Benny was a skinny kid, and his real name was then Benjamin Leiner, not Benny, and some his pals called him Dov. He was a tough little guy, maybe 5-foot-5 and around 125 pounds—soaking wet. But he was fast and had great punches, especially his jabs. I used to hit the bag and skip rope, and sometimes spar with someone, but I never would've gotten into the ring with Benny. He would've knocked me cold. Watching him, I knew he could become a champ. He was not some defenseless guy who would be pushed around or take nonsense from anyone. Worse come to worse, you knew he was the kind of guy who would go down fighting. When he turned pro, I would go to his fights. You know, his hair was always neatly combed and never seemed to get messed. He had speed and strategy. He was a smart guy, and you could see it when he got in the ring. He was always smarter than the other guy. He was wonderful to watch. He even made a few silent movies in the twenties; I think they were called *Flying Fists* or something like that. I learned even from those films.

I would go to the fights on Friday and the opera on Saturday. By 1922, I had a store to run. I still loved boxing and the opera. I would go as often as possible, but your grandmother can't stand the fights. She pretends to watch them on television, but I can see she's napping. She saw enough violence in Russia, she says. She doesn't need to watch it on TV. She likes Jack Benny and Burns and Allen. That's okay. I like to laugh, too. But you know, the saddest day for me was when Benny died. He had lost all his money during the Stock Market Crash in '29. He made a brief comeback, but his speed was gone. He looked old and like he had arthritis in his knees. His legs were stiff. He really was too old. Poor guy was in no shape to be a champ, certainly not against the Irish golden boy, Jimmy McLarnin. A real Harp. After that, I hadn't heard anything about Benny, nothing in the papers. He just vanished: another worn-out boxer.

Then he appeared again. After a few years passed, he took up work as a referee. I guess it was just to support himself. Or maybe he just liked being in the ring again. Anyway, one night, he was refereeing a fight at the St. Nicholas Arena. It wasn't that long ago. It was in '47. The crowd was excited to see the old champ back in the ring, even if he was kind of soft and going bald. Those who saw him fight in the twenties still remembered him. In the twenties, he could have been a clothing model for men's suits and coats. He had looked really sharp in a custom-made suit. He was a very smart looking guy. Anyway, there he was in the ring, just wearing dark pants and a white shirt. You could see he had gone soft around the middle and in his face. The fight started, and then during that first round Benny collapsed. Just fell to the canvas. People jumped up to get a better view. We didn't know what had happened. He was just lying there. His heart just gave out. It was his final knockout blow. He was carried out on a stretcher, and a lot of fans wept like kids. I'll never forget the day Benny died. He had a wonderful career. We all loved Benny Leonard. You know more than 2,000 mourners showed up at Riverside Chapel for his funeral—including me. It was very sad. Yup, it was a very sad day.

Abe Attell, the "Little Hebrew," was a whirlwind of ferocity. Although a mere 5-foot-4 and never weighing more than 122 pounds, he was able to intimidate his many opponents, regardless of their size. Abe was born into a poor family in San Francisco in 1883. He was one of twelve children and, from an early age, had the pugnacity of a junkyard dog. His father had died, and Abe's mother was the sole supporter of her large brood. She took in wash; she sewed clothes. She was too proud to beg, but there were times when she felt it might be the only way to feed and clothe her family.

The widow Attell would hang her wet laundry on a clothesline, hoping there would be no rain. One afternoon, when Abe was 10, he spotted an older boy using a dirty tree branch to beat his mother's wet sheets and towels, trying to take down the entire laundry line in an alley behind their shabby shack of a home. Abe went after that kid with fists flying. The two boys tumbled to the ground, rolling around, each landing punches and cursing like angry sailors. Mrs. Attell quickly arrived on the scene and pulled the boys apart. She grabbed her anger-spewing child and dragged him indoors. No sooner had she released her strong washerwoman's maternal grip than Abe dashed outside and quickly located the malefactor of his mother's laundry and launched into another battle. Again, the boys rolled around on the ground, trading punches and cursing at one another. By the time of Mrs. Attell's second interruption, both boys had bloody noses and bruised faces. Young Abe had been neither frightened nor cautious; he was all ferocity and took pleasure in physical combat. It heightened his sense of purpose, made him forget how poor his family was. It gave him a reason for breathing. It was exciting. He knew he could roam the streets and knock little tough guys like himself off of their feet. While he loved fighting, he hadn't yet thought of fighting as a career. That was just around several corners from where he lived.

Abe so enjoyed fighting that he formed a gang of hooligans who regularly indulged in afterschool fights as a form of recreation and bonding. They'd look for other gangs to fight and would have what were later called rumbles. They were often truant, and parents regularly punished them, to no avail. It would have been like putting wild dogs in a kennel and then releasing them; they would have returned to their wild ways.

Abe's mother despaired for her son ever amounting to anything respectable and self-supporting. She looked on in misery as he often returned late at night wearing his hand-me-down clothes, now torn here, ripped there. She would get out her sewing kit and attempt to mend the damage. At times, she was able to work wonders; at other times, her efforts looked like the badly sewn face of Frankenstein's monster. But it wasn't just Abe's clothing; there was an occasional black eye, a bloody nose, bruises and welts on his face, knuckles raw and bleeding. To his distraught mother, Abe was a mess. Abe, however, was indifferent to his appearance; it mattered little to him. He was a small, determined brigand, every day going into battle with his band of like-minded cronies.

The widow Attell hoped to domesticate her wild son by separating him from his wild, roaming pack and sending him south to Los Angeles, where he could live with his uncle. She hoped that Abe's uncle would be the stern disciplinarian that would remold the malleable child into a firm and steadfast member of society. Abe hated living with his uncle. He refused to wear shoes, refused to go to school, refused to learn the cornet that his uncle had laid in his hands. Abe spent most of his time in his small bedroom, sullen and mulling over his fate. He wanted to be back in San Francisco, running through the streets with his pals. The cornet, he thought, was for sissies. Real men fought with their fists, and they didn't sit back and make music so that lovebirds could dance and coo at one another. Abe spent 15 gloomy months in the "City of Angels." Frustrated by his nephew's recalcitrance, the uncle put his belligerent nephew on a train heading north to San Francisco, to home, to his pals on the streets. Stepping off that train, Abe felt as if he had been released from prison. Even the air smelled better in San Francisco than in LA. He was home, and he could return to his old ways.

One would have thought that such a wild boy would have little or no concern for the predicament of his family, but little Abe loved his mother and was determined to do whatever he could to soften the burden of her threadbare existence. He took to selling newspapers on the streets near his home in a poor section of San Francisco. By the age of 13, he was hawking newspapers on street corners and turning over his earnings to his mother. His favorite corner was at Eighth and Market. It was one of the most lucrative and desired corners, and each newsboy wanted to claim it as his own. All of the best corners were disputed, open territories that turned into battlegrounds, and only the toughest boys could claim the most prized ones. No news publisher would designate corners for news-boys. There were no franchises. No exclusives. No one owned the cor-ners, and newsboys, a tough and hungry lot, had to fight fiercely with one another to maintain their territories. Abe was no slacker; if another news-boy tried to set up on Abe's busy corner, the would-be competitor would wind up with a bloody nose, a black eye, and maybe a split lip. One boy even went home with a broken rib. Abe was relentless and feared no one.

If anything, he became the one who was feared; behind his back he was a little Jew boy, but to his face, he was respected, if only begrudgingly.

Many of the newsboys were the children of poor, struggling Irish immigrants, and they did not take kindly to Jewish newsboys, especially on Easter Sunday, when groups of Irish boys would hunt in packs for "Christ killers." Young Abe and his two brothers, Monte and Caesar, could either run or fight. If they were outnumbered, they ran to safety. If not, they fought like demons. As Abe grew, his reputation for toughness also grew. He was known as the kid who would never back down. Nothing and no one seemed to scare him. "Don't mess with little Abe" was a common warning, muttered by not only newsboys, but also by all the boys in the neighborhood. All but one, that is. It was Kid Lennett, a neighborhood boy whom Abe had regularly fought. They detested one another. And while Abe was in Los Angeles, Kid Lennett said he would beat Abe if he ever returned to his hometown. It was a challenge he would ultimately regret making.

Abe began frequenting a local boxing gym and club, the Beer Garden, run by a former middleweight boxer named Alec Greggain. Men would go there, drink beer, and watch amateur boxers slug one another in a ring at the center of the Garden. Greggain would charge men $1 to enter the Beer Garden and $2 to sit ringside and watch a boxing match in the Garden's boxing ring. Neighborhood boys would pay 25 cents to sit in the Garden's bleacher seats, where they cheered, hooted, hissed, and booed in their cheery exuberance. Being boisterous was part of the privilege of attending the fights. Most fights went on for four or six rounds, and some highly touted ones went on for 10, 15, and even 20 rounds.

To test young boys who aspired to enter his ring for the chance of winning $10 and see if they had the skills and instinct to fight, Greggain would lead a young boy into the center of the ring and suddenly whirl around and punch the surprised face. If the boy stayed down and then fled in fear and a rush of tears, he was not a prospect. If, however, the furious boy got up and returned punches, he was put on the schedule. When the test was applied to young Abe, he not only got up, but he also flew at Greggain with a fury that surprised the former boxer. Abe let go a flurry of wild punches that did little damage but impressed the impresario. Greggain laughed and hugged young Abe, telling him he was quite the young hellcat. He would put him on the schedule to fight Kid Lennett. "But be warned, Lennett has won about 10 straight fights here," said

Greggain. Abe said he didn't care, "he would knock Lennett's block off." Greggain told Abe that if he could stand up to Lennett for four rounds, he would give him $5. "I'll stand up and I'll win. I'll cream him. You'll see!" said Abe. "If you win, I'll give you $10. If you knock him out, I'll give you $15." "It's a deal," said Abe. He ran home to let his mother know that he could win $15 in less than 15 minutes.

The idea of Abe fighting for money upset his mother. She bit her lip to stop from crying. She hadn't wanted him to fight in the streets. She didn't want him to fight for money. He pleaded with her. When he said that $15 was enough to live on for two weeks and she wouldn't have to take in laundry during that time, she looked at her boy with sad love in her eyes. Abe kept pleading; he wouldn't give up until she relented. Finally, she nodded, knowing that he would fight anyway. She might as well give him her approval. Abe kissed his mother, clapped his hands, and excitedly got ready for his first big fight. He was determined to beat Lennett early in the fight. And so it went.

After the first bell sounded, Lennett rushed out of his corner prepared to flatten his upstart challenger. Abe kept out of range of Lennett's early punches, sizing up his tactics, then quickly delivered a devastating punch that sent Lennett onto the canvas. Lennett, who could hardly believe what had just happened, was dragged back to his corner. He sat there dumb and stunned for a minute, then when the bell sounded, he came out like a wild tiger. "Damn you," he cursed Abe. "I'll show you." This time he was determined to put an end to Abe's obnoxious challenge. It was not to be. The "Kid" never saw it coming: Abe had hit him with such a swift and hard uppercut to his chin that Lennett collapsed onto the canvas. The referee counted him out.

Abe was now the young hero of the Beer Garden. Everyone wanted to watch him fight. Everyone wanted to bet on him. Abe had earned his first money for fighting, and he felt exhilarated. He ran home that evening and handed his mother the $15 he had won. She wept briefly then wiped away her tears with a kitchen towel. She examined Abe's face for bruises, saw none, then hugged her boy, grateful for the money, grateful that he was unharmed, and proud that her son would put himself in harm's way for the sake of keeping food on the table for their large, fatherless family.

Abe went on to win fight after fight, often knocking out opponents within the first three rounds. By the end of one year, he had turned over to his amazed mother more than $1,000. Although she had relented to the pleadings of her young lion, giving him her permission to pursue his ambition to be a pugilist, she exacted from him a promise that he would never drink liquor and never smoke a cigar, a cigarette, or a pipe. The relieved warrior readily agreed, and for the rest of his life he neither smoked nor drank. In later years, however, gambling would become a primary vice. In fact, gambling would be a source of his notoriety.

By the time he was 16, other boys rarely challenged him. He was known as a tough guy. Those who had previously attacked him may not have liked him, but they certainly respected his prowess. Abe would regularly go to Mechanics Pavilion to watch the pros display their skills and courage. Abe had been an untutored street fighter. Now he wanted to learn the skills of a trained boxer. He told boxing interviewer Monte Cox that he had seen a "cartoon of some boxers in the *San Francisco Chronicle*," adding,

> I would like to have my picture in the paper someday, so I started boxing as an amateur; they were four rounds back then. I learned the fundamentals as an amateur, but I didn't really learn my trade until I was a pro. In the beginning I tried to knock everybody out and won my first five pro fights by knockouts. But I decided I was getting hit way too much and decided to really learn to box.[3]

Abe was fascinated by how many tricks the pros displayed. He saw how they slipped, blocked, ducked, and sidestepped punches. He understood that fighters could avoid getting hurt, if they were well trained and savvy.

Before he could turn pro, he still had to earn more money than he had been winning at the Garden. So, at his mother's urging, he became a messenger. It was a safe, easy profession, where he had plenty of freedom to pursue his boxing goals. And he enjoyed running throughout the city. As his reputation as a boxer spread among the sporting class, Abe became known as the "fighting messenger boy." He won his next 10 fights. At age 17, he agreed to fight featherweight champion George Dixon. Although no one expected him to win, maybe not even remain on his feet, fans certainly didn't expect the fight to end in a draw. "A draw," he told his mother. It was an amazing accomplishment for a young journeyman.

The following year brought the two together for a rematch in Denver, Colorado. After 15 rounds, Abe was awarded the decision and became the world featherweight champion. Fans went wild, bookies paid out more than they expected, and young Abe was now on his way to becoming the most spectacular fighter of his generation. He felt that his life had finally changed the way he had dreamed it would, and even his mother had become his biggest fan. Abe took pride in being a professional and, with a respectful grin, accepted the accolades that normally followed his victories. He developed what he called a "Fancy Dan" style that was all his own. He was 17 and determined to be champ for 10 years. His brothers Caesar and Monte, seeing what Abe had accomplished, attempted to follow in their brother's footsteps. They never reached Abe's level of pugilistic success. He was out there on his own, in a class by himself, and no one would tag him.

Although Abe continued to win fight after fight with little damage to himself, his mother—while proud of her son—still experienced bouts of anxiety that her Abe might suffer some kind of permanent damage. She saw it in some of the older fighters who hung around Abe. Hers was the concern of every mother of every boxer, for large numbers of boxers left the ring suffering from pugilistic dementia. Abe's mother did not want her son to be one of them, to become "damaged goods," as she said; however, she could not resist attending his fights. It was her maternal duty, she felt. She may have flinched when an opponent landed a glove on Abe's face, but she was also impressed by how adept he was at protecting himself while pummeling an opponent. Abe often reassured his mother not to worry, and she would smile and nod her head. In time, she learned to suppress her anxieties in his presence and just demonstrate that she was a proud supporter. She did not attend his out-of-town fights, but she was there for the at-home bouts. And if someone said anything negative about her boy, she wacked that person with a strapped umbrella, a rolled newspaper, or her handbag. "That's my boy!" she would yell. "And don't you say nothing bad about him or you'll get what you deserve." Nobody, but nobody was permitted to say a bad word about her boy—at least not in her presence.

From 1906 to 1912, Abe successfully defended his championship title. From 1909 to 1910, Abe's brother Monte, known as the "Nob Hill Terror," held the world bantamweight championship. Caesar did not fare as well as his brothers but was still a popular figure among fight fans. He was known as "Two and a Half," for that's what he gave at boxing charity events.

On a hot July 4th day in 1913, in upstate New York, Abe fought 145-pound boxer Willie Beecher. After round after round of pummeling one another in 90-plus-degree heat, the fighters, bathed in glistening sweat and breathing as hard as racehorses, were exhausted and seemed to be just going through the motions of boxing. The referee urged them on, to pick up the pace. Abe, sucking air, motioned for Willie to back up. Willie did so. And suddenly Abe let loose with a wild roundhouse right. It swooshed past Willie and landed with a thud on the referee's chin. The referee flopped onto the canvas, and the crowd leapt out of their seats and cheered. The two fighters, like mischievous delinquents, bent over the stricken ref and pulled him to his feet. Abe profusely apologized as he patted the referee on one shoulder. The ref barked, "What the hell! Why couldn't you hit Willie that hard?" Abe smiled and nodded.

It was not long after that mishap that Abe lost his title to a younger fighter, but he continued fighting. It was what he knew best, and the money was good. Like most fighters, he reached the point when he was no longer as fast and flexible as he once had been. His speed was gone, his timing was slightly off. He didn't want to be an easy target for his opponents, so, in 1917, Abe decided it was time to retire. He had fought 172 bouts and won 125–51 by knockout. It was an impressive record, and boxing historians rate Abe as one of the 10 best featherweights of the twentieth century.

Following his retirement, little Abe became a bag man for criminal mastermind Arnold Rothstein, the man who taught Lucky Luciano, Meyer Lansky, and Bugsy Siegel how to organize the gangs of New York and other cities too. Rothstein was well known as a man who plotted and executed numerous gambling scams. In 1919, using Abe as his bag man and intimidating muscle, Rothstein set out to fix the World Series. Abe gave the players of the Chicago White Sox $10,000 to lose the series against Cincinnati. The ensuing scandal became known as the Black Sox Scandal. It ended the careers of many fine players, including the legendary Shoeless Joe Jackson.

Tom, a retired doctor, delivered a fascinating account of Abe Attell during a luncheon at an Italian restaurant, Emilias, on Arthur Avenue in the Bronx. Tom had been an avid fight fan as a teenager and young man, and was privy to much inside information from his father, a professional gambler; in fact, his father controlled illegal gambling in New York for Frank Costello, known as the prime minister of the underworld. While savoring a plate of pasta vongole and a glass of red wine, Tom said,

Abe was a great friend of my dad, and I got to know him when I was growing up. He had a six-year reign as world featherweight champion from 1906 to 1912. He was known as the "Little Champ" and the "Little Hebrew"; he was a tough guy. He stood about 5-foot-4, but he was an intimidating little guy. According to my dad, Abe would stand up to guys well over six feet.

When asked to reflect on the story about Abe and Arnold Rothstein, Tom responded,

He didn't talk about it, but I asked my dad. He told me that Abe became Rothstein's muscle for intimidating the Chicago White Sox players into throwing the World Series. The players were paid off, but not all of them. Just the key players. You know, he was indicted for fixing the game. At trial, this guy showed a lot of chutzpah: He convinced the jurors that he was the wrong Abe Attell. It was another guy with the same name, and the jury bought it. Amazing!

Abe never really left the world of boxing. Tom continued,

During the 1920s and 30s, he managed a fighter named Marty Goldman, who fought in two divisions: welterweight and lightweight. Goldman was a Brooklyn guy and a pretty good fighter; he had a lot of wins by knockouts. I heard that Goldman was owned by Damon Runyon and was popular with two of the writer's friends, the columnists Ed Sullivan and Walter Winchell. Incidentally, those two guys hated each other. I used to see him fight in the Garden and at Yankee Stadium. With the columnists cheering him in print, he was a pretty big draw. Everybody connected with him made out very well.

My dad went to Abe's wedding. It was ironic: After all his fights with Irish kids who didn't like Jews back in the old days in San Francisco, Abe married an Irish woman named Mae O'Brien. It was a very happy marriage. She was a lovely woman. His first marriage, I heard, didn't turn out well, but he and Mae were good together. They opened a bar and restaurant on the east side and attracted a lot of fighters, fight fans, gamblers, athletes, sportswriters, and some Broadway hotshots. I used to see them when I went to the fights at Madison Square Garden. He was a friendly guy who couldn't stop talking. He should've had his own radio show. I once told him that, and he said his face was perfect for radio: banged up, scarred, and with a big broken nose. He was the kind of guy it was fun to be around.

A lot of people turned up for his funeral in 1970. He was 86 or 87. Most fighters are gone long before they can reach that ripe old age. But, you know, he was one of the great ones, an example for many Jewish fighters who came after him. People who knew him, when asked, always smiled and spoke kindly of him. He left his friends with many pleasant memories. Of how many people can you say that? He was one of a kind.[4]

2

THE GREAT DEPRESSION, BOXING, AND MIKE JACOBS

While Benny Leonard and Abe Attell were the prototypes for such Jewish boxers as Max Baer and Barney Ross, it was the poverty of the Great Depression that contributed to the enormous popularity of boxing, enlarging the careers of the heroes of that era. It was the golden age of boxing, the golden age of the movies, and the golden age of baseball. Heroes were writ large because the public needed large heroes to offset the small, dreary prospects for life in the 1930s. And while the glittering movie stars of the 1930s projected images of heroism and glamour onto the silver screen, their cinematic heroism and make-believe glamour did not exist outside of the darkened caverns of Depression-era movie theaters. And many of those theaters were built like gilded palaces to add to the larger-than-life fantasies that enthralled moviegoers. Escapism was a necessary component of existence during the Depression. One could dream beyond the grime and grimness, beyond the poverty and pain that engulfed so many.

Boxers, however, did not perform in movie palaces. There were no stunt men in boxing rings. Boxers often fought in hot, grimy arenas or outdoor stadiums. They sweated real sweat. They bled real blood. They experienced real broken noses, real cracked or broken ribs, real bruises, real welts. It's no wonder they were viewed as real blood-and-guts heroes; they had the same appeal gladiatorial combatants did for spectators at Rome's Coliseum. Some of them even took such severe punishment that they died. Looking at a fighter after 12 or 15 rounds, one would see black eyes, a battered nose caked with dried blood, and swollen and cut lips. Sometimes teeth would be broken or, even worse, a jaw might have needed to be wired shut. Months later those faces oftentimes featured deeply etched scars, cauliflower ears, and scar tissue—small pouches hanging over the eye sockets. For fighters, the marks of their profession were not to be hidden, not to be erased by the skill of cosmetic surgeons. None of it could be washed off after a director had yelled "cut" and "print it." Fighters took pride in the marks of their trade. It proved what they had done, what they had endured. It was part of their very identity. They were the real deal, and the deals were often for hundreds of thousands of dollars. While thousands of businesses and banks went bankrupt during the Depression, the business of boxing flourished. Money was being made hand over clenched, gloved fist.

To ensure that they got top dollar for themselves and their fighters, promoters formed cartels and promoted championship fights in such large venues as Soldiers Field in Chicago or Yankee Stadium, which could accommodate 80,000 fans. Millions of dollars were earned in a single night. While millions of people lived on less than $5 a week or government relief, thousands of fans managed to pay anywhere from 75 cents to $1 to $5 to attend a championship boxing match. In addition, they bought newspapers, binoculars, souvenirs, beer, pretzels, and sodas, and ate at diners and took taxis and trains to the bouts. They would bet a few dollars with local bookies. If they missed a fight, they could go to a movie theater and watch a newsreel of it. Following the fights, there were often large parties at restaurants and hotels to celebrate the winners. It all contributed to the local economy. The sport of boxing was economically vibrant in an era of massive economic morbidity.

If a man was struggling to pay his bills, barely making ends meet, living paycheck to paycheck just to put food on the table and keep the lights on, and hanging onto a crummy job by his fingernails, he could vent his frustrations and displaced aggression at a boxing match. He might yell and scream, "Kill the bastard! Give 'em a right to the head. Knock 'em on his ass!" He might mimic punches thrown, just missing the guys sitting to his right and left. He might raise one fist in the air and curse his man's opponent for a low blow. If his man knocked out his opponent, there would be cheers and whistles. If his man were knocked out, he might sink into utter glumness or shout at the referee for not separating the fighters when it mattered. And when his man won, by either a decision or a knockout, he could vicariously enjoy that triumph. He would share the winner's pleasure in being a champ. As the champ left the ring and walked back to his dressing room, accompanied by his cornermen and separated from the spectators by a cordon of cops, our ordinary guy would try to reach out and pat the champ on the back, tell him he had a great fight. Vicariously vindicated, a victor in his own mind, he might feel for a few moments that he was not only in control of his destiny, but also that there might be something bright and wonderful in his future. If his man had lost and was sluggishly moving up the aisle to his dressing room, his toweled head lowered in anger and humiliation, our ordinary spectator might feel that his world had collapsed. If his hero couldn't win, how could he? In his anger, he might yell that his hero had been robbed, set up, threatened by bookies to take a dive or he might wind up dead in an alley. Any excuse that worked for his fallen hero could help lighten his own burden, could mitigate his bitterness, his anger, his frustration. But he would still have to return to that dark, dank rooming house, to his dimly lit room with perhaps just a single bed, a chair, a small bureau, and a small radio to ward off loneliness. Such were the pleasures of the working man during the Depression.

For the promoters, however, life was full of bounty. Once they had formed cartels to control the boxing matches and arenas, they were in the driver's seat. While the stockbrokers of the 1920s amassed portfolios of stocks and bonds, the fight promoters of the 1930s bought, sold, and controlled portfolios of boxers. A portfolio of boxers ranged from triple-A, gold-plated champs to those who were sold short, and once their box-office value had descended to zero, they were dumped like putrid fish into the garbage can of oblivion. A portfolio of fighters included every weight class, from featherweight to heavyweight. The more boxers in a promoter's portfolio, the more money the promoter would make. And the more fights he promoted, the more he and his boxers, as well as the managers, trainers, gamblers, and doctors, benefitted. In addition, the community of local businesses, like suckerfish, was able to live off the big fights.

To maximize the dollar value of the gate, promoters instituted price discrimination, as do legitimate theaters. They would charge $5 or more for a ringside seat and $1 for a balcony seat, and maybe 75 cents for standing at the back of the balcony or bleachers in a nonchampionship bout. For a championship bout, the ringside tickets might fetch as much as $30, while a balcony seat could be rented for $5. Of course, it was the cheaper seats that brought in the large audiences. Like many mass-market merchants, for example, Woolworth, the promoters made large stacks of bills from the volume of cheap seats that Depression-era spectators warmed. There were a limited number of ringside seats, but none went unsold. Promoters, press agents, and sportswriters created so much excitement for fights that there was always a guarantee of sold-out attendances at most fights. Swells and sports, celebrities and politicians, gamblers and gangsters either paid big bucks to be near the champions or were awarded their seats to pay off favors. In the stands, thousands of ordinary fight fans were just happy to be in attendance. Looking at the swells in their ringside seats, one could view enviable opulence on display: women in furs and glittering baubles, men in fancy suits and smoking large cigars, their large, ostentatious pinky rings reflecting light. These were the men and women unaffected by the poverty of the Depression. They luxuriated in the display of their possessions. They were thumbing their noses at poverty. They were saying to the world, "Hey, look at me. Look at how successful I am! I'm no chump." They were like Roman nobility at the Coliseum.

Of all the promoters, perhaps the most innovative, driven, cold-hearted, and successful was Mike Jacobs, whom Budd Schulberg referred to as a "Machiavelli of boxing and Madison Square Garden." Jacobs saw boxing as a path to realizing his dreams of wealth. If his life story had needed a soundtrack, it could have started with "If I Were a Rich Man" from *Fiddler on the Roof* and concluded with the Beatles' "Baby, You're a Rich Man." Jacobs saw the huge crowds of fight fans who eagerly put up their meager Depression-era earnings to attend championship fights. There was a huge pile of money just waiting for Jacobs to scoop up.

The story of Mike Jacobs's rise begins in New York City in 1880. His family was poor, and Mike had to find work at an early age. Like Abe Attell, he sold newspapers on street corners; he then added candy and nuts to his inventory. He moved from street corners to the bustle of Coney Island, where he sold his goods to those venturing out on daily excursion boats. Ever ambitious, he bought concessions on the boats and hired others to run them for him. Always on the lookout for new financial opportunities, Mike began scalping tickets for boat rides and then train rides. The customers for his train tickets were primarily immigrants who were ignorant of the ticket-buying process. He overcharged them and sometimes sold counterfeit tickets. He would also sell tickets to other scalpers and then take a cut of what they had sold. It was all about the money.

From an early age, it was apparent to anyone who did business with Jacobs that he was a person without a conscience. His goal was money; it was not being liked, not being honored, not being a friend. He was in a race with himself to become a dealmaker par excellence. Money made his world go round, and he wanted as much of it as possible. His ambition knew no bounds. Wherever he espied opportunity, he was there with a strategy.

It was one thing to scalp tickets for a boat ride, but it would be quite another to own the boats and set his own prices for the tickets. For Jacobs, each venture was a stepping-stone to a bigger venture. So Mike borrowed the necessary funds and bought several ferry boats. He was not exactly the Cunard of Coney Island, but he was the captain of his own ships, turning each one into a profit center. The banks offered attractive loans for boats, and Jacobs never failed to repay those debts. The banks were his true friends, and he needed them to finance his deals. For the banks, Jacobs was virtually risk free, a well-regarded ambitious young man who was apparently going to be a good customer for years to come. He had shown the banks his books, and it was apparent to all that young Jacobs had a Midas touch: He had an outstanding record for maximizing profits.

No one could run faster than Mike Jacobs when pursuing the almighty dollar. And no one could be unimpressed by his rags-to-riches stories, especially the local bankers. He was a young man on his way up the ladder of success, a ladder that seemed to have no end in sight. Jacobs was not only a clever dealmaker and energetic in his pursuit of success, but he also had an entrepreneur's ability to think ahead, not just to tomorrow or to next week or to next month, but to next year and the year after that. Budd Schulberg, who burst onto the literary scene with his seminal novel *What Makes Sammy Run?*, could have just as easily written a companion novel entitled *What Makes Mike Run?* Instead, he wrote about Jacobs for *Collier's* magazine in 1950, but without divulging the dirty underside that Jacobs's boxing operations included. Although Schulberg wrote that Jacobs was a lonely multimillionaire living in a mansion, his was still an American dream come to life.

Like many entrepreneurs, Jacobs did not look back on his successes; he always looked ahead to the next deal. His cravings for success were insatiable; he always wanted more. And more was never enough. While others operated his network of ferry boats, Mike ventured from Coney Island to Broadway, the "Great White Way." It was the perfect neighborhood for hustlers and those who could be hustled. There, he used his expertise to become one of the leading scalpers of tickets for sports and theatrical events. As he had done with his Coney Island boating ventures, he planned on escalating his Broadway scalping to owning events. He wanted to be a player, to make a big name for himself. Soon signs began appearing, announcing "Mike Jacobs Productions." He maneuvered to control the price and availability of tickets. From there, he would control the production of high-flying Broadway events. In rapid succession, he was producing operatic concerts, charity events, circus performances, bicycle races. Whatever could be produced in a theater or auditorium, Jacobs could produce. And not just produce, but promote the events to ensure maximum profitability.

Wherever there was an opportunity, there was Mike Jacobs. And to ensure his position as a major producer, he made sure that his name was prominently displayed at all events. No one should forget that what they had enjoyed was a Mike Jacobs Production. He was particularly good at making sure that he got all possible credit for producing charity events, for nothing so polished his name and reputation as raising money for worthy causes approved by the public. The last thing he wanted was to be considered a common hustler. He wanted the rich Fifth Avenue swells to regard him as a man with good intentions, for they were also the bankers who could attest to Jacobs's creditworthiness.

It was not only ambition that had propelled Jacobs into the high realms of success, but also the example of another famous promoter, Tex Rickard. In 1906, Jacobs had met and befriended Rickard, who became the biggest and smartest boxing promoter of his time. Rickard had been a marshal in Texas, hence his name. Bored with the day-to-day tedium of being a marshal, dissatisfied with his lowly wages, and having distaste for possibly being injured, Rickard left for northern opportunities in a cold clime. He was going to stake a claim in the Klondike Gold Rush of 1897. His ambitions were not fulfilled there, so he next rushed off to the Nome Gold Rush, where he met and befriended Wyatt Earp. While Earp was known as a gambler and teller of tall tales, he was also recognized as an able referee of numerous profitable heavyweight fights. Whether he bet on his own prearranged decisions is open to dispute, but that did not diminish Earp's genuine enthusiasm for the sweet science.

Rickard and Earp's shared interest in boxing and betting was enough of a bond to establish the pair as lifelong friends. Rickard, often restless in his pursuit of quick money, set his sights on a number of various enterprises, including a few enigmatic ones in South America. He remained there briefly, his accomplishments a mystery, and then returned to the United States. He settled in New York and found his true métier: managing fighters and promoting fights at Madison Square Garden.

It was 1920, and it was the beginning of a nearly mythic career for Tex Rickard, who would be boxing's man to see, the go-to guy, who could make fighters' and managers' dreams become realities. Rickard cultivated his power, made deals, and became a last-resort arbiter. He would be celebrated as the genius who promoted the fights of Jack Dempsey, the heavyweight champion until 1926. Dempsey was probably the most popular athlete in the United States during his reign atop the heavyweight pinnacle, a champion among champions. Rickard and Jack Dempsey's manager, Jack Kearns, were able to gross $8.6 million from five fights from 1921 to 1926. It was a stunning amount, even to stockbrokers during the Roaring Twenties. Thousands wanted to get their hands on some of that boxing money, but Rickard maintained strict control of his assets. And he knew that expansion was the route of any successful business.

Not satisfied with promoting the most popular heavyweight bouts in the United States, he ventured into real estate and built the third incarnation of Madison Square Garden. One such Garden of Eden of riches was insufficient, so Rickard then went on to build the original Boston Garden. His two Gardens were lushly planted with events that bore the crop of huge success. The money was so profuse that armored cars were required to deposit it in safe havens. The two Gardens became the most successful venues for staging highly publicized boxing matches. If boxing could produce such magnificent returns, then why not venture into other sports? Be ever restless, ever ambitious, ever yearning for more. So Rickard did not stop with boxing: He founded the New York Rangers of the National Hockey League.

Perhaps Rickard ran too fast; perhaps he had run out of ideas. He traveled to Miami Beach, a magnet for Roaring Twenties land speculators, a place that would soon attract snowbirds from the north who wanted to warm themselves amid the palm trees and sand of south Florida. Rickard complained of an intense stomach pain; he clutched his lower abdomen and felt he might vomit. He was rushed to a local hospital, where doctors diagnosed the need for an appendectomy, but their scalpels were more like the cleavers of butchers. The botched operation resulted in the death of the king of boxing promoters. His reign had been short, but profitable and exciting. How appropriate that he died the same year the stock market had a near-death collapse, 1929. His pal Wyatt Earp died a month later.

It was not a good year for boxing, or so it seemed. For Mike Jacobs, a door had opened, and he was about to slam it shut behind him, although inside the world of boxing were notorious gangsters and fixers with whom Jacobs would have to come to terms. Perhaps the most spectacular of the gangsters was Owney Madden, who owned heavyweight champ Primo Carnera, who owned less of himself than the gangsters who had fixed his fights and then dumped him on the garbage heap of fistic history. Schulberg draws a fictionalized and devastating portrait of the misused and abused Carnera in his classic boxing novel *The Harder They Fall*. Carnera wasn't the only fighter owned by Madden; he owned numerous fighters in virtually every division. But when he tried to muscle in on Max Baer, he was told to pound sand, and no one was referring to the sands of Jacobs Beach.

Mike Jacobs had been standing in Tex Rickard's shadow. Some said that he was standing so close that the two men only needed one pair of shoes. Jacobs seemed to glide into Rickard's position, putting on his mentor's mantel and easily becoming respected as boxing's premier promoter. It was a natural move for him. No one would control boxing as he did in the 1930s. He was not just the Machiavelli of the ring, but also its Caesar. One could imagine him presiding over gladiatorial combat in Rome's Coliseum. In New York City, the arena had a more benevolent name; it was a Garden, and for many a boxer it was a garden in which his dreams could find root and blossom into wealth and celebrity.

Everything Jacobs did prior to 1929 had led to his being boxing's puppeteer; he pulled all the strings like the moguls of Hollywood. Boxing in the 1930s, minus Mike Jacobs, is a story without an author. He elevated the sport to its highest level of popularity, regularly competing with baseball as America's favorite athletic event. Jacobs was a visionary, not a boxer; in fact, he is known to have never thrown a punch. But everyone who threw a professional punch in New York paid his dues and a lot more to the man who pulled the strings, if not the punches in Madison Square Garden. If you wanted to be a boxer, if you were a contender and wanted a shot at the title, if you were a manager who wanted to get your man a fight at the Garden, Mike was the man to see, the man who could make it happen, and perhaps make you rich. That he would also make himself rich was accepted and understood.

The area where Mike's office stood was known to everyone in the world of boxing, not including mapmakers, as Jacobs Beach. The origin of the name has never been adequately explained, although several sportswriters of that era have been credited with creating the name. One may assume that it was a place where bookies, boxers, and managers could lounge away the morning or afternoon, as if on a beach. Jacobs Beach was located on West 49th Street, between Broadway and Eighth Avenue, opportunistically situated between Madison Square Garden and Jack Dempsey's famous restaurant, briefly seen in the first *Godfather* movie. Across the street from Jacobs Beach was the notorious Forrest Hotel. Bob Hope complained that the maids at the Forrest changed the rats once a day; for his comment, he was sued by the hotel. Such a comment could have caused its transient residents to take off for more idyllic settings. Nevertheless, Damon Runyon, who had a jeweler's eye for the demimonde, lived in its penthouse for many years without ever seeing so much as a mouse.

As America's number-one boxing promoter, Jacobs went on to promote hundreds of fights for the Hippodrome and Madison Square Garden. His abilities received widespread recognition when he organized a boxing extravaganza for William Randolph Hearst's Milk Fund Boxing Benefit at the Bronx Coliseum in 1933. He generated much more money for the event than had been generated at Madison Square Garden. The newspapers celebrated his achievement. The boxing writers lauded him as a great promoter and philanthropist. He was as much of a philanthropist as Jesse James. That didn't stop Damon Runyon from pouring accolades on Caesar's head. Oh yes, Jacobs had a Midas touch. Anything he touched turned to gold; if Jacobs was involved, could success be far behind? It was a question that didn't require an answer.

Three sportswriters, including Runyon, whose stories are the basis for the musical *Guys & Dolls*, were eager and delighted to have the privilege of forming a sports promotion company with Mike Jacobs. It was the Twentieth Century Sporting Club, which would dominate the world of boxing for more than a decade. The first bout that Jacobs and his partners promoted in 1934 was for the future lightweight champion, Barney Ross.

The following year, Jacobs became manager of the dominant heavyweight champion of the 1930s and 1940s, Joe Louis, the "Brown Bomber," whose skills in the ring brought fans out of their seats with cheers and whistles. And the fight that Jacobs later promoted between Louis and Max Baer grossed more than $1 million, a cork-popping champagne sum during the Depression.

By the late 1930s, Jacobs had decided to take his company private. He did not have to buy back any publicly traded stock. He just wanted his partners gone. Would Caesar have wanted to share his throne? Thrones are made to seat solitary monarchs, not partners, and certainly not a triumvirate. Apparently, he made them an offer they could not refuse, and he bought them out. The Twentieth Century Sporting Club was now synonymous with the name Mike Jacobs, and every champ, contender, and pug, and their managers and trainers, knew it. Jacobs now controlled every weight division in professional boxing from featherweight to heavyweight.

Looking for new territories to conquer, he would be the premier producer of boxing on the radio. In 1938, he broadcast a match to enthralled radio listeners; it was a brilliant move, celebrated by sportswriters, advertising agencies, and the fraternity of boxers. *Friday Night Fights* became one of the most popular radio sports programs on the air. Men would rush home from work or to their favorite bar and grill, and listen avidly to *Friday Night Fights* while downing their beers. The radio broadcasts increased the popularity of boxing and added greatly to the coffers of bookies. Fight fans who did not attend the bouts pulled up a bar stool and, in their saloon camaraderie, with a beer in one hand and a cigar in the other, initiated the founding of the sports bar. It was almost like being at ringside. Bartenders would call bookies on behalf of their patrons and receive a cut for their services. Betting, beer, and boxing were an irresistible combination.

As successful as boxing was on the radio, it would be even more so on television. Jacobs had immediately seen the value of television to further enlarge the audience for boxing and for increasing the dollar value of his fights. Boxing was an ideal sport for television because the three-minute rounds followed by one-minute breaks permitted the TV stations to sell advertising time during those breaks. Jacobs's first staged TV boxing match was a big hit. It was for the championship of the featherweight division, a fight between the quick-as-lightning Willie Pep and Chalky

Wright. Fight fans loved it, and so did advertisers. Television had found a new and lucrative source of revenue; advertisers had found a new audience. And bookies enjoyed boom times.

Jacobs went on from one success to another. During World War II, always eager to burnish his image and display his patriotism, he staged an enormous boxing event that generated $36 million for the sale of U.S. war bonds. The event was so popular and he was so honored that he could have run for public office and probably won a landslide victory.

But then, like his mentor, Tex Rickard, Jacobs's demise came without warning. A sudden headache, turning into a sharp, stabbing pain, became a deep groan of anguish. It was over almost as quickly as it had arrived, like a sudden, unexpected summer storm; a cerebral hemorrhage had collapsed Mike Jacobs. That stroke of misfortune permanently removed him from his throne. It was 1946. He had lived and thrived during the Great Depression and World War II. He had elevated himself out of poverty and become the most important behind-the-scenes puppeteer in boxing. But he was no longer capable of exercising his rule. He sold his company to Madison Square Garden. Jacobs lingered on in his impressive New Jersey mansion for another seven years and died in 1953. Schulberg writes, "People played up to him. But I don't think I remember any of us who could say he was a real friend. He was strictly business all the way. Totally unsentimental. And he had all the power."[1]

In his book *Ringside*, Schulberg quotes the great trainer-manager Ray Arcel, saying,

> Mike may be a hard man to love. Somehow I don't think he even wanted people to like him. He was a lone operator. He played all his cards close to the chest. I don't think he ever let anybody get close to him. After all, he's been operating in this town all his life. . . . Some of the biggest people in this city call him Mike, and yet he hasn't got a single close friend.[2]

Schulberg concludes his assessment of Jacobs by writing,

> The tallest Horatio Alger tale is mild stuff alongside Mike's upward climb from the seamiest slums of Manhattan to the palatial home in New Jersey, and only the Lord (and probably not even the Treasury Department) knows how many millions. Whether Mike's been good

for the fight game is what might be called along 49th Street a "mute pernt."[3]

One need not wonder why it took until 1982 for Jacobs to be elected to the Boxing Hall of Fame. There's no rush to eulogize a man whose very associates hardly knew him, and those who did thought he had a heart of stone. Yet, more so than any other promoter of the 1930s, Mike Jacobs was instrumental in promoting the careers of Max Baer, Barney Ross, and many other champions. They earned enormous sums of money and provided much-needed excitement during the dreary, dark days of the Depression.

Mike Jacobs's reign ended, and the new impresarios who took complete control, with their organization, the International Boxing Club (IBC), were some of the most notorious Mafia figures to ever dominate boxing: Frankie Carbo, former triggerman for Murder Incorporated, and gambler Blinky Palermo would rule the world of boxing with iron fists and mild, deceitful smiles. In his book *Jacobs Beach*, Kevin Mitchell writes that Frankie Carbo had earlier "muscled in on the operations of Uncle Mike with sledgehammer subtlety. Perceiving no resistance, he went on to formalize the relationship."[4]

3

TOUGH KID

Dov-Ber (Beryl) David Rosofsky was a tough little kid. A street fighter. Pugnacious, stubborn, afraid of no one. Although short and skinny, he stood up to anti-Semitic bullies who, looking for Jews to beat up, had invaded the Jewish ghetto on Maxwell Street in 1920s Chicago. When attacked, he would counterattack, shooting his small, clenched fists into the bellies and eyes of bullies, swinging wildly but connecting with chins and noses. He looked like an easy target, a scrawny figure out of Oliver Twist, an artful dodger, but one who could quickly dodge, duck, and sidestep, while shooting well-aimed blows at a less skillful opponent. A quick right or left to the jaw of a bully ended a fight, the bruised opponent learning the painful lesson not to mess with the little Jewish kid.

Beryl, as he was known before becoming the world famous champ Barney Ross, ran with an informal gang of other teenage delinquents in their Twentieth Ward neighborhood. It was during Prohibition, and adult gangs were fighting for territory and shooting those who got in the way. It was the era of the tommy gun and the Molotov cocktail, of the car bomb and the bombing of uncooperative speakeasies, gambling and bookie joints. And the Twentieth Ward was one of the worst locales in Chicago; in fact, it was so notorious for the number of dead bodies tossed from speeding cars onto its streets that it was known as the "Bloody Twentieth." It was in the Twentieth Ward that the notorious Genna brothers operated outside of the law. Their base of operations and their bootlegging factory was located there at 1022 Taylor Street, in what was known as the "Patch." From there, they processed alcohol for distribution to speakeasies, and it was from there that they issued their monthly payoffs to the police of the Maxwell Street precinct. The Rosofskys lived cheek by jowl to some of the most notorious killers in Chicago. Among the more famous Chicago gangsters of the time were Al Capone, Paul Ricca, Frankie Yale, Johnny Torrio, Sam Giancana, Tony Accardo, Bugs Moran, Machine Gun Jack McGurn, and a host of other public enemies.

In such an environment, it was not surprising that Beryl would fall in with a group of aspiring and enterprising thugs. His closest pal was Jacob "Sparky" Rubenstein (aka Jack Ruby, the assassin of Lee Harvey Oswald). Sparky was known for his volatile, hair-trigger temper. When offended, he would explode, pummeling the offender. He seemed to have no fear and would attack anyone regardless of size or strength. He was a boy who hit first and didn't ask questions later. Sparky and Beryl were an intimidating team; if you were not a resident of Maxwell Street, you would have wanted to cross the street when you saw those two coming at you. It was a wise move to stay clear of their path. They were said to have rolled drunks, offered protection to peddlers (and in some cases it was not just an offer, but insisted upon, or else), and run errands for Big Al, known to the world and history as "Scarface," Al Capone. He was one of many who made notorious and bloody contributions to Chicago and beyond. In addition to the previously noted Chicago gangsters, the Maxwell Street ghetto was famous for nurturing a number of others, including Samuel "Nails" Morton, Louis "Two Gun" Alterie, and Jake "Greasy Thumb" Guzik, who would rise to become Capone's money man and run the Outfit while Capone was in prison. While many criminals emerged from the Maxwell Street ghetto, there were even more prizefighters there.

The atmosphere of the Maxwell Street ghetto molded tough young men, for they felt you had to be tough to survive. Like calluses, their toughness grew hard and protective throughout time. For them, life on the streets posed the perils of a wild jungle populated by desperate predators. Attacks and counterattacks were actions of the day and night. You had to be on your guard, be prepared, walk with clenched fists, and look tough. Any sign of weakness in the jungle was an invitation to be set upon as a wounded animal is set upon by a lion. Police sirens and the sounds of shootings were often the soundtrack for the activities of the ghetto. In such an environment, close friendships were necessary to create bonds of protection. Two boys standing back-to-back were a better defense than one boy standing alone. Three or four boys were even better, certainly less easy to threaten than a single boy. The bigger the gang the more control they had of the streets.

From such protective necessities developed deep and lasting friendships, and the bond of friendship that Sparky and Beryl created in boyhood lasted a lifetime. There were other members of their gang, but they are the only two who made a mark on history. Ross and Ruby were considered by neighbors and friends to be good candidates to grow into professional hoodlums who would find their true home in prison. Others thought they might qualify for membership in the Outfit, which could protect them from prison, since cops and judges were on the Outfit's payroll. Since members of one gang often killed members of other gangs, service in the Outfit was no guarantee of a long life; however, unlike many institutions of corporate America at the time, the Outfit did not have a quota on Jewish admittance. In fact, the Outfit was primarily made up of Jews and Italians. When Big Al was sentenced to Alcatraz, the "Rock," it was no surprise to anyone that his empire was run by a Jew, "Greasy Thumb" Guzik. (When Guzik died in 1956, there were as many Italians as Jews at his funeral service, which was held in a synagogue.)

Like many poor delinquents, young and brazen, Beryl had dreams of being a gangster, wearing elegant suits, driving a fancy car, and having beautiful babes, one on each arm. He had already showed how tough he was; scared of no one, fearing neither the law nor the Old Testament scripture contained in the Ten Commandments, Beryl asked one of his Italian friends to introduce him to Big Al. To be introduced to Big Al, for a street kid, would be like an ardent Catholic kid asking and being granted an audience with the Pope. Although his requests were regularly ignored, Beryl wouldn't give up. Big Al held the key that could open the doors to a world of wealth and excitement. Beryl was as relentless in pursuit of an invitation as he would later prove to be in going after an opponent in the boxing ring. He kept coming back like a dog to a hidden bone, and he would not stop until he was granted that introduction. He would not take no for an answer. Days and weeks of trying finally led to admission into the presence of the big man, the "Don," the "Godfather" who controlled Chicago, the man who controlled the importation and distribution of illegal liquor throughout Illinois.

Big Al, a connoisseur of tough young talent, had finally learned of Beryl's fast-flying fists as a street fighter; he had heard the tales of Beryl being challenged and erupting with a furious rapid-fire display of fists that knocked a challenger to the pavement. On Maxwell Street and in other ethnic enclaves, Beryl was known as "One-Punch Rosofsky" and "Beryl the Terrible." Big Al had nodded and paternalistically smiled at this persistent young tough guy; he was impressed with the kid. The kid had heart and guts, and could not be intimidated. The Outfit was always on the lookout for young tough guys who could be its soldiers, its muscle. The Outfit didn't need recruiting posters. The word was always out on the street: If you're a small-time crook, stay away; if you have the makings to be a big earner, the Outfit will always be interested in your services. If those who signed up had brains, as well as muscle, they might pull off big scams. Brains, muscle, and creative schemes were the best ingredients for getting profitable results. Al could always find a use for such a young man.

So, he finally summoned the tough kid who had wanted to meet him. Al smiled like an indulgent older brother or a pleased uncle meeting a distant nephew; he gently slapped Beryl's cheek, then squeezed a fold of skin. "So tell me about yourself," he said. Beryl told him the story of his brief life up to that time, and Al questioned the eager young thug, just to make sure the kid was on the level. Capone offered Beryl low-level employment—a test. He could start out as a messenger, maybe become a runner for Al's bookie joints, and perhaps eventually a bagman. Beryl passed his initial test of delivering envelopes of money and never opening them. The kid could be trusted. He wouldn't steal from the hands that paid him. In addition to running errands for Capone, Beryl ran errands for Capone's brothers, for the Fischetti brothers, for the Genna brothers, for Bugs Moran, and for Machine Gun Jack McGurn. It could have developed into a mob-owned messenger subsidiary run by a talented young junior executive on his way up the corporate ladder. By the time of the St. Valentine's Day Massacre of 1929, Beryl had run errands for all the victims. The cops never thought of the kid as a witness or someone who could give them leads. He was never questioned.

Al kept an eye on the kid as weeks and months passed. He liked the kid, was really fond of him, and decided not to promote him as a runner for bookies. There were plenty of other young, aspiring mob guys who would work as messengers, each trying to get his nose in the door of the executive suites. Maybe Big Al liked the kid too much and wanted to protect him, thinking there might be a better career path for the young thug. Based on his ability to read people, to intuitively delve into their motives, to size up their talents, Capone decided that Beryl was not cut out for the mob. He could fight all right, but he didn't have a killer instinct. He didn't enjoy hurting people. His fists were more defensive weapons than offensive ones, not to be used for cold-blooded adventures. The kid may have thought of himself as a thug, but he was basically just out to protect himself and prove that he could survive better than his compatriots. You wouldn't want to use him to muscle some recalcitrant speakeasy customer into paying his bill or to blow up the refinery of a competitive bootlegger.

So while Capone initially dismissed Beryl, telling him to get a legit job and support his family, and handing him some money, he would come to think that the kid had the makings of a boxer. Capone got in touch with Beryl and directed him to a boxing gym. He made sure that Beryl didn't have to pay for training. Capone would collect on his investment at a later time. The kid would learn the skills of a professional boxer, learn that boxing was a sport of skill and that if you mastered those skills you could protect yourself from getting badly hurt. Facing opponents who had differing styles, you could adopt tactics to outwit those styles and develop a strategy for winning. It was no different than what the kid had been doing on the streets of the ghetto. And who wouldn't want to bet on such a boxer?

Beryl, the tough guy of Maxwell Street, the Outfit's messenger boy, was not what his father Isadore had expected or wanted. He wanted a boy who would follow in his footsteps. He was an Orthodox Jew, a Talmudic scholar and teacher. He should have had his own synagogue; however, as a poor immigrant with little money and several children and a wife to support, he settled for running a tiny grocery store, Rosofsky's Dairy, where he was only able to eke out a small income. The store was so modest that no more than four or five customers could fit inside at one time. Its prices were modest, the margins of profit even more modest. Yet, it provided the Rosofsky family with a sense of security; it was their small lifeboat in an economically precarious sea of poverty. Isadore hoped to provide the support and example that would be an impetus for his children to have a better life than he struggled to maintain. Poor Isadore.

When Beryl would come home with a black eye, a bloody nose, or a cut lip, his father's dreams of a better life for his children exploded into a nightmare of such intense disappointment that it horrified him. His face would turn red with frustration, anger, and disappointment. Fighting was not for Jewish scholars. No self-respecting Jew would permit his son to wander the streets with clenched fists, ready to punch the first kid who called him a dirty Jew, a sheenie, or a kike. Although Beryl would claim that he tripped and bruised his face or bloodied his nose or cut his lip, Pa Rosofsky did not believe such tales. For him, Beryl had descended to the level of a bum, a tramp, and (he could barely bring himself to admit) a hoodlum. The boy had disgraced his heritage, violated the values that his father had attempted to instill in him.

Pa Rosofsky would take his leather belt and, with a swishing sound, rapidly pull it through the loops of his pants and tightly wrap it around his angry hand. It was refashioned as a whip; in fact, Beryl referred to it as a "cat o' nine tails." It was supposed to break the boy of his wild ways, break his spirited rebellion, make him obey, make him into an honest student of the Talmud, not some wayward warring waif. As Isadore angrily whipped his son, the belt rising and falling with a crack of pain on naked, reddened flesh, he cried out that Beryl had forgotten his background and was ignoring his heritage, which went back thousands of years. Beryl, gritting his teeth, refusing to cry or whimper, would stoically receive the beating. Although the belt raised welts on young Beryl's bottom, he never complained, never cried out for his father to stop, and he refused to change his ways, refused to desert his pals. Yes, he loved the Torah, but he also was a street kid. Why not adhere to codes of both worlds? Well, at least some of them. He was a boy of the streets and could never be like his father, an ardent biblical scholar. But he could be a good Jew, even an observant one. He admired his father, dearly loved the man, but he could not follow his example. He could not become his father. Poor Isadore, frustrated and angry, even after beating his son, his anger at high volume, would yell that Jews were not to be fighters or street thugs. Jews were not trained to be fighters. Let gentiles fight. A Jew should study and learn from the Talmud. Jews were born and raised to be scholars of the law, not lawbreakers. Beryl should be a good Jew, not a hoodlum from the streets.

But for Beryl, the street was his universe and his university. He learned to defend himself against the Italian and Irish kids fighting for territorial advantage. He learned the tough ways of the world. Yes, he loved his father and appreciated how hard he worked to earn a small living for the family. But the life of a grocer, especially a grocer scholar, was not the life for him; who would want to work 16 to 18 hours a day in a tiny grocery for little money? He had to work every day, except on the Sabbath. Beryl understood his father's anger. But it would have no effect on the choices he would make. They lived cheek by jowl, but in two different worlds. What Beryl wanted from life his father would never be able to understand. There was a big, glittering world beyond Maxwell Street that Isadore would never experience, and even if he did, he would not be able to comprehend or evaluate it, except in the terms of the Bible. His father was more familiar with Sodom and Gomorrah than what went on in Al Capone's Chicago. For the Rosofskys, their world was the synagogue, the home, and the grocery store. It was a poor, confined world, but it was one in which they felt safe. They were glad not to be in Russia, not to be victims of drunken Cossacks who started pogroms and beat, raped, and killed Jews.

But it was that small, confined world of the Maxwell Street ghetto that felt so constricting to young Beryl. He wanted out. He wanted the big, wide, exciting world that he imagined the bootleggers inhabited. It was a world where the flashes and smoke from gunfire made one take notice; danger was exciting and to be close to those who committed violent acts could be exciting. The benefits of a well-executed crime could be exciting. It was a world of its own laws, laws that intimidated the lawful, leaving them at the mercy of strong, violent men who went their own way and flouted the rules of society.

Nevertheless, it would be irrational gunfire that would blast holes in Beryl's world. Gunfire would be the sound that ended the past and brought about the future. Two black hoods, desperate thieves with angry eyes and hair-trigger tempers, entered his father's store, pulled out pistols, and demanded cash. Impetuously, the daring, righteous grocer rushed at the robbers; they could not take the money that he worked so hard to earn, the money that put food on the table for his family and kept a roof over their heads and clothing on their bodies. And so they shot him in the chest, the bullets penetrating his heart. His yarmulke flew off his head, and he collapsed onto the floor with a thud. His head fell back onto the floor, and his open mouth gurgled blood. He clutched his chest; the pain was excruciating, his shirt and apron covered with blood. His heart pumped the blood out of his dying body. He was rushed to a local hospital, but he had lost a tremendous amount of blood. His pulse was as faint as a whisper, his skin pale, cold, and clammy. The paralyzed look on his face was that of a man who was shocked and furious. He died angry. His son would live on anger.

In the furious estimation of Beryl, his father died a hero, a man who had been obedient to his principles and the rules of the Talmud, a man who slaved to support his family, a man who never complained of his fate, a man who accepted his responsibilities, for that was what he expected of himself. His father died a hero, trying to save what little security he had been able to provide for his family. Beryl would never stop loving his father, would never need to forgive him for those beatings, for he knew that his father could not understand the world and did not know how to deal with his wayward son. His father, in his limited way, thought he was doing the right thing. It was the way he had been raised and probably the way his father had been raised, generation after generation.

Beryl wanted to track down and kill his father's murderers, hunting them down as if they were wild game. He wanted to break their heads, to beat them until they could no longer stand. But the thieves had vanished, fleeing into anonymity. Beryl was propelled by his need for revenge; it was more than just an eye for an eye, a tooth for tooth. He wanted to plunge his hatred like a dagger into the heartless hearts of the assassins and turn that blade over and over. He wanted to exact the revenge called for in Exodus—an endlessly repeated echo in his mind:

> If any man hate his neighbour, and lie in wait for him, and rise up against him, and smite him mortally that he die, and fleeth . . . then the elders of his city shall send and fetch him thence, and deliver him into the hand of the avenger of blood, that he may die. Thine eye shall not pity him . . . if a man come presumptuously upon his neighbour, to slay him with guile; thou shalt take him from mine altar, that he may die. . . . And he that smiteth his father, or his mother, shall be surely put to death.

His father would have been surprised that Beryl knew the Bible, for he truly was his father's son, more than either father or son had realized.

While Beryl's anger boiled inside of him like lava waiting to erupt from a pressure-filled volcano, he could not satisfy his need for revenge. There was talk that Big Al would take care of it. Whether he did, no one knows. Beryl hoped that the big guy would throw the punks who had killed his father into a river of sharks. That only would have been good enough for Beryl if he had been one of the sharks. What did, in fact, happen only served to make Beryl even angrier and more determined to seek revenge.

After much questioning, threats, and some roughing up of people who might have heard the two murderers talking about the crime, the killers were finally caught. A reward had been posted, and one of the thieves' neighbors wanted the money more than he wanted to see justice done. The thieves were treated roughly by the cops. They were punched and shoved, and tightly handcuffed, the skin on their wrists pinched tight. They were taken to the local police precinct, undergoing an intense interrogation that included the use of blackjacks, punches, and threats until they confessed. The suspects were arraigned, jailed, and scheduled for trial. Beryl, when told of what had transpired, yelled at the cops for not being given the opportunity to address the killers himself. He wanted the pleasure of slowly killing them, watching them suffer as his father had suffered. A friendly neighborhood cop, Officer Murphy, took Beryl aside and assured him that justice would be served. It was out of Beryl's hands. The state would fry them as crisp as chicken in "Old Sparky," the electric chair.

But it was not to be. Because the killers had made oral confessions, their lawyer told them not to sign subsequent written confessions. In court they testified that they had never confessed to holding up the grocery or to shooting anyone. They said they had been beaten and threatened by the cops. The police, however, had an eyewitness, a fragile, frail, frightened old lady from the neighborhood. When asked to identify the killers in a lineup, she hung her head in fear, trembled, and mumbled that she couldn't. She said that if she identified them, she would be killed. She did not want to die. She knew from reading the paper that stool pigeons were killed and that sometimes their tongues were cut from their mouths. She wanted to do the right thing, but what would it get her? A bullet in the mouth?

As Beryl and others begged, urged, scolded, yelled, and fulminated that she had a duty to do the right thing, she wiped tears from her eyes and shook her head. Her breathing was hard and swift, like a cornered animal frightened that it would be killed. She held a hand to her chest as if she was going to have a heart attack. She closed her eyes and used the thumb and forefinger of her right hand to massage her forehead. She said she never should have come and wanted to go home and be left alone. A few months later, she died of a heart attack. Beryl and his siblings thought it was God's will; the poor old lady had been cursed by them, and she paid the price.

With no evidence and no witnesses to testify against them, the killers were set free and never seen or heard from again on Maxwell Street. Officer Murphy thought their luck would run out one day. Maybe sooner rather than later. There were always people who were willing to see that justice was done. Beryl doubted it, but there was nothing he could do.

There was a funeral to plan. There was family to help. For Beryl's mother Sarah, who had attempted to throw herself into Isadore's grave during the funeral service, revenge should be left to God. She yelled out her husband's name as if he could still hear her. She then said the Kaddish and hoped that God would hear her prayer and honor the life that Isadore had lived. The thought of life without Isadore filled her with panic. Who would run the store? She knew nothing about buying and selling groceries. She had been a housewife and mother, not a grocer. Who would pay the bills? Who would discipline the kids? She felt a void. The emptiness was like a black hole that would grow larger until she finally disappeared inside of it. The hole, like a large mouth, would swallow her pain. But for now, she could only endure that pain. Her soul was shattered without her soulmate. Isadore had been her rock, her anchor, her friend, her guide, the interpreter of her universe, her lover, the breadwinner, the moral guide for their children. How could she possibly replace him?

They were an old-world couple with old-world values. Yes, Chicago was their home, but it did not represent the traditional Jewish values they had brought with them from the old country. Like many Orthodox Jewish women, Sarah had relied on Isadore to make many of the decisions that defined how they lived. She could not imagine living without him. His death was too much to bear; it led her to despair. Having sole responsibility for her four children was too much to bear. She felt bent over, crushed. Her deeply religious husband had seeded her with those children. Why wasn't he here to help her? What would happen to them without the guidance of their father? She could not stop crying. She fretted; she yelled at God. She banged her fists on the kitchen table. Her condition was diagnosed as a nervous breakdown. She felt herself sinking like a bag of cement tossed into the ocean. Down and down she went, until she was institutionalized. Beryl's three younger siblings, two brothers and a sister, were scattered, either being sent away to live with a cousin or to an orphanage. Beryl would eventually rescue them, bringing them out of the fetid darkness of their depressing lives and into the fresh air and sunlight of a new, better day.

The flame of anger that had been ignited by the indignities of poverty and anti-Semitism, by feeling like an outsider, had turned Beryl into a highly determined young man. Religion was no longer for him. He gave up attending Hebrew school and never went to synagogue. When his rabbi asked why, Beryl asked what God had done for Isadore, a holy man, a good man gunned down by a pair of lowlife punks who escaped their punishment. Yet, every day, for 11 days, Beryl said the Kaddish, the mourner's prayer for the dead. He did not want his father to turn to dust and be forgotten. Beryl would make enough money to rescue his family. He would find a way to reunite his family. But first he would become even more of a thug.

In school, he was such a troublemaker that he was frequently suspended. In the neighborhood, he was running illegal craps games. He ran a variety of scams and, one day, was invited to join a new gang and participate in a robbery. He thought for days about whether he should. He avoided seeing the gang's leader so that he wouldn't have to decide. On the night of the robbery, he didn't show up, a wordless answer that saved him from a life of serious crime and its consequences. A few days later, the gang leader told Beryl that he had missed out on a great score. There were sharp new clothes, beautiful babes, and smooth booze (not that rot-gut stuff). They had been dancing, cutting loose, and raising hell. Beryl just smiled and nodded. He was not prepared to go so deep into a life of crime. Maybe Big Al had been right that Beryl wasn't really cut out for a life of crime. He also had some of his father's values in him now. Beryl was having second thoughts, and he was right, for the path that the gang would tread for the next few years would not be one of easy riches. Several members were killed, while others were sentenced to long prison terms. Beryl had, indeed, made a wise decision. But he didn't know what his next move should be.

One may have to ponder various alternatives before deciding on a course of action. What was Beryl good at? What could he do to earn money? When he reached the decision to fight, it seemed like the only solution. What else was he going to do? Work as a clerk in a store? Be a shipping clerk on a loading dock? Dig ditches? He decided to fight to earn enough money to buy his mother a house and give her the warmth that comes from feeling safe and secure, and he would ransom his deracinated siblings from their abandonment.

Again, Big Al had been right. Beryl confessed his intentions to his pal Sparky, who offered to do whatever he could to help. Theirs was a friendship as close as that between two siblings born out of the same womb of ghettoized poverty. And now that it was time to venture forth, it was Big Al who launched Beryl's career as Barney Ross, future lightweight, light welterweight, and welterweight champion of the world. He would become one of the greatest fighters of the twentieth century, the heir to Benny Leonard; he didn't yet know it, but he was on his way to becoming an iconic figure who would be applauded for his heroic rise from poverty to become a millionaire, a war hero who would be awarded the Silver Star by President Roosevelt in the Rose Garden at the White House, a drug addict who would become clean and sober in record time and serve as a mentor to kids, an author of a best-selling autobiography, and a hero in a Hollywood movie. Barney Ross would be the proud young man, a son and a brother, who fought for sums small and large so that he could rescue and reunite his family. That was his ambition. And his ambition and drive to succeed would take him to the top of the world of boxing.

4

FISTS OF FURY

From Rosofsky to Ross. From Beryl to Barney. The initials were the same, but he was no BS. He was the real deal. A tough young fighter with lightning-fast fists and a granite chin. He was the first Golden Gloves champion to become a pro—and not just a pro, but a champ. While his name change briefly kept his overprotective mother from identifying her son as a boxer and aided in his assimilation into the world of popular American sports, his fans knew he was a Jew, regardless of what he called himself. And those fans loved him, cheering him on from one fight to another. They marveled at his fast fists and steadfastness in never being knocked out. It was his anger at his father's murder that first fueled those fists of fury; then it became all the rewards: the money, the adulation of the fans, the women who proposed marriage, the good times with his new pals, whether boxers, politicians, or movie stars. He was a sport, and the world loved him.

Because of his association with the Chicago Outfit, he would be their boy. They put their money where their cigars were: on Barney to win. Big Al, the Outfit's CEO, would make sure that Barney's first pro fight would be properly financed. Al arranged to have his minions buy up the tickets for Barney's first pro fight. It would be a full house. And if some of the guys wanted to make a little money on the side scalping tickets, that was okay with the boss. Money in and money out. It was all an investment. And the bookies paid handsomely. There was plenty of backslapping, cigars, champagne, and prostitutes.

That first fight for money was fought against Ramon Lugo on September 1, 1929. Lugo, who had his first professional fight in 1926, was a lightweight. He had fought in 51 bouts, winning 29 and losing 15, while recording 6 draws. After six rounds of skillful boxing, Barney won by a unanimous decision. He went on to win his next 10 fights, suffering his first loss against Carlos Garcia by a decision after 6 rounds. Garcia was an extraordinary boxer: he fought from 1923 to 1949, retiring at age 46, an old man for a boxer. Maintaining a career for 26 years as a prizefighter takes an enormous amount of willpower and perseverance. It also requires a fighter to withstand and absorb a tremendous amount of punishment. Garcia was an indefatigable fighting machine, fighting 10, 15, 19 times in a single year. He was one of Barney's toughest opponents.

Learning from his loss and being an excellent student of both himself and his opponents, Ross won 32 of his next 35 bouts. It was an impressive record, one that captured the attention of eager promoters whose eyes blinked dollar signs. On March 26, 1933, Ross signed a contract for his first shot at a world championship title; he would go toe-to-toe with the world lightweight and junior welterweight champion, Tony Canzoneri, who was a three-time world champion and held a total of five world titles. (Canzoneri and Ross are members of an exclusive group of world champions, fighters who have won titles in three or more divisions.) Canzoneri had become a three-division world champion by knocking out Jackie "Kid" Berg in the third round of their fight in April 1931. Next would be Canzoneri's two fights with Ross.

Those two fights were fought for both the lightweight and welterweight titles. Of their first 10-round encounter, held on June 23, 1933, at Chicago Stadium, the *Chicago Tribune* writes, "The fight was razor-sharp close and was replete with action. . . . No title fight in Chicago was better fought."[1] Ross certainly landed many more blows than his opponent, for his left jab never ceased. It was like a jackhammer. And his defensive maneuvers proved an excellent defense; Canzoneri may have been the harder hitter, especially with his right fist, but Ross was the better strategist and tactician. Ross had mounted a ferocious defense.

It was reported that Canzoneri couldn't believe he had lost his first fight and his lightweight title to Ross. He was a hero in the Italian community of New York, and they were angry, mystified, and frustrated by the decision. Those who were at the fight booed the verdict and felt the judges and referee had been paid by the gamblers to give the decision to

Ross. The referee had scored the fight as a draw, but the two judges, Edward Hintz and William A. Battey, scored the fight in favor of Ross. Canzoneri, until the end of his life, had no doubt that he had won the fight. Ross, the happier of the two, knew he had won. In fact, many fans could see that Ross was confident that he was winning, as he began coasting during the last few rounds.

Ross had fought fiercely and brilliantly during the early rounds, and rather than punching himself out during the final rounds, he simply did enough to ensure his victory. Both combatants had demonstrated excellent skills: Canzoneri was the faster fighter, with punches that seemed attached to hair-trigger reflexes, while Ross was the more classical boxer, using a left jab as a tactical weapon combined with long punches to create a formidable strategy. He was the pugilistic progeny of Benny Leonard, whose style Ross had brilliantly mastered.

Regardless of the opinions of Canzoneri's fans, no one could deny that the men had fought well: Their faces—featuring bruises and welts, as well as puffy, swollen eyes and lips—showed what they had endured. Canzoneri's left cheek was cut, and Ross had a cut over his left eye. It had been a fast-paced bout, as exciting and enthralling as any athletic duel between two superb performers of the manly art. Canzoneri's partisans were surely disappointed by the outcome, but Ross's were overjoyed. And neither group could gainsay that it hadn't been worth every dollar they paid; it would be remembered as a great showdown.

For their second, 15-round encounter, held at the Polo Grounds in New York on September 12, 1933, Ross—as champion—was to be paid $35,000, a huge sum during the Depression. Sitting at ringside was Ross's mother, hoping her son would be declared the winner. And Ross was indeed favored to win, but Canzoneri was determined to take the title from Ross. Canzoneri thought he was the more skillful fighter and that he should have been awarded the win in their previous matchup. Ross was slightly taller than Canzoneri, so his reach was longer, a distinct advantage for a fighter.

Looking at their individual fighting stances, it is surprising how low Canzoneri held his fists, while Ross—more conventionally and protectively—held his up near his face. With his fists down at his midsection, Canzoneri seemed to offer his chin as an open target to Ross, who took full advantage of every opportunity Canzoneri offered. While Ross boxed as classically as his hero Benny Leonard, Canzoneri attempted to turn the fight into a brawl. Many of Canzoneri's punches seemed to be aimed at mauling Ross with powerful left hooks. Ross won most of the early rounds, and it was not until the 12th round that Canzoneri seemed to have had his batteries recharged: He was the energetic aggressor, taking the fight to Ross, whose energy level seemed to be dropping. Canzoneri easily outpointed Ross in the last three rounds of the fight, but it was not enough to make up for his poor performance in the earlier stages. In addition, or by subtraction, Canzoneri had lost several earlier rounds for landing below-the-belt blows. Once again, Ross won by a decision.

That second fight had been no less exciting than the first. Each man had set a fast pace and rapidly traded hard-hitting punches. Canzoneri had wanted to knock out Ross, but Ross was able to duck and sidestep many of his foe's punches. Canzoneri seemed to be boxing with more spontaneous wit and tactical intelligence than he had in the first go-round with Ross. His speed and endurance were a match for Ross. Although his fists were unusually small for a fighter, Canzoneri had a powerful right punch. As Mike Casey writes for the premier boxing website Boxing.com,

> Against Ross, Canzoneri brought to the table all the excellent qualities that made him one of the genuine greats. He possessed outstanding speed of hand and foot, had stamina in abundance and a granite chin. His straight right was an accurate and formidable weapon, and he was a wonderful pressure fighter. He was no less proficient defensively, even though he carried his left hand very low. . . . But Tony thought he was cruising against Barney, and the clown came out to play. Canzoneri began to dance around and stick out his chin invitingly, while Ross paid attention to his boxing and started tagging Tony with solid shots. Canzoneri sensed the danger and got back to serious work as he opened up with two-fisted attacks in the seventh round. In the eighth and ninth rounds, he tried to turn the bout into a slugging match, but Ross kept jabbing and finding Tony's chin with left hooks.

Years later, Canzoneri said, "Sure it was worth it, every drop of blood and every stitch of it. I wouldn't have it any other way."[2]

The title was lost. Ross was still champion, having defeated Canzoneri on points. Even if Canzoneri had refrained from striking low blows in three early rounds, he would not have won those rounds. Ross had proven to the world that he was more than capable of mounting a serious defense against one of the greatest fighters of the 1930s. He had become a two-division world champion when he beat Canzoneri. The following year, *Ring Magazine* named them Fighters of the Year.

In writing and speaking of the two bouts, sportswriters agreed that the fights had been fiercely fought by two evenly matched opponents. Canzoneri had a particularly powerful right fist that, if it had connected with Ross's chin, would have delivered a fight-ending knockout punch. The men were highly regarded as two of the most impressive and imposing pugilists who few others would be able to beat. That opinion would be tested by the famous Ross versus McLarnin trilogy of fights.

Many years later, it was revealed in a book by Mafia scion Bill Bonanno that Tony Canzoneri was a Capo in the Bonanno family. Tony's mother's maiden name was Schiro, and she may have been related to Nicolo Schiro, a Mafia boss. Using the money he earned in the ring, Tony bought a resort hotel in Newburgh, New York, not far from Joe Bonanno's upstate farm. Although he retired from boxing in 1939, it is not known when he joined the Mafia, but he was reported to be a Capo by the 1950s. He operated a restaurant in New York City, lived in a hotel near Broadway, and died at age 51 in 1959. It is unknown whether Ross knew of Canzoneri's mob connections, and perhaps it would have made no difference in the outcome of their fights, for Ross was connected with his own mob, the Outfit in Chicago.

After Canzoneri, the most dangerous opponent Ross fought was hard-hitting Irishman Jimmy McLarnin. McLarnin was born in Hillsborough, County Down, Ireland, into a large family that went to live in Vancouver when Jimmy was three. Like many newsboys of the time, including Abe Attell in San Francisco, McLarnin had to defend himself against other newsboys—and he was good at it. He had fast fists that broke through the wild, unsystematic flurries of his young opponents. In fact, he was so good at fighting that he decided, at age 10, to learn the sport of boxing. By the time the youngster was 13, his pugilistic talents had been recognized by a former boxer named Charles "Pop" Foster. Pop put together what passed for a gym and proceeded to train his young protégé. He was convinced that he could produce a champion. The two men developed a father–son relationship, as well as a profound friendship based on trust, admiration, and respect for one another's talents. Their relationship endured until Pop's death.

When Pop thought that McLarnin was ready to turn pro, he took him to San Francisco, where boxing officials said he was too young to enter the ring and fight older pros. McLarnin then lied about his age and got a match. He was now the "Baby-faced Assassin." The young fighter was small and slight, although heavily muscled, and could deliver stinging blows with both fists, especially his right one. And it was that right fist that would eventually cause prospective opponents to sweat with anxiety, if not fear, in their dressing rooms just before a fight. That right hand became a crowd pleaser. It was not unusual to hear fans shout, "Hit him with your right! Finish him off! Give him the right! To the chin, to the chin!" It was as if McLarnin's right fist was a lethal weapon that he brought into the ring, and to many fans it was a knockout rocket.

That right fist was celebrated by not only fans, but also sportswriters, who never failed to write about it when describing a McLarnin fight. Those who suffered from that powerful right felt they had been hit with a sledgehammer. McLarnin's reputation, from his debut in 1928, was built on that powerful right hand, which knocked opponents out as soon as they showed weakness. Many fighters dreaded getting into the ring with McLarnin. In the first round of his debut fight, he knocked out Sid Terris, a top-ranked lightweight. McLarnin went on to beat a gaggle of impressive fighters: In addition to Terris, he knocked out Ruby Goldstein in two rounds and Al Singer in three. McLarnin could hit harder and aim more accurately with his right than any other fighter. Jackie Fields, who had been a formidable opponent of many top boxers, with a record of 82 wins and 9 loses, was no match for McLarnin. In their bout, McLarnin broke Fields's jaw after knocking him down five times, and when Fields could no longer see straight, his corner threw in the towel.

McLarnin was not only known as the "Baby-faced Assassin," but also, more disturbingly, the "Hebrew Scourge" and the "Jew Killer." Those epithets were appended to him following his wins over a series of Jewish opponents that included Louis "Kid" Kaplan (a former featherweight titleholder), Sid Terris, Sergeant Sammy Baker, Al Singer (a former lightweight champion), Joe Glick, Jackie Fields, and Ruby Goldstein. When it came to his fight with Barney Ross, ethnic and religious rivalries were at a boil. Promoters and sportswriters further turned up the heat. It was good for the gate; get ethnic fans riled up and they would turn out in droves to shout for their man. While McLarnin was not an anti-Semite and later said he was not happy about the anti-Semitic epithets that hung like stinking, rotten fish around his reputation, he did nothing to put an end to what was a volatile subject, especially in the 1930s, during the rise of

Nazism and vicious anti-Semitic speeches by public figures in the United States.

In addition to having defeated those seven Jewish fighters, McLarnin had ended, by a sixth-round knockout, the once-illustrious career of legendary Jewish champion Benny Leonard, who, in 1932, seven years after his retirement, was slow of foot and fist, paunchy, and obviously well past his prime; when Benny entered the ring, fans could not believe their eyes. The pride of the ghetto looked less like a lethal avenger and more like a world-weary accountant who had wandered into the wrong environment. A bow tie, a white shirt, and baggy slacks would have been more appropriate attire than boxing trunks. Leonard had signed to fight McLarnin for the money, for he had been financially wiped out when the stock market crashed. Secondarily, he wanted to avenge the humiliating defeats suffered by fallen Jewish fighters. But Leonard had deluded himself into thinking he was the man to do it. Too many heroes live on the memories of their golden exploits. It would be Ross who would be the symbolic Jewish avenger, replacing a hero of bygone days. While fans judged the bout between McLarnin and Leonard in terms of ethnic and religious rivalry, McLarnin was saddened by his defeat of Leonard, who had been not only a hero to Jews, but also a fighter admired by everyone for his skills and gentlemanly demeanor.

McLarnin and Ross were evenly matched contenders. They were fine athletic specimens. They had flat, strong stomachs; muscled arms; and strong, flexible legs. They had the hearts of young lions. They trained to the highest level of pugilistic proficiency. Any additional training would have been superfluous. They were scheduled to fight on May 28, 1934, at the Madison Square Garden Bowl in Long Island City, Queens, New York. Going into the fight, each fighter had an impressive record, although Ross's was slightly better: McLarnin had 51wins, 8 losses, and 3 draws; Ross had 52 wins, 2 losses, and 3 draws.

The fight was scheduled for 15 rounds, and many fans, sportswriters, and money men thought that McLarnin's powerful right fist was the surefire weapon for driving Ross to the canvas before the end of the first round. Sixty thousand fans, mostly Jewish and Irish immigrants and children of immigrants, bought tickets to attend the fight. That so many people, impoverished by the Great Depression, would pay to attend the event was evidence of the intensity of the ethnic and religious rivalry that existed at that time. The fight was more than an athletic event; it was a symbolic test of political import. It was also an opportunity to escape, if only briefly, from the destitution and deprivation of the Depression and shout for one's hero, to identify with a gladiator who was untouched by the darkness of poverty and prejudice, and the claustrophobia imposed by the contemplation of a dreary future. For those fans, it was worth the little bit of money they had, for they got to witness one of the great boxing bouts of the decade, a fight they could recount to their grandchildren.

While men of meager means sat far away from the ring, ringside seats had been reserved for the wealthy and some of the year's most popular celebrities. Seated there were the Marx brothers, Jack Dempsey, Mayor Fiorello LaGuardia, Benny Leonard, Gene Tunney, and some mob figures and their girlfriends. Seated nearby was Father Charles Coughlin, who would go on to become a vicious anti-Semite who spouted hate-filled commentary on his popular radio program.

Ross weighed 10 pounds less than McLarnin, but he made up for it with faster movements and smarter tactics. McLarnin repeatedly shot his powerfully devastating right fist at Ross's chin, but Ross deftly avoided the blows. Had any of them connected with the button of his chin, Ross would have sunk into a pool of unconsciousness. In the ninth round, McLarnin came close, landing a stunning off-center left hook that sent Ross to the canvas, but Ross sprang back up like a jackrabbit, and the referee didn't even have time to start his count. In that compressed moment, fans for one side cheered and then the fans for the other side cheered. It was repeated again, only in reverse, when Ross sent McLarnin to the canvas and he too sprang up before the referee could begin his count. Neither Ross nor McLarnin wanted to show any weakness. They didn't want to hear the referee shouting out numbers that announced the impending end of time. It would be the only time that Ross would be knocked down.

The two fighters engaged in a flurry of rapid-fire blows, throwing lefts and rights. Each was pummeling the other. It was attack, counterattack. Ross was the more scientific boxer, while McLarnin threw big, crowd-pleasing punches. Throughout the rounds, the attacks and counterattacks continued with undiminished energy. Ross and McLarnin were in such good shape that neither man seemed to tire. At the final bell, the fighters broke apart and retreated to their corners. After a decision was announced, Ross invariably put his arm around his opponent, for his bouts had been a test of skill between two highly trained and proficient athletes.

While the fans may have been shouting for blood, the boxers were of a different breed.

The ring announcer, in his flat New York accent, told the crowd that the judges had split the decision (one judge awarded McLarnin nine rounds, while a second judge awarded Ross 11 rounds), and the referee (who had scored it 13 rounds for Ross) had made Ross the new welterweight champion. McLarnin's fans either were silently glum or booed the announcement; Ross's fans cheered, whistled, and hooted with approval. A Jew had finally avenged the multiple losses suffered by his tribe. Ross was also the first boxer to simultaneously retain the welterweight and junior welterweight titles.

Upon his return to Chicago, Ross was given a hero's welcome. Thirty thousand fans greeted him when he disembarked at Union Station; a forty-piece band played "Chicago, Chicago." He was cheered as he rode in an open limousine through the Loop and escorted by a hundred policemen on motorcycles. He was saluted at City Hall by the governor and the mayor. When it came time to speak, Ross said,

> I just won the welterweight championship from an Irishman with the good name of McLarnin. I was escorted from the station here by a hundred policemen with Ireland written all over their faces. Now I am receiving cheering words from the mayor, blessed with the grand name of Kelly. The Irish are the greatest of sportsmen. I'm almost ashamed that I licked one![3]

Wherever Ross went in Chicago, he was wined and dined. His photo was splashed throughout the local newspapers and appeared in store windows in his old neighborhood, the Maxwell Street ghetto. Unbeknownst to his fans, he was now devoted to gambling and had lost a large amount of his winnings betting on horses that could not win championship titles.

Ross and McLarnin signed for a return bout, to be held on September 17, 1934. It drew the same enthusiastic crowd as the first fight. In fact, shortly after the two fighters signed, fans rushed to buy tickets, McLarnin's fans hoping that their man would whip the new champ and Ross's supporters looking for a repeat performance. The political climate for Jews had worsened. Jews throughout the world were apprehensive about the growth of anti-Semitism. In some quarters, it was rampant. *Der Stürmer* published a crazed article alleging that Jews were killing Christian children and using their blood to make Passover matzohs. In New

York City, which had the largest Jewish population in the country, more than 20,000 Nazi supporters held a raucous rally in Madison Square Garden. Many of them carried and waved Nazi banners and flags as they goose-stepped up and down the aisles of the Garden. They repeatedly raised their arms in the Nazi salute, and shouts of "Sieg Heil!" echoed off the rafters.

Eleven days later, the "Hero of the Ghetto" and the "Fighting Irishman," with an image of a golden harp sewn onto his robe and a bright, bold shamrock on his trunks, stepped into the ring for a suspense-filled rematch. In the world of boxing, there was something known as the "welterweight jinx": Twelve consecutive welterweight champions had been dethroned when defending their titles. And that included McLarnin. Would he be able to regain the throne? Would Ross prove to be the exception and keep the title? And which group of fans would be cheering the outcome? The odds kept changing, but Ross was favored to win.

Ross entered the ring in his usual striped robe, which had become somewhat tattered around the edges. It looked like an old household robe that one might wear on a Sunday morning while reading the newspaper. The referee made his standard introduction and gave the boilerplate instructions, and the fighters went to their respective corners.

The onset of the fight offered no clues. The fighters were again in superb shape, keyed up for another title bout. Both men started off vigorously, each aware of the other's strengths and weakness. As usual, McLarnin seemed loose limbed, holding his guard low. Ross, in contrast, held his guard high, seeming tightly strung and compact. Flurries of hard-hitting punches kept fans on their feet. McLarnin threw many left jabs. And Ross used his right more frequently than in the first fight. McLarnin's left hook was powerful, and when it connected with Ross's chin or head, it momentarily stunned him, although Ross would quickly recover and issue a powerful, long right. The fighters often wound up in clinches and then exchanged volleys of rapid-fire punches after being separated.

The fight was proving to be as brutal and intense as the first one. McLarnin seemed to be in much better physical shape than during the first go-round. He was not at all tentative and was often the aggressor. He had a neat, oft-repeated trick of lowering his left shoulder and feinting a punch to draw his target in for a fierce blow. It didn't always work, however, for Ross was adept at deciphering McLarnin's tactics and rarely fell victim to them. Nevertheless, it was apparent to everyone, including

Ross, that McLarnin was piling up points in the first four rounds. He lost the fifth round due to a low blow. There were several of those, but oftentimes the referee didn't see them.

McLarnin, who had the face of a choir boy and the mind of an assassin, seemed well on the way to taking the title. But then a cut opened over his left eye, and his cutman had to use his skills and magic to stop the bleeding. Coming out of his corner, he repeatedly threw his devastating left hook. And though Ross's face was badly bruised, he kept coming at McLarnin with the determination of a bull. The fighters were often going at one another, toe-to-toe, head-to-head. Ross knew he had to make up for the rounds he had lost, and he battled fiercely during rounds 10 and 11, both of which he won.

It went on round after round. Each fighter was relentless in his drive to win. By round 12, McLarnin's left eye was red, swollen, and closed. Ross aimed his punches at that eye, as well as at McLarnin's other eye. Yet, McLarnin not only withstood those, but also released his own flurry of punches. In round 15, the final round, Ross bashed McLarnin with a hard right. McLarnin tripped, but some fans thought he had suffered a knockdown. McLarnin quickly righted himself, and the two fighters went at one another with every ounce of strength and determination they could muster.

The final bell sounded, and the 25,000 fans applauded a tense, fast-paced fight: It was just what they had paid to see. McLarnin regained the title. The judges split their decisions, one for Ross and one for McLarnin, and the referee decided in McLarnin's favor. By the end of the fight, McLarnin's face looked more battered than Ross's. Both fighters were bruised and sporting the occasional welt; their torsos were covered in red blotches from the powerful body blows they had exchanged. McLarnin's left eye was severely swollen, black and blue, and closed, needing a few stitches. He certainly looked worse than Ross, but he had been determined and put up an impressively relentless fight against the man he would fight yet again. Twenty-two of 29 sports reporters thought that Ross had won. Some were speculating that one of the judges and the referee, both Irish, did not want to see McLarnin suffer another defeat. Ethnic rivalry was alive and fierce.

A rematch, or rubber match, was a promoter's dream. It would take place one year later, on the anniversary of their first encounter. It would be a big-money match to determine the more skillful fighter. Fans could hardly wait. It was slated to take place on May 28, 1935, at the Polo Grounds, the home field of the New York Giants baseball team before they migrated to San Francisco. Again, tens of thousands of New Yorkers lined up to buy tickets to the third fight in the most exciting boxing trilogy of the 1930s. To add even more excitement to the event, former heavyweight champ Jack Dempsey would be the referee. Ross's managers were worried that their man had been robbed of a decision in the previous fight, so they insisted that one of the judges be a Jew. Abe Goldberg was chosen, with no objections.

The night was unseasonably hot and humid, and the weather would take a toll on the fighters. Fighting for 15 rounds at full speed is exhausting enough; doing it in debilitating heat and drenching humidity can easily cause a fighter to fade into slow motion or faint. It had happened before and would happen again years later during a heavyweight bout at Yankee Stadium.

Ross and McLarnin would have to fight through their heat-induced exhaustion and draw from their reservoirs to maintain stamina, grit, and speed, which would determine the winner. The winner would be the welterweight titleholder: McLarnin wanted desperately to beat the jinx and keep the title, and Ross wanted it as much for himself and he did for his family, in attendance that night. He also wanted it for the Jewish community, which had turned out in large numbers once more to cheer him on. They needed a symbolic answer to the stereotype being tossed about by anti-Semites that Jews were pale-faced cowards.

For this match, Ross came in at 137 pounds and McLarnin at 142. Ross was 5-foot-7, and McLarnin was 5-foot-5. The slight advantage that Ross had in height, he lost in weight. The differences were so small, however, that sportswriters and promoters thought the two fighters to be evenly matched. Ross had fought 77 fights and McLarnin 74. The two men had trained rigorously and were in excellent shape—lean, hard, energetic, and raring to go.

And so the two men, who would grow to become friends, came out of their corners for the first round much as they had in their two previous contests. It was just the kind of gladiatorial combat fans had come to see, and they wouldn't be disappointed. Ross and McLarnin fought with an intensity that revealed their determination to win. Early in the fight, McLarnin landed his powerful left hook on Ross's jaw, which seemed as hard and impervious as stone. Ross shook his head and continued punching, drawing on ever-present resources of energy. In the sixth round, Ross, jabbing with his left fist, broke his thumb and was in excruciating pain. He winced, but that was about all he could do. He would have to maintain that flitting jab, for without it the fight would surely be McLarnin's to win. He threw a hard left into McLarnin's gut and briefly doubled him over. The pain, which briefly staggered both fighters, must have been intense, but neither of them gave into it. Their endurance seemed limitless. They were indefatigable.

The 12th round was the most dramatic of the fight. Ross feverishly outpunched McLarnin, hitting him repeatedly with rapid jabs and hooks. The crowd cheered, calling out for their man to punch this way, that way, to sock him in the jaw, to get him, to flatten him. They must have yelled themselves hoarse. The fighters looked like they were running on high-octane adrenalin. Their bodies gleamed with sweat. Their torsos were reddened from body blows. Their faces were masks of bruises and welts. Their eyes were swollen; their lips were cut. In the 15th round, it was apparent that Ross had outpointed McLarnin. He knew it was going his way, and he wouldn't stop until that final bell sounded. Just to make sure, Ross landed two powerful right punches that nearly knocked McLarnin off his feet.

The judges and referee conferred, wrote their decisions, and unanimously gave Ross back his title. Jack Dempsey, the referee, awarded Ross five rounds and McLarnin three rounds, and he declared that seven rounds had been even. Judge Abe Goldberg awarded Ross eight rounds and McLarnin six rounds, declaring only one as even. George LeCron, the third judge, awarded Ross nine rounds and McLarnin four rounds, and he declared that two were even.

It should be noted at this point that Pop Foster decried the choice of officials before the fight. He said that Goldberg was obviously a Hebrew and that Jack Dempsey had admitted to having Semitic blood. And to the amused derision of the press, Pop said that LeCron was hiding his Jewish identity under a phony name. He added that Ross, a Jewish fighter, was fighting in front of a crowd of Jewish fans in the city with the largest Jewish population in the country; there was obviously pressure for Ross to win. He further claimed that McLarnin was viewed as a foreigner from Vancouver, an outlier, as someone to be rejected by the big-city boys. Foster yelled himself hoarse arguing that his fighter had been robbed.

"Robbed I say!" He insisted that McLarnin had won nine rounds and should have been declared the winner.

The sportswriters agreed that Ross had won the fight. Damon Runyon, perhaps the most famous of the writers covering the fight, thought there was no doubt that Ross had dominated McLarnin and won the bout. Foster, however, claimed that Dempsey had wanted Ross to win well before the fight. He supposedly made it known to his entourage. Foster's accusation of bias outraged Dempsey, who complained to the press that he had been friends with Foster and McLarnin, and would not permit his judgment to be affected by his friendship with either fighter.

The brouhaha grew, like an ever-increasing windstorm, to such an intensity that Foster was required to state his accusations and evidence before the New York State Athletic Commission. Foster claimed that Dempsey's friend, Abe Lyman, had bet $10,000 on Ross to win; he was supposedly overheard making the comment in Dempsey's own restaurant. He further claimed that many of Lyman and Dempsey's friends also put money down on Ross. Lyman was outraged at the charge, and he told Foster that he would bet $10,000 on Ross to beat McLarnin for a fourth match. He would even let Foster be the ring referee. Foster sneered at the suggestion and did not back down from his accusations. Lyman, believing that his reputation had been sullied, brought a legal action for defamation and libel. He sued Foster, asking for $500,000 in compensatory damages. The case was settled out of court for an undisclosed amount.

None of this mattered to Ross's fans, for they had cheered as if a vital victory over bigotry, parochialism, and stereotypes had been won by Ross's bloody courage and relentless aggression. Robert Sussman, the author's father and a fight fan who attended the fight, said that it seemed as if the fans were not only cheering for Ross, but also for themselves:

> They had lived vicariously through Barney's stamina, skill, and determination to win. He was as determined to win as a bulldog; he wouldn't let go of the opportunity to be the champ, and we applauded his willingness to risk the poundings on his brain to become champion. There were few in the crowd who would have gone to the lengths that Barney did to win the title over a fellow who many had perceived as an anti-Semite. Though a lot of people in the boxing world thought that McLarnin was not anti-Semitic; they thought the promoters had ginned that up to increase attendance. And you know? It worked! I was a great fight, an exciting fight. And I later learned from one of the columnists

that Ross was the first fighter to win back a title twice on the same date.

In his dressing room after the fight, McLarnin agreed with Foster's assessment that he had won nine of the 15 rounds. He seemed genuinely stunned that he had not been awarded the win; however, there was nothing he could do about it. He earned a lot of money from the fight, and that was the motivation for him to step into the ring. Fighting was a tough game, one that exposed fighters to the dangers of death and dementia. McLarnin was getting ready to hang up his gloves. Thanks to Pop Foster he had made and saved a substantial amount of money, unlike many other fighters, who spent their winnings almost as quickly as they earned them.

Years later, McLarnin, speaking about entering professional boxing, commented,

> I started to make money: When I was 19, I had $100,000 in the bank—so all of a sudden I realized boxing is for me, and I put my entire mind into it. There was no romance in it. It was a tough, tough ordeal, but as the years went by and I got to know boxing, it wasn't as hard as I thought it would be, although it isn't the easiest game in the world. I'm glad I was a boxer.[4]

McLarnin said he was particularly unhappy that he had been labeled the "Jew Killer" and the "Hebrew Scourge." Although he always insisted that he should have been declared the winner of that third fight, he and Ross went on to become friends, exchanging Christmas and birthday cards each year until Ross's death in 1967. The 1930s were a bad time for Jews, and fight promoters took every opportunity to set up rivalries to garner publicity from the latent and overt prejudices of fight fans. The flames of prejudice would not be turned to embers until the outbreak of World War II and the subsequent revelations of the Nazi Holocaust.

McLarnin retired in November 1936, having won his last two fights against tough opponents, Tony Canzoneri and Lou Ambers. His final record stood at 54 wins, 11 losses, and 3 draws. The editors of *Ring Magazine*, a premier boxing publication, declared McLarnin the fifth-greatest welterweight of all time. He retired to Glendale, California, where he bought a large house and where he and his wife raised their three daughters and one son. McLarnin joined the prestigious Lakeside Club and became a popular golfing partner of such Hollywood stars as

Bing Crosby, Bob Hope, Fred Astaire, and Humphrey Bogart, among others. One day Bogart, affectionately known as "Bogie," said that he didn't believe anyone could be knocked unconscious with a hard blow to the stomach. McLarnin assured him it could be done; Bogie bet $500 that he couldn't be nicked out with such a blow and offered up his gut as a target. McLarnin, with one quick and solid punch, knocked Bogie onto the fairway, where he lay comatose for several seconds. He arose with a sharp pain in his stomach, rubbing it as he looked at McLarnin with reluctant admiration. That blow did not sever their bonds of friendship, however; Crosby remained McLarnin's chief celebrity golfing partner, with the sense to never challenge McLarnin to a demonstration of his pugilistic abilities.

While many boxers had their money stolen by unscrupulous managers and promoters, McLarnin was shrewd with the money he had won: It was sagaciously invested by his manager, Pop Foster, allowing the former champ to retire to a life of wealth and leisure. In his book *Baby Face Goes to Hollywood*, Andrew Gallimore quotes McLarnin saying,

> But there's only two reasons why a man should fight, Pop said. One's because he likes it, and you stopped liking it a long time ago. The other's for money, and you know you don't need money. . . . Boxing's a very hazardous business, and I'd always felt that anybody that goes into it for fun has got to be out of their cotton pickin' mind.[5]

Then, like many other boxers, active as well as retired, McLarnin heard the siren call of Hollywood and was cast in several movies. In 1937, he appeared in a MGM film called *Big City*, starring Spencer Tracy. It is considered a less-than-stellar movie, a typical 1930's melodrama, about rival taxi drivers. In addition to McLarnin, other members of the boxing fraternity who appear in the movie are Slapsie Maxie Rosenbloom (who would later partner in movies with Max Baer), Jack Dempsey, Jackie Fields, and Jim Jeffries. The following year, McLarnin had a small background role in another MGM film called *The Crowd Roars*, starring Robert Taylor, a movie also populated by famous boxers the likes of Abe "The Newsboy" Hollandersky, Joe Glick, Maxie Rosenbloom, Jack Roper, and Tommy Herman, among others.

McLarnin had one final part in a movie in 1946, when he, along with Joe Louis, Henry Armstrong, Ceferino Garcia, and Manuel Ortiz, appeared in *Joe Palooka, Champ*, a film about a young boxer and his girlfriend doing all they can to resist the influence and entreaties of gangsters who want to corrupt young Joe while he trains for a championship bout. While McLarnin enjoyed appearing in movies, he did not feel well suited for them since his thespian abilities were somewhat subpar; he much preferred the golf links to the silver screen.

Although a good golfer and a once great boxer, he was no one's idea of a sagacious businessman. He was led astray by several greedy acquaintances who had gotten him to invest in businesses that turned out to be surefire losers. Each one went belly-up. McLarnin lost some of his much-valued and painfully accumulated savings, realizing too late that the offers to invest, while sounding reasonable at the time, were too good to be true. Yet, like many intuitively smart people, he learned from his mistakes and rebuffed many future offerings to invest in what he considered speculative enterprises. To recoup some of his losses, McLarnin joined a hotshot Beverly Hills travel agency, where he booked trips for his Hollywood pals, especially Bing Crosby, who gave most of his travel business to his golfing buddy.

The financial event, however, that returned McLarnin to his previous prosperity was the death in 1956 of his longtime manager, mentor, and friend Pop Foster. Foster had bequeathed to McLarnin $200,000, a considerable sum in the mid-1950s. McLarnin bought an electrical appliance store that provided a steady stream of revenue and continued to have sufficient free time to golf regularly with his celebrity friends.

Ross's life followed a different path. He would go on to have more fights, but none as devastating as his defeat by the windmill-spinning gloves of the amazing Henry Armstrong, one of the greatest fighters of the twentieth century (and a role model for the inimitable Sugar Ray Robinson) who held three championship titles simultaneously. The fight with Armstrong took place on May 31, 1938, at the Madison Square Garden Bowl in Long Island City in front of 35,000 fans. It occurred three years after Ross had taken the title from McLarnin. Ross may have been overconfident. He was two inches taller and almost 10 pounds heavier than Armstrong, and his reach was slightly longer than his opponent's. Having held the title for three years, Ross may have felt it was his to keep. Complacency is not unknown to those who have grown accustomed to wearing a crown. Ross should have considered his options and studied Armstrong more closely. After all, Armstrong was known as

"Hurricane Henry" and "Homicide Hank"; such sobriquets were bestowed on him for a reason.

In the early rounds, Ross put up a formidable defense and periodically offered an impressive flurry of punches. He seemed his old talented self during the first three rounds. His jabs were right on target; he was fast on his feet. Then it all ceased, as if a spigot of adrenaline had been turned off. Ross was no longer the young tiger who could take apart opponent after opponent. Nothing he did seemed to deter Armstrong. He was an aggressive force of nature who would not quit. How does one stop a hurricane? By the ninth round, Ross seemed nearly helpless. He was taking a terrible beating.

When Ross's managers wanted to throw in the towel, he told them he would throw it right back at them. He said that he would never talk to them again if they submitted. He was furious that they would even consider it. He was no quitter. He felt he owed it to his fans to stay in the fight. He took punch after punch and refused, through sheer willpower it seemed, to fall down. His face was a bloody mess. By the 13th round, Ross's position had only worsened. Yet, he would not give up. He attempted to hold off Armstrong with his normally effective left jabs. Armstrong reacted as if Ross's left jabs were nothing more than the flicks of a flyswatter. Barney's combinations proved completely ineffective. When the referee said he would stop the fight, Barney refused to let him do so. He promised the referee that he would quit fighting, if only the referee would let him finish this one fight. It would be his last fight. Ross was up against the ropes, absorbing one punch after another, his face a bloody mass of raw beef, but he refused to go down—if he was going to lose, he wanted to do it standing on his feet.

In the final round, the 15th, Ross gained the admiration of the entire crowd because of his sheer courage, his determination to remain on his feet. Never fall down. He lived by the maxim that a Jew never quits; he fights to the end, win or lose. His lip was split, a tooth had been knocked out, his eyes were swollen and puffy, and his face was soaked with blood. Still standing, Ross—as was his custom—went over to Armstrong and gave him a hug after the final bell sounded. He always respected the courage and skills of his opponents. For him, the fights were never personal. There were no revenge matches, no vendettas. The crowd admired Ross. How many men could withstand such a beating and refuse to quit? As he left the ring, Ross was met with total silence, the silence of fans who stood in amazement and admiration for a heroic figure who refused to surrender.

In his autobiography, Ross writes about leaving the ring following this brutal beating, relating,

> I kept walking. Funny, I thought. I don't hear any shouting. I don't even hear talking. How come they're not raising the roof for the hero of the night, the new champ? I saw faces and they were all looking at me, not up at the ring, and in the whole arena, 35,000 people were sitting in silence. And then I suddenly realized that this unbelievable, fantastic silence was the most wonderful tribute I had ever received. It spoke louder than all the cheers I had heard since the day . . . I won my first fight.[6]

The promoter, Mike Jacobs, offered Ross $50,000 to fight Tony Canzoneri again. He thought the fans would love it. He told Ross that he was still a great fighter and the fans would happily pay to see him in the ring again. Ross turned him down. He turned down offers to fight second-raters in states throughout the country. He had promised his mother that if he ever got badly beaten, he would quit the world of boxing. She didn't want him to suffer brain damage. In addition, his two managers, Art "Pi" Pian and Winch, said they never wanted to see him so badly hurt again. It wasn't worth the money they all could have made. "Don't do it," they advised.

Ross reflected, years later, that he was glad he hadn't wound up like so many other former champs, for instance, Joe Louis, Henry Armstrong, Benny Leonard, and Jack Dempsey, each of whom fought well past his prime and suffered humiliations simply because they did not know when to call it quits. When his pal, undefeated heavyweight champ Rocky Marciano, asked Ross whether he should continue to fight, Ross advised him to give it up, advice Rocky took to heart and so retired as heavyweight champion. Ross, although also retired from boxing, would have other battles to wage, all of which would require an extraordinary amount of courage and determination.

5

HERO AND DRUG ADDICT

Barney Ross spent a lot of time lounging in his own dark and smoky cocktail lounge, with popular music playing from the jukebox. The bar was always filled with men and women sipping drinks, smoking cigarettes, and laughing congenially. Every so often they would cease chatting and pause mid-laugh and turn their heads as Chicago celebrities dropped by to shoot the breeze and have a few drinks with the former champ. Guys from the Outfit made it one of their hangouts. They were always the best-dressed men in the joint. Al Capone's brothers frequently came by for a drink or two. No one would dare stare at them, but they would stretch their ears to try and pick up gossip. They might hear Big Al say to Barney, "You need anything, just let me know." Ross would say he was fine, didn't need anything, but if he did, he would let the big man know. Politicians ranging from the aldermen to the mayor would stop by. Barney Ross was beloved, a fun guy, a charmer, the toast of the town. His company meant a convivial night, a night of jokes, laughter, and booze. He had hung up his gloves, but for Chicago sports fans, a fraternity of pols, hoods, and journalists, Ross was still the champ. Life for the former champ was easy, profitable, and pleasant—light-years away from the hardships of Maxwell Street.

Ross was also light-years away from his marriage. He had long ago stopped loving his wife, Pearl. She was a nice woman, but she inspired neither ardent love nor powerful lust in him. His marriage to her would soon end, and he would feel relieved. For him, divorce was something that just happens. He was ready to move on, but he wasn't on a hunt for a new woman. If he met a beautiful, sexy, fun-loving, and intelligent woman, he would welcome her into his life, if, of course, she agreed. But he had yet to meet a woman who could occupy his attention, who he could dream about at night. He didn't know that he was fated to meet such a woman, one who would satisfy his needs and to whom he could be devoted. And that woman, who was just across town, wasn't on the lookout for a new lover. Cathy Howlett, beautiful, svelte, athletic, and smart, was an independent woman with a satisfying career as a dancer. She liked men and enjoyed the pleasure of their company, but she wasn't ready to marry.

One night, having grown bored with the quotidian routines of his cocktail lounge, Ross went to see a show called *Boys and Girls Together*, starring incomparable comedic actor Ed Wynn. Ross was enraptured. And there, in his field of vision, was a woman to whom he immediately felt drawn. He focused on her like a guided missile. He looked at no other performers. He wanted to meet her, to speak with her, to learn if she might be the kind of woman that he desired. Following the final curtain and encores of applause, Ross quickly left his seat and made his way backstage, ostensibly to congratulate Wynn on his delightful performance. But Ross was distracted. He kept looking for the dancer who had captured his imagination. And there she was in his peripheral vision: a beautiful, long-legged dancer striding elegantly and confidently across the room. He slowly turned his head, like a turret on ball bearings, his eyes drawing a bead on her torso.

To Ross, she was a poised thoroughbred, femininity at its best—rarely, if ever, seen on Maxwell Street, and never in the boxing gyms and training camps that were his fetid fitness factories. She was tall and slim with just right amount of curve and muscle in her legs—she excited him. She had a beautiful, chiseled face on a swan-like neck with large, cool but friendly eyes. His own eyes lingered over her and continued to follow her. When she was no longer in sight, he turned to Wynn, who had been standing there with a slightly baffled smile, and asked, "Who's that beautiful woman?" Before Wynn could respond, Ross asked him to introduce him to her.

It was strange that such a bold, aggressive man needed a formal introduction and that he hadn't simply approached her and introduced himself. Wynn, now with an avuncular smile, unlike a referee introducing two opposing fighters, acted the matchmaker. "This is Cathy Howlett, the sweetheart of our show. Watch out for this guy, Cathy. He used to be a tough hombre with his fists—though personally, I think I could have licked him with my pinkie."[1] The introduction did more than open Cathy's dressing room door to Ross, it began a new chapter in their lives.

Ross was smitten, and Cathy was pleased and flattered to have his attention. An intense courtship followed. Ross could not get her out of his mind. He dreamt of her at night and couldn't wait to see her during the day. Bearing flowers, perfume, or a dinner invitation—or all three—he showed up in Cathy's dressing room every night thereafter for 16 weeks, the full run of the show. He fell in love fast and hard, and knew this was the woman he would marry. Cathy may not have fallen as quickly, but when she did her love for him was just as intense. Theirs was a marriage made in heaven, although not a Jewish heaven, as Ross would soon learn.

Ross had to overcome one obstacle before he could marry the woman of his dreams. Mama Ross was a force to be reckoned with, as unmovable as an iceberg. In Mama's eyes, Cathy was not Jewish. She may have been her boy's shiksa fantasy, but in reality she wasn't kosher. Mama Ross had lived her life among Jews in a Jewish ghetto. It was a tight-knit and insular world, where Jews did not marry gentiles, did not marry goyish women, no matter how exotic and beautiful the shiksa. Ross knew his mother would be upset, but he was determined to marry Cathy. He would be as steadfast as he imagined her being immovable.

When he told her of his plans to marry a non-Jewish woman, Mama Ross's mouth fell open, her brow furrowed, and her eyes welled with tears. She asked how he could betray his heritage. What would his dear old father, now in heaven, think? Ross assured his mother that he would not betray his heritage, would not do anything to tarnish the memory of his father. "Mama, I'm a Jew and always will be. There's nothing to worry about," he said. He also told her that regardless of what anyone thought or said, he was going to marry Cathy. "I can't tell you how much I love her Ma . . . I'll never love anyone else. Ma, I can't live without her," Ross declared. He stared at his mother beseechingly, and her expression began to soften. What had been a hard, hurt look was now a thoughtful, pensive expression. The iceberg was melting. He could see that. After a few moments, the look on her face became one of maternal warmth; she brightened, smiled, and told him that if that's where his happiness lay, he had her blessing. "Then marry her Beryl," she said, "I want you to live, not die."[2]

The future now looked sweet. Ross was going to marry Cathy and be a father to Cathy's daughter, Noreen. Business at the cocktail lounge was running smoothly and producing a nice income. It was frequently noted in the gossip columns and had a steady traffic of regular customers. Ross would no longer have to endure the brutality of the boxing ring. His defeat by Henry Armstrong had been the defining conclusion to an otherwise heroic and illustrious career. It could have been the perfect retirement. But then came Pearl Harbor—the bombs being dropped, the ships catching fire and sinking, the sailors being blown apart or drowning. It infuriated Ross. The United States had been good to him. He loved the country and had a deep sense of gratitude. He wanted to pick up a weapon and defend his country, the country that had provided him with an opportunity to soar out of poverty, rescue his family, become the champ, and make millions of dollars.

Ross decided to enlist in the U.S. Marines. He chose it because it had a reputation as the toughest of the military services. A tough outfit for a tough guy. Its men were celebrated in history and legend. Ross wanted to be one of them. When he told friends and associates that he would enlist and take the fight to the Japanese, they tried to talk him out of it, telling him he was too old to enlist. Ross wasn't deterred. When some local politicos and Outfit guys told him they could get him a commission, a soft berth stateside, Ross said no. He didn't want some cushy assignment that kept him away from the fighting; he didn't want special treatment. He wanted to enlist like an ordinary patriot. Yes, he was a celebrity, a former champ; his name was known by millions, but as an American he was just like every other citizen who was outraged by a sneak attack on his country.

Still, he was no kid just out of high school, itching to get into the fight. He was 32 years old, a guy who knew he wasn't immortal, a guy who had seen and heard about boxers being killed in the ring. He could easily imagine the dangers of war. He was not some romantic kid who pictured himself festooned in ribbons and glory, being hailed as a hero. Ross was willing to put his life on the line. It didn't matter to him that he might have to take orders from a drill sergeant 10 years his junior. He could take being called "Pops" with a smile and a nod. He was not so proud that his ego could be damaged by some good-natured kidding.

As might have been expected, the Marines said Ross was not only over the hill as a prizefighter (a gratuitous insult issued by an anonymous man in uniform), but also too damn old to go through grueling basic training. He just wouldn't make it. He wouldn't be able to keep up with 18-year-old kids. Ross was indignant and insisted he could keep up with anyone. He thought he was in great shape. So, he requested a waiver; for 60 days, he wondered and waited, paced the floor of his cocktail lounge, and read the newspapers for the latest war news. As he saw it, every day he waited was a day he was absent from the war, a war that he felt was his own, and as a son of America, he felt he had both the right and the responsibility to fight. And then it came: His waiver had been granted. He smiled, laughed, and yelled, "Hooray!" He waived the document around as if it were a flag of victory. He could now join the Marines.

His mother thought he was crazy. As Ross explains in his autobiography, "[S]ince the country had been so good to me, since it had given me the chance to come up from the ghetto to become a champion and win all kinds of fame, I simply had to fight for it in a time of war."[3] He assured his mother he would be all right. And, not unexpectedly, when he told Cathy the news, she cried bitterly. She had finally found the man with whom she wanted to spend the rest of her life, and now he was going to be target practice for Japanese shooters. Ross tried to calm and reassure Cathy, saying he would return to her and they would get married as soon as his divorce from Pearl was finalized. "Don't worry. I'll never leave you," he promised. Their departure was full of tears, hugs, and promises to write. Cathy dried her tears; she and Barney hugged one another, and he gave her a long good-bye kiss.

When Ross arrived for basic training, he was treated as an oddball, an interloper. Greeted by a sneering corporal at the outset of basic training, he was told that the Marines didn't need any grandpas in their ranks and the recruits didn't need any babysitters. And if he couldn't keep up with the younger men, he would be out of the service. "One, two, three, gone. You can go back to your grandkids," was what he heard. When the corporal learned that Ross was a celebrity and a former boxing champ, his dislike for him only increased. He informed his new recruit that he would not only not be given special treatment, but also that he would have to prove he was better than soldiers 10 years his junior. To make sure that Ross understood exactly what the corporal meant, he was given a series of dirty jobs just to shrink his supposedly big ego.

Ross had not trained in years. Exercise was not part of his daily routine, and when he began basic training, he was surprised to find himself out of shape. His muscles had gone slack, his belly looked like a pouch of beer, his energy level was diminished. Put through his paces with the other younger recruits, he did push-ups and sit-ups, and ran obstacle courses with a full pack on his back. He started off slowly, slightly out of breath, but soon regained muscle tone and stamina. The Marines were whipping Ross into fighting shape, and he was determined to be part of the battles that lay ahead. He had become one of the most "gung-ho" men in his outfit.

But when his basic training was complete and he thought he would be shipped to a battle zone, his commanding colonel told Ross he needed him to train recruits in the fundamentals of boxing for six weeks. "But, I enlisted to fight the Japs, not teach boxing," Ross complained. The colonel said he appreciated Ross's attitude and patriotism, but he thought he could be more valuable to the service by teaching soldiers to defend themselves when in close contact with the enemy. The boxing lessons would also give the Marines a sense of self-confidence, a feeling that they would be able to handle themselves when a rifle, grenade, or bayonet were no longer useful. Ross understood the importance of what he was being asked to do, but it was not the duty that he had imagined performing. It was not the reason he had gone through such rigorous basic training. But it did give him the time and opportunity to marry Cathy. They would be able to live stateside, off base, for a six-week honeymoon.

Ross and Cathy enjoyed their time together, but Ross kept counting the days when the six weeks would be over and he would be able to enter the fighting. He got a Jeep and drove to his colonel's office. He was welcomed with a salute, a handshake, and an expression of appreciation for what he had been doing. He requested that he be sent into a battle zone. Ross's earlier requests had been frequent, prolonged, and intense. It was apparent to the colonel that Ross would not cease requesting an overseas assignment and would be miserable if he were not put into battle. The colonel agreed, and Ross's face beamed with pleasure as he extended his thanks. Much to Cathy's distress and disappointment, Ross was shipped off to fight the enemy. From that day onward, her anxiety about her husband's safety continued and was only occasionally abated by the thought that he would one day be back in her arms. She kept a photograph of him on the nightstand beside their bed. It was the last thing she saw each night before closing her eyes and the first thing she saw each morning.

Ross's final destination, after a journey on rough seas, was Guadalcanal in the Solomon Islands, where the First Division was fighting a bloody battle with the Japanese. The Marines were greatly outnumbered and were fighting long and hard to maintain control of Henderson Field, the only U.S. airfield on the island. Ross was a member of the Second Division, sent to augment some of the First Division's troops and relieve the remainder of them.

Like most sensible middle-aged men, Ross knew of the dangers that lay ahead and expected that he would be cautious going into battle. He was torn between his desire to be in the middle of the fiercest battles and his anxiety about possibly dying, a conflict endured by many soldiers. Most men forced themselves to do as they were ordered, while a few attempted to wound themselves by shooting off a toe or a finger so they could be sent to hospital and perhaps home. Ross never gave into those kinds of fears. For him, the war was something that had to be fought, and fears had to be conquered. He was about to endure a battle that would be far more dangerous than any fight he had faced in the ring.

Ross was assigned to B Company, Second Battalion, Eighth Regiment, Second Marine Division. His platoon consisted of 10 men, each scared of the unknown that awaited him in a jungle of enemies. They canvased the jungle, remaining alert for the smallest signs of an enemy, worried that they could be taken out by an enemy ambush. And there it was: a hard-bitten platoon of Japanese soldiers willing to sacrifice themselves for their homeland and their emperor. Bullets, mortars, and machine guns erupted like a sudden storm without warning. As the Marines dove for cover, their fears were erased, supplanted by heavy doses of adrenaline. Their will to fight and survive became paramount. This is what they had been trained for, this is what they knew they might face, and they were prepared. They reacted without thinking, like the well-trained soldiers they were. They fought ferociously and intensely, a single unit of determined men. The fighting went on and on: the ricochet of bullets, the explosion of grenades, and the whistling of mortar shells.

By the time the Marines had killed their Japanese attackers, they were exhausted. Their bodies were drenched in sweat, their hearts pounded, and the muscles in their arms suddenly went slack. A sense of relief engulfed them. But one of Ross's buddies had been shot in the forehead. He had silently collapsed like a marionette with cut strings. Ross looked at his friend, blood still flowing from his head. Ross took a breath and then vomited. The expression on his friend's face was hidden by a red mask of blood. It would take days for Ross to accept the reality of a landscape of bodies ready to be harvested for funerals—young men with their limbs blown off, some with butchered guts and intestines spilling out like uncooked sausages in a slaughterhouse, and heads that had been battered by blasts, looking like splattered rotten melons. There were faces of shocked death, eyes wide open in horror and disbelief, and mouths that had once emitted screams, now silent and smeared with blood. Was this what they had signed on for? One had to go on. One could not submit to this. There was horror and terror, but there was no turning back. The alternatives were humiliating.

As Ross relates in his autobiography, there suddenly came a new barrage of bullets whizzing through the humid, insect-infested air. Mortar shells again began whistling and exploding. A machine gun, sounding like a jackhammer, tore open plants and scattered splinters of branches. There was a cry of agony from a man who had been cut in two. Another battle raged in the sky overhead. There was the roar and buzz of fighter planes, the screech of planes diving at hundreds of miles per hour, machine guns blazing. For the men on the ground, it was a diversion. All eyes, amazed and perhaps disbelieving, were turned toward the sky. American fighters were met in a blazing air war by 32 Japanese Zeros, 31 of which were shot down. It was a spectacle so real it seemed unbelievable. Ross was amazed that not one Japanese pilot bailed out of his terminally wounded aircraft, spiraling to the sea and a final burial. The battle overhead provided a brief relief. But hell on Earth continued.

Ross's platoon continued to move forward, not knowing what was in store for them. Their eyes were sensitive to every movement, their ears sensitive to the slightest crack of a branch or the sound of a boot crushing a soft, watery plant. And then it happened again: The rat-tat-tat of machine-gun fire announced their unwelcome arrival on enemy ground. It was immediately accompanied by rifle fire and the explosion of hand grenades; it sounded as if an entire Japanese battalion had gone on the attack. It was relentless. "Oh! Ahg!" The soldier nearest Ross had been hit; he went down and continued to moan. Ross looked over at him and saw that he suffered three severe wounds. His groans were faint compared to the explosive roar and whistle of artillery. The mortar shells alone were enough to cause havoc, but there was no escape. They were surrounded by a hurricane of enemy fire. Another Marine gasped and then groaned in pain. He was hit, and Ross could see that his midsection was awash in blood. The poor guy murmured something about his mother and fell silent. For a few minutes he seemed to come alive and then painfully rolled over into a shell hole. Two more soldiers were wounded and crawling; they too sought protection in the shell hole. A dead, rotted tree had fallen like a corpse in front of the shell hole, bullets penetrating its soft, moist flesh, providing cover from the painful sting of gunfire. A well-aimed grenade, however, could blow the soldiers into ragged pieces.

Ross, amazingly, was the only one who wasn't wounded; he had no choice but to defend himself and his comrades. If not, they would all be slaughtered. The Japanese were not about to take prisoners and honor the Geneva Convention of 1864, which established the treatment of prisoners of war. Indeed, for them, war was war. And winning was the only goal they aimed to achieve. Wounded men would probably be given a coup de grâce, a quick beheading, or a bullet in the head. A live prisoner was sure to be mistreated. The Marines knew their lives depended on Ross holding off the Japanese onslaught. As he fired his rifle, the two wounded Marines loaded other rifles and handed them to Ross, who kept firing at the enemy. The metal barrels of the rifles felt like hot pots just off a stove. As he kept clutching the gun and firing, Ross's hand grew red and sore, and the muscle behind his thumb began to spasm. Yet, he kept on firing. He could see the Japanese soldiers as they moved about, yelling at him and firing. Their movements were meant to draw Ross's fire away so that other soldiers could advance on the beleaguered Marines. Ross kept firing at the main body of Japanese soldiers, round after round.

Although his bladder felt like it was about to burst, he kept firing. He figured it was better to wet himself than to pause for even a minute. It was only his bullets that were keeping the Japanese soldiers at bay. He was firing hundreds of rounds, and it was not until that battle was over that he realized he had fired more than 350 rounds of ammunition. It was all they had. The last bullet was fired, and it echoed for a moment in Ross's ears. Would he and his comrades be put on their knees and beheaded? Would they be lined up in front of a firing squad? Not as long as Ross had something to defend himself with.

Each of the Marines had hand grenades. Ross gathered them up and proceeded to throw one after another in the direction of the machine-gun fire. His shoulder felt as if bone were rubbing bone. Each throw lit a fire of pain in his shoulder and elbow. The pain was becoming excruciating, but he kept throwing grenades while lying on his stomach. He could hear enemy bullets sinking into the rotted tree trunk and shrapnel pinging like hail against his helmet. Lying prone and throwing grenades was also straining his back muscles. The pain he felt was worse than what he had experienced in his fight with Henry Armstrong. And just as he had refused to give in to Armstrong, he would not stop throwing grenades. He counted them. He had 22 grenades left. How long could he hold out? Would those grenades be enough to keep the enemy away? Maybe another battalion or platoon of Marines would come to his rescue.

Ross was about to pull the pin on another grenade when he realized that the enemy had stopped firing. Was it a bluff? Were they, too, out of bullets? Could he really have blown them to bits? Did they retreat, only waiting to regroup? Would they attack from another direction? Were its desperate shooters dead? Ross waited and waited. There was no sound other than his heavy breathing and intermittent groans from one of his wounded comrades. Ross's shoulders, elbows, and back ached. He swallowed, but his mouth felt as dry as dirt. He waited a few minutes and then rolled over onto his back. He looked up at the sky as if he were about to say a prayer. His pain was not from sore muscles alone. He realized that he had also been wounded. Shrapnel had pierced his side, tearing through one arm and one leg like red-hot splinters, and his entire body was spasming in pain. A heavy rain was falling, and it briefly cooled the hot pain of his wounds.

Ross thought the fight was over, but then bullets started flying again. Another machine gun was raking their position. One of the soldiers was hit a second time, and a bullet dove into Ross's ankle, shattering bone and tearing flesh and tendon. Desperate to survive, cursing the enemy and the pain in his ankle, he painfully twisted his body and rolled back onto his stomach. He began throwing grenades again, 1, 2, 3, until he had thrown 21 altogether. With fear and adrenaline fueling his desperation, he kept cursing as his supply of grenades grew smaller and smaller. Ross had been under attack for 13 hours, and now he had a single hand grenade, which he was holding for the suicides of himself and his comrades—just in case the Japanese soldiers overran their position.

From behind him, Ross heard a mortar shell being fired. He thought the Japanese soldiers had caught them in a cross fire. The mortar shell landed between the wounded Marines and what had been the Japanese position. Marines, their boots pounding the wet, mushy ground, rushed en masse to save the remnants of their division. Ross nearly cried and then sighed with relief, moaning as the pain in his ankle grew worse. "Thank God," he said. It would be a few moments before Ross learned that he had killed 22 Japanese soldiers. He was a hero, a bleeding, wounded hero, but a hero nevertheless. His accomplishment would be celebrated in newspapers throughout the United States and in military publications being circulated to American soldiers.

At base, Ross was greeted by his good friend, Father Frederick Gehring, a Catholic priest who was the division's chaplain. The two had met and become friends on Guadalcanal. Prior to Ross's night in the jungle, he and Father Gehring had, for the entertainment of the troops, put on boxing gloves and gently sparred a few rounds. Gehring had been a cheering fan of Jimmy McLarnin, sitting ringside and urging on his favorite Irishman to win. Shortly after meeting Ross, however, he became one of Ross's closest friends. Years later, he would say the Lord's Prayer at Ross's funeral. Gehring could read Hebrew and helped conduct Sabbath services for Jewish Marines on the island, and Ross played the organ for Father Gehring's Christmas Eve Mass. Soldiers of all faiths attended the Mass.

Upon seeing Ross's wounds, Father Gehring knelt in prayer and asked God to save his friend. He crossed himself and rose to his feet and bowed his head. He accompanied Ross to an ambulance and waved as Ross was driven to an infirmary, where the shrapnel was removed from his wounds. The wounds were cleaned and bandaged. Ross was experiencing intense pain, and so the doctors gave him regular injections of morphine. From the infirmary, he was shipped to a hospital in Auckland, New Zealand, where he continued to receive regular injections of morphine. Finally, he was shipped back to the United States, by which time he was addicted. Several hours without the drug proved unbearable. Ross was able to appear at a war bond rally with Eleanor Roosevelt and receive an award from the Boxing Writers Association. No one knew that he was as high as a kite. An even more important event awaited Ross. He was awarded the Silver Star for his bravery and for saving the lives of his comrades. It was an honor that filled him with enormous pride, but he also knew that without morphine he wouldn't be able to attend the ceremony. He had himself surreptitiously injected.

(One can only wonder, as perhaps Ross did, why he wasn't awarded the Congressional Medal of Honor. While the Silver Star is an important medal, it is the third-highest military decoration for valor awarded to members of the U.S. Armed Forces. It is awarded for gallantry in action against an enemy of the United States. The Medal of Honor is the highest military honor a member of the U.S. military can receive, awarded for personal acts of valor above and beyond the call of duty. Ross's actions on Guadalcanal certainly qualified him for the higher medal.)

Ross certainly would not turn down the Silver Star, and he traveled to Washington, DC, for the presidential presentation ceremony in the Rose Garden of the White House, where he received from the president's hands a Presidential Citation for bravery and devotion to his comrades. The president thanked Ross for his commitment for helping to defeat the enemy and said he was an example to all Americans.

Ross had been a boxing champion, and he was now a national war hero. Hollywood was eager to make a movie about him. Few people at that time knew that Ross was a slave to his drug habit, certainly not John Garfield, who was prepared to play the lead in *The Barney Ross Story*. Drug addiction was a taboo subject in the movies during that era and would not have been approved as a film topic by the industry's self-appointed censors. When Garfield learned of Ross's addiction, he cancelled the production of *The Barney Ross Story* and hired a writer to come up with a fictional script that was loosely based on the outline of the Ross story. It was to be called *Body & Soul*, and it was one of Garfield's most successful and popular films, along with *The Postman Always Rings Twice*. When Ross saw the film, he was outraged that aspects of his life had been lifted and included in the movie. He felt as if his autobiography had been pirated and reproduced as a clever facsimile, but a poor roman à clef. At Ross's urging, his agent sued, and the suit was settled for $60,000.

While $60,000 was a substantial sum in 1947, of far greater value than it would be today, it would rapidly vanish into Ross's veins. As his drug addiction came to control his life, he was a slave to not only his addiction, but also a series of heartless drug pushers whose only interest was in squeezing as much money out of the former champ as possible. Although Ross had attempted to hide his identity from them, the pushers ultimately discovered who their regular customer was and doubled, tripled, and quadrupled their prices. As in any free market when the demand is insatiable and the supply plentiful, the price of will rise. The pushers had opened a vein to Ross's bank accounts, and they were bleeding him poor and dry. He could not go more than a few hours without a fix. "If you can't pay, then steal the money," they told him. He couldn't do it. He was not the delinquent of his youth. He perceived himself as a responsible man, a former world champion and a war hero.

Instead, he depleted his bank accounts. When he no longer had money for his fixes, he ran to friends. Initially, they gave Ross the money he needed, and he was able to keep himself stoned. The loans from friends, however, were not repaid, and so the spigot of money was turned off. Ross became increasingly desperate. He thought again of the words of the pushers, advising him to steal the money. He thought of getting a gun and committing a holdup. It was a desperate man's fantasy. He could not commit the same kind of cold-blooded act that had resulted in his father's death. He was so desperate for his next fix that he even thought of putting on a boxing exhibition. But that was ridiculous: He was a wasted version of his old self.

Just as Ross was feeling he had no place to turn, he ran into Abner "Longy" Zwillman, a Jewish gangster who controlled all of New Jersey until he was killed and his domain was taken over by Willie Moretti, friend of Frank Sinatra. Zwillman, who had befriended Ross during his boxing career, was a member of the "Big Six," who controlled organized crime (aka "the syndicate") throughout the United States. In addition to Zwillman, the Big Six included Lucky Luciano, Meyer Lansky, Frank Costello, Tony Accardo, and Jake "Greasy Thumb" Guzik. Zwillman was known for his generosity to friends, and so when Ross said he was desperate for money, Zwillman simply handed him several thousand dollars. He told him not to worry about repaying the loan, for Zwillman had made plenty of money gambling on Ross's fights. The money was a life raft, but soon Ross would feel as if he were again drowning in desperation.

In addition to his attempts to hide his identity from drug pushers, Ross didn't want Cathy to find out he was a drug addict, so he decided to stay in New York while she lived in California, working in films as a dancer. In New York, Ross accepted a job as a public relations consultant with his old friend Blackstone, who owned and operated a successful advertising and public relations company. In his small office, Ross kept his needle and syringe locked in his desk. He found it increasingly difficult to perform the tasks that Milton had hired him to do. His mind was always on his next fix. For Milton, Ross had become a charity case. Ross moved into the Edison Hotel, just off of Broadway, and got to know many of the neighborhood pushers. While he was drawing a weekly salary, it wasn't enough to support his habit, and he had to borrow money from an evaporating pool of New York friends. After that pool dried up and was only a mirage in Ross's fevered imagination, and with no other options, he started borrowing money from loan sharks. His indebtedness ran into the thousands of dollars. When the sharks would no longer lend him money, his condition went from precarious to dire. His presence at the advertising agency had become less than that of an employee down on his luck and more like that of a terminally ill patient. His pale, skeletal presence portended a sad, pitiful end that was quickly approaching.

Not wishing to kill himself and realizing he had no place left to obtain a fix, he felt caged, and that cage was getting smaller and smaller. If he stayed in it, he would shrivel and die. Some desperate men do desperate things. And for a drug addict who has reached the end of the line, the most desperate thing he can do is to search for a cure. Channeling the massive willpower he had demonstrated on Guadalcanal, Ross made up his mind to fight and survive, to find a cure for his addiction, no matter how painful. He learned of the Public Health Service, which ran a detoxification hospital in Lexington, Kentucky. He told his friend Milton Blackstone that he was going to turn himself in and be sentenced to a year at the hospital. Blackstone told him not to worry; he was proud of Ross's decision and arranged to fly him to Lexington on the private plane of Grossinger's Resort Hotel, one of Blackstone's clients. While on the flight, Ross gave himself one last shot, his pathetic going-away present. Blackstone watched sadly as Ross prepared the syringe and injected a vein. After the plane landed, Blackstone bid Ross good-bye and said he would see again him in a year. While it would normally take a year to affect a cure, Ross was determined to undergo whatever stress and agony were necessary so that he could get clean and return to his beloved Cathy. He endured the torture of going cold turkey, painful as it was, with the determination to be cured. After four months, he was released and never turned to drugs again.

The story of Ross's drug addiction and subsequent recovery is told in his touching autobiography *No Man Stands Alone*, and less so in a sentimental movie entitled *Monkey on My Back*, starring Cameron Mitchell as Barney Ross. The following statement appears just after the film's title: "The story of Barney Ross, one-time lightweight champion, twice world's welterweight champion, ex-corporal U.S. Marine Corps awarded

Silver Star for Gallantry in Action."[4] The title of the film was a common expression used by addicts in the 1940s, 1950s, and early 1960s, to express that their drug habits were like having a monkey on their backs; a burden that could not be removed. The monkey always had to be fed.

Because many films of that era were given what are generously called "Hollywood endings," referring to the optimistic, uplifting, cheerful "take-homes," the film does not state "The End" but instead reads "The Beginning." And Ross's recovery from drug addiction certainly was a new beginning for him, as well as for Cathy. They happily reunited and had a successful marriage that lasted until his death. While Ross's drug addiction is explicit in the movie, his Judaism is only implied. Hollywood producers feared alienating a large non-Jewish audience with a Jewish main character. Although the 1947 film *Gentleman's Agreement* deals with the subject of anti-Semitism, its star is the WASP-y Gregory Peck, whose character only pretends to be Jewish to expose anti-Semitism.

In addition to avoiding Ross's Judaism, *Monkey on My Back* does not delve into his relationship with the Chicago Outfit, nor does it deal with the murder of Ross's father during a robbery. The film portrays only one of Ross's three fights with Jimmy McLarnin and his terrible loss to Henry Armstrong, and it does not portray his important fights with Tony Canzoneri. The film does depict his enlistment in the Marines, his heroics, his being awarded the Silver Star, and his dependence on morphine while in the hospital suffering from malaria and various wounds. The film shows the hardships and humiliations of morphine addiction and creates fictional and stereotypical drug pushers. It also portrays Ross checking into a federal medical facility and his subsequent cure from addiction. It was discovered after the film's release that Ross's good friend from Guadalcanal, Catholic priest Father Gehring, had convinced Ross to let a film of his drug addiction be made. He thought it would serve as a warning to young people to stay away from drugs. The all-too-implicit message was, "Don't let this happen to you."

It is interesting to note that the original producer and director of the film had attempted to sign Marlon Brando to play Barney Ross. Brando had never played a fighter, but he had the physique and athleticism of one. That became apparent in the movie *On the Waterfront*. Whether Brando rejected the role or was ultimately not given the part has not been reported. One person who did belong in the film was Ceferino Garcia, who had, in fact, fiercely fought Ross a number of years before the film was produced. His part is a small one, but it adds a touch of verisimilitude.

Both *Monkey on My Back* and *The Man with the Golden Arm*, starring Frank Sinatra as a heroic, addicted jazz drummer, were denied seals of approval by the Production Code Association (PCA) because of scenes depicting drug use. As reported by Turner Classic Movies,

> In April 1957, after the film was completed and submitted to the PCA for approval, it was denied a Code Seal, even after a second review [was] requested by [the director and the producer] for the following reason: "The scene in which Barney Ross is shown injecting morphine into his arm with a hypodermic appears to be in violation of Paragraph d, Section 9 of the Production Code, which states that no picture shall be approved by the PCA if it 'shows details of drug procurement or of the taking of drugs in any manner.'"[5]

One would have thought that the Catholic Legion of Decency, which was noted for wanting to ban films that it felt could have a corrosive effect on morals, would also have objected to the movie, but it gave the film a B rating: It was objectionable, but Catholics could view it without fear of going against Catholic teachings.

Regardless of the controversy aroused by strict moralists, the film was neither banned nor censored. None of it mattered to Ross and his siblings. They hated the film; they felt that it presented Ross as a craven degenerate, a heartless hustler, corrupt, dissolute, immoral, and cowardly. According to the *Hollywood Reporter*, an angry Ross referred to the film as "filth, bilge, and cheap sensationalism."[6] The family was particularly displeased with the film's advertising campaign, which—they believed—showed Ross as a lowlife creature, as something that crawls in alleys late at night. The enormous letters on a billboard advertising the film were meant to scandalize the public, while appealing to their interest in sleazy, lowlife behavior: "THE BARNEY ROSS STORY! JUNKIE! IT MEANS A DOPE-FIEND! THE HOTTEST HELL ON EARTH!"[7] This was hardly the uplifting message that Ross and Father Gehring had wanted to send to vulnerable youth.

So, Ross decided to take a new route: He began lecturing to high school students, letting them know how drugs could ruin their lives and destroy any chance for forming happy families and achieving success. His message was a powerful one, and students listened to the once triple-title-holding champ with rapt attention. He was still the champ. And he was finally able to expiate the feelings of guilt that had also been a monkey on his back.

6

FROM RANCH HAND TO POWERFUL RIGHT HAND

Max Baer, a fun-loving teenager, shy around girls, fearful of fighting, came of age on his parents' ranch in Livermore, California. The town is east of the San Francisco Bay Area and has a pleasant, almost Mediterranean climate, which is what had attracted Baer's parents, Jacob and Dora. Livermore was known as cowboy country, where thousands of acres of ranches held vast herds of cattle. The Baers raised both hogs and cattle. Today, Livermore is still a small town with a population of slightly more than 85,000 people. For the Baer family, it was an ideal place to breathe fresh air, raise a family, and operate a ranch.

As a result of hours of hard, manual labor on his family's ranch, Max developed the chiseled muscles of a weightlifter and the stamina of a dray horse. His older sister said that he looked as if he had taken a Charles Atlas course in bodybuilding, but he had the flexibility of a gymnast. That physique would later ignite the admiration and, in numerous cases, arouse the sexual desires of female fans; for men, he would become an ideal of a Lothario as a great athlete who could successfully defend himself against any opponent. His clenched and gloved right fist would become legendary and inspire fear in other boxers. A now-forgotten Greenwich Village sculptor named Marie Rodman once told this author's father that she wished Baer could have posed for her, saying, "He could be the second David," referring to, of course, Michelangelo's heroic sculpture. Yet, as a teenager, Baer had no idea what fate had in store for him.

At age 17, he stood six feet tall and weighed 190 pounds. By the time he began pursuing a career as a boxer, he had shot up another four inches. Nat Fleischer, editor of *Ring Magazine*, writes in his book *Max Baer: The Glamour Boy of the Ring*, "Six-foot-four in height, with a tremendous span of shoulders, curled lignite for hair, topping a countenance radiant with smiles, dimples, and flashing white teeth, a picture-fighter if there ever was one, is it any wonder that ladies loved him as voluminously as he loved them?"[1]

Throughout town, ranchers, housewives, store owners, and high school students speculated that Max must have taken one of those courses advertised on the back page of magazines for bodybuilding. When he heard such talk, he laughed and waved it off. Baer was modest and likeable, easygoing and eager to make others laugh at his jokes, some of which were self-deprecating: "I have a million-dollar body, but a 10 cent brain."[2]

He told his older sister, who was six feet tall and weighed 200 pounds, and who often protected him from bullies, that people liked to tease him. "Don't pay no mind to them," she would say. Her kid brother would smile and agree with her.

One night at a weekly dance, when Baer was 17 years old, he and a group of friends made off with several jugs of homemade wine that belonged to a local lumberjack. It was during Prohibition, and alcohol was hard to get for teenagers. Wine and other alcoholic beverages were often made in people's basements, barns, and garages, away from the prying eyes of police. The boys marveled at their find and proceeded to consume the wine as if it were a magic elixir. As they drank, they laughed and whooped, drawing the attention of onlookers as they consumed the contents of one jug after another. While Max refrained from drinking the wine, his pals left the jugs dry. They were having a great time, that is, until the lumberjack spotted his stolen wine being consumed by a bunch of rowdy teenagers; angry and shouting, he took off after them.

The boys turned and ran. Baer was at the back of the pack, and the lumberjack caught up with him and violently jerked him back by the collar of his shirt. Baer spun around and faced the lumberjack, who reached out with his big, square fist to hit the boy in the chin. The punch made a solid landing, and Baer had a surprised look on his face. The lumberjack had expected his target to collapse to the floor, but nothing happened. The punch had no effect. Baer looked at the lumberjack for a moment and then clenched his big right fist, the biggest fist the lumberjack had ever seen. Baer let it fly with the full power of his muscled right arm and shoulder. The lumberjack's head snapped back as if attached to a rubber neck. The lumberjack crumpled to the floor, his head bouncing off the wooden planks and landing again with a soft thud. His eyes rolled up in his head like symbols on a slot machine and then came to rest. He opened his eyes in surprise and wonder: Who was this oversized lad who could pack such a wallop?

Baer stood over the chagrined lumberjack and smiled, amazed by his own power and pleased with himself. It was the first time he hadn't needed to rely on his sister for protection. He had never punched anyone. He looked at his fist as if seeing it for the first time, as if it were a newly received gift. He looked at the crowd that had gathered. Onlookers were staring at the young gladiator. He smiled at them. He would do something special with that right fist. A few nights later, he tried it out again on a cowboy who had offended him. Once again, his powerful right fist flattened his astonished opponent. Fleischer writes, "He knew now that he possessed a talent worthy of recognition. He could hit and how!"[3]

Baer attributed the power in his right fist to carrying hog and cow carcasses, and wielding a butcher's axe, which his father had taught him to use when killing a cow or hog. On his way home that night, he wondered if perhaps a career as a boxer might be in his future. It seemed a lot more attractive and romantic than spending his life on a ranch. After all, he had quit high school after his freshman year and had few professional opportunities. He had planned on being a rancher, a factory worker, or some sort of laborer. He thought of Jack Dempsey, the reigning American boxing hero at the time, and how he might be able to follow in the great pugilist's footsteps. In addition, his mother, who was a fan of boxing, encouraged him to pursue a career in the ring. She had originally thought that her younger son Buddy would pursue a boxing career, for he was the more aggressive of the two brothers.

In fact, Buddy did follow in Max's footsteps, but he never achieved his older brother's prominence, although he had a record of 57 wins and three losses. In 1937, he fought and beat Abe Simon, a professional heavyweight boxer who would go on to challenge one of the greatest fighters of the 20th century, Joe Louis, for the heavyweight title of the world and lose, not once, but twice. Buddy Baer's final bout was also against Joe Louis, and Baer was obviously no match for the hard-hitting, skillful heavyweight. After being knocked out by Louis, Buddy retired from boxing. Although two of the hardest punchers in the brutal world of professional boxing, the Baer brothers were known as the "genial giants of the ring" and "professional good guys." Many people both in and out of the world of boxing thought the Baers should have been in a more amiable business than boxing, say show business.

The day after knocking out the lumberjack, Baer decided he would train himself to become a professional boxer. To develop his skills, he purchased a pair of boxing gloves and a punching bag. He worked at it daily and then introduced himself to a local amateur boxing promoter named J. Hamilton Lorimer. Max pleaded, begged, and importuned Lorimer to represent him. Lorimer was initially annoyed by Max and thought he would cure him of his "crazy" desire to be a fighter. Lorimer didn't think Max had the right technique to succeed as a boxer; in fact, he had little technique other than swinging wildly. Lorimer also thought Baer was too good looking to be a fighter and would be reluctant to have his nose broken, his ears pummeled, and his face scarred. "He was big and powerful, but I thought him too good looking to go in for fighting,"[4] Lorimer said. To Lorimer and others, the young Max looked more like movie-star material than ring material. And while Max would become a movie marquee name in later years, even starring in a film built around his career as a boxer, he just wanted to box, to be another Jack Dempsey.

To cure him of such an ambition, Lorimer arranged for Max to fight a local heavyweight named Chief Caribou. Prior to the match, a thirsty Baer consumed several bottles of soda until his belly was inflated like a balloon that would burst when hammered by the first body blow of the fight. The two adversaries pummeled one another; as expected, Baer swung wildly, flailing away at Chief, who managed to duck or skip away from the onslaught. A couple of times, Baer managed to land his powerful right fist, and Chief went over like a large oak; dazed and shaking his head, he would get up. He began to notice the effect of his body blows on Baer and pounded away at the bloated, swollen target. Baer would belch and suppress the desire to vomit by continuing to swing wildly at Chief's head. Finally, Baer's right fist made a perfect landing on Chief's chin, and his opponent went over like a sacrificed oak and lay on the canvas like a dead tree trunk. When Baer, gulping air, made it back to his dressing room, he proceeded to vomit into a bucket. He had learned his first lesson about eating and drinking before a bout. Lorimer was impressed by

Max's strength, determination, and power but insisted he would never be anything other than an ordinary pug unless he was taught the necessary skills and tactics to become a first-rate pugilist.

Baer was paid $35 dollars for the fight. His son, Max Baer Jr., said,

> My dad used to get up at 2:30 or 3:00 in the morning and go around town collecting the garbage from restaurants. He would bring it back to the ranch and slop it to the pigs. The pigs would root through the garbage, eating anything that was edible. My dad did that seven nights a week. And for that he got paid 35 cents a night. So boxing was a big deal: He could make in one night what would have taken him three months to earn. And don't forget that was the beginning of the Depression. So my dad asked for more fights. He would have been happy to fight several nights a week. He just wanted the money. He never loved boxing.[5]

Having already invested in Baer's future, Lorimer enlisted a highly capable middleweight named Bob McAllister to tutor the young fighter, who turned out to be a good, although impatient, student. He would absorb what he thought necessary and discard the finer points. Nevertheless, from 1929, when he first fought Chief Caribou, to 1930, he won 23 fights, 19 by knockout. He lost two fights to more skillful opponents, Les Kennedy and Ernie Schaaf, both of whom he would defeat years later. He was not only developing a reputation as a fighter who could pack a wallop (the "Livermore Larruper," the "Livermore Butcher Boy," inter alia), but he was also becoming a magnet for beautiful young women who wanted to take the handsome hunk into their arms and beds. Fleischer writes, "For the girls were beginning to gang up on this enticing combination of Hercules and Adonis in the first of the amorous dramas, staging him as a 'Squire of Dames.'"[6]

Throughout his boxing career, Baer was the guy who always wanted to party, to have a good time. He loved joking with both men and women, and could stand at a bar entertaining the crowd with humorous stories and comedic quips. Although a party animal, he was not a drunk. Max Baer Jr. said that his father would hold a drink in his hand, take a few sips, and never finish it. He would have the same glass in his hand at the end of a party that he had been holding at the beginning.

While bevies of nubile young women kept Baer's testosterone flowing, he suffered an emotional defeat in August 1930 that almost KO'd his career. He was scheduled to fight Frankie Campbell for the Pacific Coast Championship. (Frankie's real name was Francisco Camilli, and he was the brother of Dolph Camilli, a future brilliant first baseman for the old Brooklyn Dodgers who would be recorded as one of the best first basemen of the 1940s.) Campbell was well aware of Baer's powerful right fist and diligently avoided extending his chin as a target. He managed to sidestep, duck, dance, bob and weave, and jerk away from most of Baer's wild swings. At one point early in the fight, Campbell landed a solid punch that sent Baer to the canvas; Campbell then turned and walked back to his corner. There, he grinned and waved to his cheering fans.

Max scrambled to his feet and rushed at Campbell, who—hearing the pounding steps of his opponent coming from behind him—began to turn his head. It was too little, too late. Baer landed a powerful blow to one side of Campbell's head. Campbell crumpled, like a dead marionette, to the canvas, lay there for a moment, and then regained his strength and slowly managed to get up just before the referee could count him out. Back in his corner, he said to his manager, "I feel like something has snapped in my head." Nevertheless, using quick jabs and well-aimed rights, he skillfully outpointed Baer in the next two rounds. Before the fifth round began, Campbell's trainer, Kid Herman, who had been Baer's friend and trainer, flung ugly and derogatory insults at Baer that pierced his sense of pride. He insulted not only Baer, but also his family. Enraged and hurt, although far from deflated, Baer angrily rushed at Campbell as soon as the bell tolled the beginning of the next round. His right fist, fueled by defiance and fury, landed powerfully on Campbell, forcing him against the ropes, where Baer relentlessly pounded his helpless opponent. Baer's fists flew, rights and lefts, delivering hammer blows that bewildered and devastated Campbell. Baer was shooting angry punches that should have been aimed at Kid Herman for his nasty, provocative insults.

While his fierce retaliation was misplaced, Baer could not step back. It was as if Herman had flipped a switch in Baer's psyche that could not be turned off. Baer viciously pounded Campbell against the ropes. Campbell was trapped: He could not fall down. He was a helpless punching bag. When Campbell's head began to droop and it became apparent that the beating was leaving him helpless, the referee—after much hesitation—finally separated the fighters, ending it.

For Campbell, the end came too late, as he collapsed onto the floor of the ring. Although massaged and gently shaken, he could not be revived.

His cornermen knelt over him, the fate of their fighter apparent on their distressed faces. Doctors were called. After examining Campbell, one of the doctors, in response to the referee, just shook his head. An ambulance arrived and attendants carried off Campbell's limp body on a stretcher. A few worried murmurs could barely be heard. The crowd stared at the stretcher as it passed by them on the way to the ambulance. Campbell was carried out in the stunned silence of the arena. Baer, a witness to his own power and a perpetrator of another man's doom, was reduced to tears and remorse. He had signed up for boxing to earn money, not to kill someone. As far as he was concerned that was never in the cards. He rode silently in the ambulance, staring helplessly at his unconscious former opponent.

Once at the hospital, Baer rushed over to Campbell's stricken wife Elsie. He knew his words would be inadequate, but he could do nothing but tearfully apologize to her. Over and over again, he said how sorry he was. It was not meant to happen. Elsie replied, "It even might have been you, mightn't it?" Baer looked at her with deep sorrow, almost wishing that it had been him. His remorse was nearly overpowering. Yet, Elsie seemed to forgive him, as if understanding that one enters the ring knowing the chances. When two men are slugging one another with all their skill and power, how can they not be hurt?

It came as no surprise to Elsie or Max when Campbell was pronounced dead the next day. They had seen his condition in the hospital. They didn't need doctors or medical examiners to confirm what their eyes had recorded. Nevertheless, when he heard the news, Baer fell to his knees and could not stop crying. He pounded the floor with his enormous fists. He said he never wanted to fight again. Killing a man in the ring was not what Baer had imagined or wanted; for him, boxing was a means of making money and a test of skills—who was the better athlete, who was better at protecting himself, who had faster reflexes, who had the best tactics? He admired and liked his opponents. He respected their courage and tenacity. It takes guts to step into a boxing ring and be prepared to give and receive punishment.

California authorities, on a mission to outlaw boxing, did not view it as a sport, but as brutal, primitive combat. They did not view pugilists as consenting adults with the right and freedom to engage in fistic combat. It was still a form of primitive gladiatorial combat. The state was prepared to have Baer arrested for manslaughter. An indictment, an arrest, and a trial would certainly intimidate the boxing community, they believed.

Yet, it did not come to pass, for there was too much interest and influence to permit the banishment of boxing. Baer did not need the state to tell him what to do, what to feel, and how to act. He felt a moral, if not legal, obligation to Campbell's widow and children. He contributed money to the Campbell family and offered them whatever assistance he could. For the rest of his life, Baer felt an obligation to them and would choke up and sometimes cry whenever he recounted the awful outcome of that bout. For many years, he could not sleep through the night without suddenly awakening to the image of Campbell lying dead on the canvas. It haunted him for the rest of his life.

For managers and promoters, however, Baer had demonstrated the ingredients of a champion. After the Campbell fight, Lorimer thought that Baer, with the right kind of training, could indeed ascend to the title and dominate the heavyweight class, earning millions of dollars. Lorimer also realized that he did not have the necessary time to manage the young dynamo. He would still own a piece of him, but he would turn over the management to a professional. He chose Ancil Hoffman, a thoughtful and effective manager who could guide Baer's career to the top. Now Hoffman and Lorimer would each own a piece of Baer, and that would lead to some friction and disputes as Baer earned larger and larger sums of money. For the time being, however, the arrangement pleased all parties.

When Hoffman took over, he thought a change of scenery would help to alleviate Baer's despondency and guilt about the death of Campbell. New York, with its bright lights, was Hoffman's choice of destination. There would be enough nightclubs, an abundance of beautiful women, parties, and Broadway shows, as well as a lineup of tough boxing opponents, to keep Baer's mind off the death of Frankie Campbell. And once in New York, Baer indeed threw himself into the high life of the city. He loved Broadway, the bright lights, the beautiful chorus girls, the nightclubs, the dance bands, and all the fun that was available to a young, handsome athlete. It was a new world for him, and he dove into it like a boy who had just learned to swim and loved diving into a pool of water. For many on Broadway's "Great White Way," Baer was Mr. Bon Vivant, a great sport, a good-time Charlie (to use an expression of that era). To be in his company was a guarantee of fun, laughter, and charming company. In his book about James Braddock and Max Baer, entitled *Cinderella Man*, Jeremy Schaap quotes a double limerick about Baer in New York City:

> There was a young scrapper named Baer
> Who had the most beautiful hair
> He could flirt, he could fight,
> He could dance all the night
> That fantastic fast puncher, Max Baer!
> That frivolous fighter named Baer
> Had the ladies all up in the air,
> He could love 'em and leave 'em,
> And blithely deceive 'em
> That bewitching young biffer, Max Baer! [7]

Baer was no snob when it came to dating beautiful women; he dated not only showgirls, Broadway stars, and debutantes, but also waitresses and shopgirls. To use a cliché of the time, he was "feeling his oats."

While Baer seemed the life of every party he attended, he was still haunted by the death of Frankie Campbell. When alone at night or early morning, he was still floating like a dead man in a pool of despondency. He needed to force himself to look to the future, to swim with the current, swim against the current, but stop floating in self-pity. Ancil Hoffman, like an army drill sergeant, thought the best way to engage Baer in a life of purpose was for him to have another professional fight. First on the list would be tough young boxer Ernie Schaaf, who had racked up numerous wins in his brief career. Schaaf was an exceedingly skillful boxer who trained rigorously and with determination to be the best man in the ring. Baer, guided by another set of values, was still a fun-loving bon vivant who thought little of rigorous training. Yes, he would go to the gym, hit the body bag, hit the speed bag, skip rope, do a little sparring, but his mind was on other things, for example, a stunningly beautiful socialite named Dorothy Dunbar. He needed to be with her around the clock. He had never known a woman like her back in California. She was beautiful, sophisticated, and smart. She made him feel 10 feet tall.

But Baer was a boxer and had to focus on his career. He could not earn money dating the beautiful Dunbar. He could only earn cash from fighting. And it would be a lot of cash. Once in his hands, he would spend it without concern. He would have given it all to Dunbar. To keep the cash flowing, he would next have to fight the formidable Schaaf, who, like all good boxers, had studied the strengths and weaknesses of his opponent. He knew that Baer didn't have much of a jab and relied on his powerful right hand to overwhelm an opponent.

The fight went as Schaaf had predicted and as Hoffman had feared. Schaaf proved to be the more skillful boxer, fast on his feet, ducking punches, slipping punches, jerking his head out of the axis of Baer's swinging right arm. Schaaf outboxed Baer round after round. After each round, the judges awarded the majority of points to Schaaf. At the beginning of each round, Baer went after Schaaf but was unable to tag him with that powerful right. Baer absorbed punch after punch. His face was proving to be a slow-moving target, one that Schaaf repeatedly jabbed and jabbed. It was amazing that Baer was able to absorb so many punches and keep going. He was like a bull facing the taunts of a matador. At one point, Hoffman looked at Baer's swollen face, blood here and there, and thought his man was finished. Yet, Baer kept attempting to deliver that powerful right punch. It was his brand, his trademark, the fist that had killed Frankie Campbell and inspired newspaper headlines and betting odds. That handsome face that women wanted to kiss and fondle now looked more like uncooked hamburger than the visage of a Greek god. Adonis was nowhere to be seen. But how about Hercules? Had he, too, abandoned the once-undefeated hero of the ring?

Baer swung that powerful right again and again, but Schaaf easily danced out of range, frustrating Baer. If there was one person Baer did not want to embarrass himself in front of, it was the woman who filled his dreams and satisfied his desires, Dorothy Dunbar. She was sitting ringside, her face showing no emotion, neither smiling nor frowning, neither proud nor aghast. She looked like a model of porcelain beauty. Of course, she wanted her lover to win, to be seen in society on the arm of a handsome victor as he squired her into the best nightclubs and Broadway shows. But how would it look, her arm encircling his, if he gazed at her with an adoring smile, but with a bruised, swollen face?

Baer didn't merely lose the fight, he was massacred. It was Custer's Last Stand in the ring. Dunbar did not say anything at the time, but she must have been appalled. Baer would have to redeem himself. He would have to win another fight. Another loss and his value would dissipate, not only according to Dunbar, Lorimer, and Hoffman, but also as prescribed by the world of boxing, which needed to have Adonis/Hercules back on top. Another loss would mean that the climb to the top of the mountain would grow increasingly steep; furthermore, as a Lothario among pugilists and at the head of the line of Dunbar admirers, Baer did not want to lose his allure to her. He was not only smitten with her, but also captivated, enthralled, and imprisoned by his unrelenting desire for her.

Dunbar had been a star of silent films and one of several women who had played the part of Jane in a Tarzan film (*Tarzan and the Golden Lion*, 1927). Baer was her Tarzan, and he wanted to swing with his Jane. To succeed with her, he would have to train, duck, and swing. Of the three, training was the discipline he was least inclined to pursue. Dunbar had given up her cinematic role as Jane by the end of 1927, and Baer did not want her to also give up her role as his ardent lover. He knew that once she had given up her film career, she was focusing her attention on an assortment of possible trophy husbands. Baer did not want to become a has-been in that long line of losers. She had increasingly become Baer's fantasy of what a femme fatale should be. She wrapped men around her finger like pieces of putty. She toyed with them the way a cat would toy with a mouse; as dangerous as she was to susceptible married men, they were irresistibly drawn to her. And once in her embrace, they became addicted to her charm, beauty, and sexual skills; she was a drug that sent her lovers soaring to heights they had not previously known. From the late 1920s to the late 1930s, Dunbar married seven times. When Baer proposed, Dunbar accepted. Baer was joyful. His was a dream fulfilled. He did not know that he would only be number three.

Their once-joyful marriage soon turned volatile, tumultuous, and acrimonious. It would last a mere two years, from 1931 to 1933. Yet, during the good days, Baer could barely keep his mind on boxing. His interest in training was negligible. Hoffman despaired of his fighter's marriage. He felt that if Baer and Dunbar had sex before a fight, Baer would lack the energy and stamina to go 12 rounds. Trainers believed that sexual activity sapped the strength from fighters' legs and left them devoid of the fighting spirit. Hoffman could see that Baer, something of a country bumpkin, was out of Dunbar's league. He would never be entirely accepted by an elite group of socialites, women who had gone to the best finishing schools and whose husbands and fiancés worked on Wall Street. Dunbar's friends were married to bond brokers, bankers, and financiers— captains of industry. As handsome and daring as a fighter might be, he was still just a fighter, a pug, a palooka, a man who might not know which fork to use. They might regard him as a curiosity or a court jester. Hoffman knew that Baer's animal magnetism would eventually lose its luster for Dunbar, that sooner or later the two would part ways; of course, Hoffman hoped it would be sooner rather than later.

Regardless of Dunbar's hypnotic presence and Baer's enthrallment, Hoffman knew he had to keep the pressure on Baer, had to turn up the heat, had to fill Baer with the drive and ambition to be a champ. Hoffman arranged for Baer to fight again just four weeks after his ignominious defeat by Schaaf. Baer's opponent this time would be New Zealand heavyweight Tom Heeney; he was less skillful than Schaaf and regarded by many as something of a plodder in the ring. He did not have Schaaf's dance steps and speed. Hoffman was not going to take any chances. He would get Baer to train hard for this fight, to do it for his future, and, although Hoffman neither liked nor approved of Dorothy Dunbar, he didn't think that Baer would want her to see another loss. He knew Baer did not want to stand in his own corner as the referee lifted the arm of his opponent in victory. Another such loss would be a humiliation that Baer would not want to endure. So, Baer followed Hoffman's advice. He trained for hours, day after day. His speed improved. He developed a better left jab. He was in far better condition than he had been for the Schaaf disaster.

The first two rounds went as Hoffman hoped, with Baer doing a good job of going after his opponent and landing solid blows. In the third round, Baer came out of his corner like a tiger, determined to put an end to the fight. He wanted a dramatic win, not by points, not by a technical knockout, but by showing the world that he had not lost his powerful right-hand punch. Like the loyal weapon of a fierce gladiator, Baer threw that right fist directly at Heeney's chin. It landed and quickly put Heeney to sleep on the canvas for an official knockout. Baer felt redeemed, Dunbar smiled and applauded, and Hoffman's view of the future brightened. This time, it was Heeney who was led off in defeat.

Even though Baer had demonstrated the power and skill that fans had admired, he had sufficient self-realization to know that his fundamental style of fighting had limitations that would prevent him from becoming a champion. With 20/20 hindsight, he saw those limitations in his bout with Schaaf. In comparison with Schaaf, Heeney had been a pushover, and Baer knew it. Hoffman would not be matching him with a series of Tom Heeneys again. Heeney had served as a confidence builder. His next fight would determine his future. He would fight Tommy Loughran and finally garner a clear self-awareness of his limitations, of how far his strengths would carry him, and how much his weaknesses would hurt him.

Tommy Loughran was one of the most highly rated fighters of his time. A loss to him would be of inestimable value to Baer, and it was a loss that Baer had to have if he was going to be a better fighter. In *Cinderella Man*, Schaap writes, "Loughran danced, jabbed, flitted in and out of Baer's reach, and avoided a lucky punch at all costs."[8] Baer did land one hard punch in round two, and Loughran thought he suffered a broken rib. It was not enough. Loughran's defeat of Baer would be unanimous; even Baer's manager agreed with the decision. He hoped that Baer would now understand that he had a lot to learn: He could not ascend to the championship without greater skills and more rigorous training. Loughran, too, could see that without the proper training, Baer would never rise above being a mere contender. With the proper training, however, he would be able to use his devastating right hand with uncommon effect. If used strategically, he could use it to punch his way to the pinnacle of boxing fame and fortune, the heavyweight championship of the world.

While Baer took pride in himself, he was not so proud that he was blind to his shortcomings. Neither pride nor false modesty kept him from wanting to learn from a fighter who was more skilled than he was. He was like any thoughtful student who knows he needs a little tutoring to pass tests. And what better tutor could there be than the man who had so deftly defeated him? Thus, Baer approached Loughran in his dressing room. He was neither bowed nor arrogant. He simply asked, almost matter-of-factly, but with a charming smile, for advice. Loughran, a natural teacher who would not withhold his knowledge from another professional, suggested that they meet the next day, and he would give Baer some pointers that would make an enormous difference in the outcomes of future fights. Baer thanked him and looked forward to their meeting.

Loughran generously taught the man who owned one of the most powerful right fists of any fighter in the business how to use his left fist for disarming jabs that would keep opponents on the defensive. Loughran taught Baer the art of the successful left jab, an essential punch that Baer had virtually discounted in his previous fights. Jack Dempsey, who saw something of himself in the hard-hitting fighter from the west, also gave Baer a few lessons. If Baer could learn what Loughran and Dempsey had demonstrated, "you just might become a champion," Dempsey told him. Baer smiled and nodded.

With his newly developed skills and to undo a humiliating loss, Baer was again matched to fight the formidable Ernie Schaaf. Schaaf was a highly regarded fighter, and if Baer could defeat him, he would overcome a formidable obstacle on the road to a shot at the championship. Baer's newly developed skills made him a more threatening opponent than he had been in his earlier fight with Schaaf. He had also trained somewhat harder for his rematch. Yet Schaaf expected a repeat performance of his earlier bout with Baer. But it was not to be, and Schaaf almost felt as if he were fighting a different man.

Throughout the match, Baer dominated, throwing and landing more punches than Schaaf. He used his left jab effectively, winning round after round. Schaaf could hardly believe what was happening. The judges scored each round for Baer. At the outset of the 10th round, as he had done in the third round with Heeney, Baer rushed from his corner like a tiger, determined to end the fight with a sudden knockout. He saw an opening in Schaaf's defenses and unleashed his powerful right hand with the force of a sledgehammer. It landed solidly on Schaaf's chin, sending the surprised and blurry-eyed fighter to the canvas. Schaaf lay there comatose while the referee counted him out. Schaaf had never been hit with such a powerful punch, and it took him several minutes to recover. He rolled his head to one side and gazed through the ropes. His turned his head again and stared up at the lights above the ring. He was nearly motionless, and so a doctor entered the ring to examine the supine fighter.

Baer suddenly felt sick at the possibility that he had killed another opponent. "No, no," he muttered to himself. Were these his alternatives: to lose in a humiliating defeat or to kill his opponent? He wanted neither one. If he killed another opponent, he was ready to throw in the towel, to call it quits. He was not a killer; it was the last thing he wanted to be. Yes, he wanted to be rich and famous, and be a celebrity, but he did not want to pay for it by killing another man. Baer was a lover, a bon vivant. That's how he wanted to be regarded. Fortunately, Schaaf regained consciousness, a little wobbly on his feet and a little dazed, but he was apparently okay. He was not quite himself, but who is after being knocked out? He responded correctly to questions and didn't complain about any unusual pains, so he was judged to be in good shape. He believed that he would soon feel like his old self.

A few weeks later, Schaaf felt fully restored to his good physical condition and was prepared to fight again. His manager and trainer gave him a green light. He needn't worry. Yet, once in the ring, he was not the bobbing and weaving pugilist he had been. His performance surprised and disappointed onlookers, especially those in his corner. He seemed sodden, often slow moving, and nearly flat-footed; he seemed to be going through the motions of a boxer like an actor who was playing a part that he had recently learned. The fire that had once burned so fiercely in him was now an ember that only periodically flamed. He couldn't fan the sparks from his past into the flames of energy, exuberance, and fast-moving skills that were necessary to score a win.

Nonetheless, he kept going. He was, if anything, relentless. It was what he had been trained to do. He was still a box-office draw, and his handlers continued to make money off of him. He wasn't going to sit in his corner and refuse to come out at the sound of the bell. His reputation had not yet died. He was a different man, and six months after his devastating defeat by Baer, he fought the mountainous, mob-controlled Primo Carnera. Carnera was an easy, slow-moving target and was never known as a hard puncher. In fact, it was suspected that his mob handlers had fixed his fights against second- and third-rate opponents to create a reputation that he was indomitable. Because of his towering height (6-foot-6) and large, melon-like muscles, Carnera looked more dangerous than he was. He was the perfect picture of a circus strongman, which is what he had been in Europe before being induced to become a professional fighter.

In the 11th round of his bout with Schaaf, Carnera tagged his adversary with an unimpressive right to the chin. Some said it was a powder-puff punch, or a mere whisper of a punch. But Schaaf went down. And he went down hard. This time, Schaaf did not get up. The press had a field day, blaming Baer for Schaaf's death and reasoning that Carnera's punch was little more than a light smack, a tap, a soft blow, not powerful enough to knock an ordinary man down, never mind kill someone. Schaaf's death, they claimed, was the result of the beating he had suffered at the fists of a killer, the viciously unrelenting and sadistically mad Max Baer.

While the world of boxing could have lived for months on the negative publicity accorded Baer, he once again found himself deeply conflicted. How could this be? Boxing was how he made his living; he was good at it. He never wanted to kill anyone. He didn't have a homicidal thought in his head when boxing. He just wanted to win, to be a fun-loving celebrity who was admired far and wide. The publicity came like a tidal wave that would carry an ocean of cash into the hands of promoters who could put together the next Max Baer fight. It would be like selling tickets to a Roman gladiatorial combat where death was the outcome. Baer, the powerful, the killer, was now being touted as the next likely world champion.

For Baer, it was not the way he hoped his career would develop. He had no intention of killing an opponent, regardless of what the fans wanted or expected. The fans had known the kind of fighter he was; they had laughed along with his antics, laughed at his quips from the ring. When he waved at his fans, they waved back at him. Many regarded him as a clown, someone who would rather make an audience laugh than engage the crowd's lust for violence. In many of his fights, he would turn to the fans and play the part of a smiling vaudevillian comedian, not a killer. But could such a fun-loving entertainer discipline himself and train rigorously to become the world heavyweight boxing champion and not kill anyone in the ring, or would he be haunted for the rest of his life by the deaths of Frankie Campbell and Ernie Schaaf? In numerous subsequent fights, fearful of causing life-threatening injuries, he would back off after landing a powerful blow, glance anxiously for a moment at his opponent, and then proceed, sometimes with undo caution. He was determined to avoid doing permanent damage to an opponent.

Baer's next fight would be against the pugilistic powerhouse of Nazi Germany, Max Schmeling, a symbol of the Aryan strongman that every Jew wanted to see defeated. What would Baer do? Would he, with the Star of David on his boxing shorts, spare the Nazi stooge, or would he go for the kill? Would the most dangerous European heavyweight fight the clown or the student of Jack Dempsey and Tommy Loughran? The world waited. The bookies took the bets. The Nazi hierarchy wanted a decisive win over what they considered to be a mongrel Jew, and the Jewish community wanted to show the Nazis that they had a champ, not a clown, who exemplified tough Jewish resistance to the coming bestiality.

Benny Leonard and Annette Kellerman, 1922. *Courtesy of National Police Gazette Enterprises, LLC.*

Abe Attell. *Bain News Service. Courtesy of the Library of Congress.*

Abe Attell. *Bain News Service. Courtesy of the Library of Congress.*

Jack Dempsey, Harry Houdini, and Benny Leonard. *Bain News Service. Courtesy of the Library of Congress.*

Barney Ross and Phil Furr, 1936. *Photo by Harris & Ewing. Courtesy of the Library of Congress.*

Barney Ross, 1938. *Courtesy of the Library of Congress.*

Max Baer, 1940. *Courtesy of the Library of Congress.*

Max Schmeling, 1938. *Photo by Wm. C. Greene. Courtesy of the Library of Congress.*

Primo Carnera, 1933. *Courtesy of the Library of Congress.*

James Braddock, 1935. *Photo by Alan Fisher. Courtesy of the Library of Congress.*

7

JEW VERSUS NAZI

Many people both inside and outside of the world of boxing did not consider Max Baer to be an authentic Jew, for they believed, as many still do, that a Jew must have a Jewish mother. Baer's mother was not Jewish, and his father was the son of a Jewish father and a gentile mother. When Max Baer fought Max Schmeling, he wore a Star of David on his boxing trunks. If a non-Jew thinks of himself as a Jew and joins the Israel Defense Forces, does he fight as a Jew or a gentile? That is a question of personal identification, not for others to say.

Under the Nazi Nuremberg Laws, passed in 1933, the year that Baer fought Schmeling, a person with only one Jewish grandparent was classified as a Mischling of the second degree, that is, a mixed-breed or mongrel Jew. It was colloquially known as the "First Racial Definition." The decree stipulated that a person would be regarded as a racial Jew for purposes of the law if he had one Jewish parent or one Jewish grandparent. Had Max Baer, the Mischling, lived in Germany or one of the Nazi-conquered countries, he would have been shipped off to a concentration camp, if not immediately killed. If there had been an Israel in 1933, and if Baer had wanted to become one of its citizens, he would have been accepted because he had one Jewish grandparent.

In defense of self-proclaimed Jews like Max Baer, Israeli author Amos Oz writes in the magazine *Tikkun*, "A Jew is anyone who chooses or is compelled to share a common fate with other Jews." He adds, "Who is a Jew? Anyone who is mad enough to call himself or herself a Jew is a Jew."[1] Hence, according to not only Amos Oz, but also Israeli immigra-

tion policy and the Nazi definition of a Jew promulgated by the Nuremberg Laws, Max Baer was a Jew. Perhaps Baer's mother should have the
last word, as quoted in Jeremy Schaap's *Cinderella Man*: "You can tell
those people in New York that Maxie has got a Jewish father, and if that
doesn't make him Jewish enough for them, I don't know what will."[2]

And what about Max Schmeling? Although he was briefly Hitler's
favorite athlete, Schmeling may have been one of the least enthusiastic
Nazis celebrated by the Nazi hierarchy. He started his professional boxing career in 1924 and came to the United States in 1928, to fight for
bigger purses than he could earn in Germany. New York, however, did
not greet Schmeling with open arms. Few in the boxing world were
willing to deal with his German manager. Schmeling could have shadowboxed and skipped rope on Fifth Avenue and no one would have cared.

If he was going to earn the kind of purses he had dreamed of back in
Germany, he would need an American manager. And that person turned
out to be the inimitable and irrepressible Joe Jacobs. Joe was the son of
poor Hungarian Jewish immigrants who had settled on the Lower East
Side of Manhattan. He spoke a strange language of his own invention, a
curious and at times humorous mixture of English and Hungarian (what
one of his friends referred to as Engarian). It didn't matter, for Jacobs was
a superb negotiator, whether speaking the King's English or his own
patois, and his contacts in the world of boxing were second to none.

Jacobs, as a young man, had started out knowing next to nothing about
boxing, but by the time he had evaluated Schmeling's possibilities, skill,
and athleticism, he knew he might one day have a champion as a client.
Schmeling writes in his autobiography that Jacobs was "as nice as he was
clever."[3] And Schmeling was further impressed when Jacobs refused to
take the standard manager's commission from Schmeling until the fighter's contract with his German manager had expired. Yet, Jacobs got to
work immediately. Through his creative publicity efforts, he made sure
that Schmeling's name appeared in newspapers almost every day. Press
releases flowed from Jacobs's typewriter. He designated Schmeling the
"Black Ulan of the Rhine." He had him photographed against tall buildings, visually implying that Schmeling was a skyscraper of boxing: tall,
solid, and indestructible. And since Schmeling bore a striking resemblance to Jack Dempsey, Jacobs had posters printed with side-by-side
images of the two pugilists. The world knew Jack Dempsey as one of the

most ferocious boxers of his time; certainly Schmeling would follow in the former champ's footsteps. It was just a matter of time.

For the Nazis, Joe Jacobs presented a problem that could not be ignored. The Jew Jacobs was like a painful splinter in the psychopathology of Adolf Hitler. There, it festered. Schmeling, the great Aryan specimen of physical strength and power, could not be managed by a Jew. It was ridiculous. Impossible. Laughable. An embarrassment to the theory of Aryan superiority: A superior being could not be managed by an inferior one. Who could believe such an insane arrangement? Hitler naturally demanded that Schmeling fire Jacobs. Schmeling, however, had a strength that went beyond the physical; he had sufficient strength of character to say no to the Führer. Few men, even high-ranking Nazi officials, would have dared to openly disobey one of their Führer's commands. One can imagine Hitler's surprise, anger, and disgust; however, he did not insist, for Schmeling was a highly valuable commodity, a symbol and potential propaganda tool for the Nazi dictator. Besides, Schmeling was getting matched against important opponents thanks to Jacob's keen negotiating skills and wide range of contacts. Each time Schmeling won, he won for the Reich. Films of his winning bouts were de rigueur throughout Germany. Hitler had merely turned away in disgust.

And so Jacobs continued to negotiate deals for Schmeling. Finally, they were both getting wealthy. The publicity that Jacobs engineered for Schmeling meant that all the seats for his bouts were sold out and for top dollar. Jacobs had told Schmeling at the beginning of their relationship, "Not a single day can go by without your name being in the papers." And Jacobs did not disappoint: He proved to be one of the great boxing publicists of the era; he was a relentless PR dynamo, a PR juggernaut, resourceful, skillful, and relentless. After several years, however, Jacobs's PR stunts began to annoy the boxing commission, which wanted the public to see its sport as a manly endeavor free of gimmicks.

After Jacobs had "Two Ton" Tony Galento appear in the ring with a beer barrel, the commissioners suspended Jacobs before Schmeling's second and critical bout with Joe Louis. It didn't matter that Galento trained by throwing beer barrels on the sidewalk outside his bar in New Jersey. That was Jersey, not the hallowed arena of Madison Square Garden. A disappointed and suspended Jacobs was not permitted to be in Schmeling's corner for the Louis rematch, and his absence made Schmeling nervous and fearful of the revenge-seeking "Brown Bomber." Having lost to Schmeling in their first encounter, Louis was determined to show the world that he was the superior boxer. In the first round, Louis disposed of Schmeling first with a hard blow to the latter's liver, which resulted in Schmeling yelling in pain, and then with several quick shots to the head. Schmeling's cornerman threw in the towel, and Louis was awarded a technical knockout win.

Jacobs always knew that the key to big paydays lay in generating so much publicity for a fight that all available tickets would be snapped up, often for more than the face value. Several years before Schmeling's historical encounters with Joe Louis, Jacobs had rented a hall in one of Berlin's working-class neighborhoods during the Christmas season, 1929. He engendered so much publicity about his superman that he filled the hall to capacity, including standing room, and left hundreds of disappointed fans outside. In New York, for Schmeling's 1930 championship fight against Jack Sharkey, Jacobs arranged to donate a portion of ticket sales to the Hearst Milk Fund, one of the Hearst family's favorite charities, thus guaranteeing extensive coverage in all of the Hearst newspapers. According to the news stories that Jacobs produced, Schmeling was not only a great fighter, but also a kind and charitable man who loved children. A picture of the fighter with a slum-dwelling child painted him as one of boxing's most sympathetic and kindly pugilists. The public ate it up.

In addition to being a superb boxing promoter and publicist, Jacobs was also a creative and astute businessman, seeing opportunities that others passed up. For example, during Prohibition, aboard an ocean liner with Schmeling to Germany, Jacobs discovered a lucrative opportunity that would have won the admiration or envy of Al Capone. Prohibition had dramatically inflated the price of alcoholic beverages, whether bootlegged or homemade. A bottle of champagne sold for $50 on the black market. When Jacobs toasted his great fighter with a shipboard bottle of champagne, he was given a bill for a mere $3. Astonished at the low price of a single bottle, Jacobs asked the wine steward how many bottles were in the ship's inventory. The ship's entire stock of champagne amounted to 20,000 bottles. Jacobs smiled and bought the entire lot for $3 a bottle, turning a $60,000 dollar investment into $1 million

It was not boxing, however, that generated the most publicity for the clever publicist. It was an act of satirical irony that raised the ire of Nazis

and Jews alike. Jacobs had gone to Germany in 1935, when Schmeling
was to fight Steve Hamas in Hamburg. Schmeling won the fight, and an
enthusiastic crowd of 25,000, unable to contain themselves, rose in uni-
son and started to sing the Nazi anthem, known as the "Deutschlandlied,"
with the infamous opening lines, "Deutschland, Deutschland über alles."
As they did so, they gave the stiff-armed Nazi salute. Jacobs, meanwhile,
rushed to the center of the ring, where he congratulated Schmeling. As
the voices of the crowd grew in volume and enthusiasm, Jacobs seemed
momentarily bemused. He looked at the crowd, not knowing what to do,
then smiled and winked at Schmeling; much to Schmeling's surprise,
Jacobs spontaneously raised his right arm and gave the Nazi salute. But
rather than an outstretched hand, fingers as straight as a board, Jacobs
held up a cigar between his bent forefinger and middle finger. The large
cigar seemed a prosthetic substitute for his middle finger. He smiled and
winked again as if inviting Schmeling to participate in the joke. News
photographers recorded the scene with their cameras, and when the Nazis
saw the photographs they were irate, outraged, and disgusted, with many
of them spewing anti-Semitic epithets and ranting about that damned
impertinent Yid. A Jew was not only giving the Nazi salute, but he also
seemed to be giving them the finger with his outstretched, vertically
raised cigar.

   In New York, however, people weren't laughing, although perhaps
they should have been. Jews thought it outrageous that a fellow Jew had
given the Nazi salute; for them, there was no irony in such an act. It was
not defiant, it was craven. In the *New York Daily News*, Jack Miley
writes, "Up in the Bronx the good burghers agreed that the little man with
the big cigar was no credit to their creed. In the Broadway delicatessens
and nighteries . . . the waiters were conspiring to slip Mickey Finns in his
herring."[4]

   For a few satirists, however, it was a gesture that brought smiles to
their faces. It preceded by years Woody Allen's *Zelig*, but it was the real
thing, not a cinematic contrivance. It could also have been a scene in Mel
Brooks's movie and play *The Producers*. Charlie Chaplin could have
used it in his satirical comedy *The Great Dictator*. And even the Three
Stooges had altered the title of the popular song "I'll Never Fall in Love
Again" to appear "I'll Never Heil Again." For that, the Stooges had been
put on Hitler's death list, which was dependent—of course—on the Nazis
conquering the United States. Dictators cannot tolerate being the subject

of satire. It certainly took no small amount of courage for Jacobs, a Jew, to stand up in front of a crowd of 25,000 cheering and singing Nazis to satirize the Nazi salute. The guy gets credit for chutzpah.

And that was the man who engineered Max Schmeling's successful career, and he did it as well as a film director who creates a work of art worthy of praise and awards. But while Jacobs could generate a seemingly endless ream of newspaper clippings for Schmeling and negotiate profitable deals for his fights, Schmeling still had to win fights. A series of losses would have left Jacobs's efforts stillborn. When Schmeling won the heavyweight title, it was not by a knockout; in fact, it was not because of any of his efforts. Schmeling became the world heavyweight champion because his opponent, Jack Sharkey, delivered a powerful below-the-belt blow. Sharkey was known for such tactics, but this time the referee refused to overlook it or even give Sharkey a warning. He declared Schmeling the winner, pointing out that Sharkey's punch was a foul and not in keeping with the stated (but often ignored) rules of the Marquis of Queensbury. It was the only time that the outcome of a championship fight had been decided because of a foul punch. The public called Schmeling the "low-blow champion." Jacobs told him that he must defend his title in the next fight. It would demonstrate to the world that he deserved the championship.

That was in 1930, and Schmeling's tepid glory was short-lived, as he and Sharkey met for a rematch in 1932, and Sharkey won the title, following a controversial and disputed decision. It had seemed as if Sharkey could barely stand up after being on the receiving end of blow after hard-hitting blow delivered by an apparently impervious Schmeling. The crowd did not approve, and the sportswriters smelled a judicial payoff. Jacobs insisted that his fighter had been robbed of the title and that the judges had been paid off.

Things only got worse for Schmeling, for Hitler now headed the most powerful political party in Germany. The following year, 1933, Hitler would ascend to the chancellorship. For Hitler and his PR guru, Joseph Goebbels, Schmeling was worth cultivating and presenting to the world as an ideal Aryan specimen, a superman of the superior race. It was not surprising then that the public came to view Schmeling as a hateful Nazi puppet.

A little more than four months after Hitler attained the chancellorship, there was a fight that sparked and fired the animosity and adoration of boxing fans. The German-American Bund was nearly rhapsodic about their superman. The Jewish community in New York and other cities not only excoriated the so-called superman, but they also turned their adoring attention on the man who could represent their strength and determination—Max Baer. The excitement riled up by the upcoming bout was palpable. The scene was set, the actors were in place, and the curtain was about to go up on a momentous bout between the reluctant Nazi puppet and the Jew who was not considered an authentic Jew.

Famous boxing writer and editor of *Ring Magazine* Nat Fleischer declared that Baer had been circumcised a Jew just for the fight. It was an argument that continues in some quarters. It didn't matter to Jewish fight fans, for they had hoped and prayed that Baer would send a message to the Third Reich that Jews could not be pushed around, that they would fight anti-Semitism and defend their rights. For Jews, and for many others, the scheduled heavyweight bout between the two Maxes (which foreshadowed the more famous bouts between Joe Louis and Max Schmeling) would be a microcosm of a battle that many foresaw taking place between two armies, one representing the forces of bigotry, repression, and murder, and the other representing the tolerance and opportunities provided to citizens by liberal democracies. Going into the fight, Schmeling was a 4–1 favorite to beat Baer. The bookies were doing a brisk business: There were few fans willing to bet on Baer, but those who did would clean up nicely. Fleischer writes in *Max Baer: The Glamour Boy of the Ring*,

> You couldn't quite blame the dopestars . . . for Schmeling had just won a high reputation as a dependable, if somewhat plodding gladiator. The German was a sharpshooter, with plenty of endurance and equipped with a sure-enough kayo wallop. Whereas, Baer, though brilliant, was rated erratic and just as apt to make a mediocre showing as he was to score a quick victory. [5]

Erstwhile heavyweight champ Jack Dempsey, who had a Jewish grandmother but had never—even remotely—been considered a Jew, was promoting the fight and playing up Baer's Jewishness. The excitement grew more intense as the date of the fight, June 8, 1933, approached. Well before that date, Dempsey had already sold $250,000 worth of tickets, a large sum considering that 1933 was one of the worst years of the Depression. The promoters and fighters, whether out of charitable goodness or for the PR benefits, agreed that 10 percent of the proceeds would be donated to Calvary Hospital in the Bronx, which remains one of the most respected hospices in New York City. Seats for the fight at Yankee Stadium would range from $1.15 to $11.50; however, scalpers were able to get as much as $50 for ringside seats. Those were filled by senators, governors, mayors, movie stars, and a few mobsters and their showgirls. By June 8, there would be 60,000 fans warming every seat in Yankee Stadium, and ticket sales topped $300,000 and reported being $1 million. It was the kind of purse that Jacobs and Schmeling had dreamed about, whereas Baer cared little for money, spending it as fast as he earned it. For him, money was a passport that opened borders to lands of pleasure.

Baer's fans and his manager were worried that Baer would not take the fight seriously, that he would play the clown in the ring, lose interest, and perform so badly that Schmeling would walk away the winner. To avoid that disaster and fire up Baer's anger and ferocity, his manager, Ancil Hoffman, repeatedly told his fighter that Schmeling was a Jew hater, just like all those other Nazis, and that he wanted to show the world that Jews are sniveling cowards. Hitler was the kind of guy who would have kicked the Baer family into the gutter and let them rot. Hitler would use Schmeling's victory to propagate the idea that the Nazis were truly a race of supermen and that Schmeling was the best of the best, more super than super. It was therefore up to Baer to teach the Nazis a lesson and prove Hitler wrong.

Baer entered the ring sporting a Jewish star on his boxing trunks. It was the first time he had done so, and Joe Jacobs, Schmeling's manager, was disconcerted by it. It portended Baer's determination to not just win, but also pummel his opponent into ignominious defeat. When the largely Jewish crowd saw the star, they applauded, whistled, and cheered enthusiastically.

Jacobs, like Hoffman, thought that Baer would clown around in the ring, as he usually did. He would probably get bored midway through the bout, leaving himself open to being outpointed by a superior pugilist. And Baer was also taken aback when Schmeling entered the ring, for although he had seen plenty of photos of Schmeling and met him, it had all taken place out of the ring. Now Schmeling looked like Dempsey's younger brother. The resemblance was startling and perhaps portended a devastating defeat for Baer. Dempsey had been the most brilliant, persistent, feared, and brutal fighter of his era. To this day, many think of him as the greatest heavyweight boxer of the 20th century. For affirmation of that opinion, one need only read Roger Kahn's excellent book *A Flame of Pure Fire: Jack Dempsey and the Roaring Twenties.*

Baer was one of Dempsey's favorite boxers, as the former champ saw himself in the powerhouse that could be awakened in the joyful Baer. Dempsey thought that Baer had one of the most powerful right fists in the business. Yet, Baer might never achieve true greatness, said Dempsey. One of Baer's characteristic problems was that he disdained regular training and preferred seducing beautiful women and making people laugh at his clownish antics rather than impressing them with his fistic talents. Even though Dempsey was fond of Baer, he also enjoyed the company of Schmeling. While Schmeling trained for the fight, Dempsey appeared at his training camp and offered to spar with him. Once in the ring, Dempsey asked Schmeling not to hit his nose, because he had gotten a nose job to improve his looks for his new career as a screen actor. The sparring matches, reported by major sportswriters, added further excitement to the upcoming bout. Was Schmeling another Dempsey, or was Baer going to be the new ring titan?

And then there was the fight: The fighters were brought to the center of the ring, received their instructions, touched gloves, and returned to their corners. When the bell for round one clanged, Baer rushed from his corner like a tiger about to seize its prey. Schmeling was taken aback, got off to a slow start, and seemed bewildered by Baer's ferocious rapid-fire punches. It was a devastating round for Schmeling. He looked shaken, but Baer provided him with an opportunity to recover, for Baer's intense fire seemed to cool to a warm glow. He now seemed bored, distracted, and uninterested, and Schmeling was racking up points. He was outboxing Baer and even landed a powerful right to Baer's head. Following the end of the round, back in his corner, Baer complained that he was seeing three images of Schmeling. "Hit the one in the middle," said Dempsey. Still, round after round was being won by Schmeling; when Baer returned to his corner at the end of the eighth round, Hoffman told him he was losing the fight. "Go out and get him. Finish it!"

Hoffman had lit a new fire in Baer, who rushed out from his corner and pummeled Schmeling as if he wanted to kill him. Schmeling was once again caught off guard, as Baer wildly threw punches, including backhanded ones and a few rabbit punches. He was thrashing Schmeling but could not finish him; Schmeling was saved by the bell. Back in his corner, Baer was told to go out and end the fight. He needed a knockout, because he had fallen behind in points. As the bell clanged for the start of the 10th round, Baer rushed at Schmeling and landed a hard right to his chin, knocking him to the canvas. Schmeling lay there for a moment, stunned, dazed, and looking bewildered. In slow motion, he managed to stand, his rubbery legs barely supporting him. Before Schmeling could get his bearings, Baer rushed him again, knocking the confused fighter about the ring. Schmeling looked like a drunk who couldn't understand what was happening to him and had no place to hide.

Fearing that he might kill Schmeling as he had Frankie Campbell and perhaps Ernie Schaaf, Baer asked the referee to end the fight. His conscience could not bear the burden of guilt that would have consumed him if he killed another opponent. The referee agreed that Schmeling was unable to defend himself and mercifully ended the fight, declaring Baer the undisputed winner. The crowd, with the exception of those representing the German-American Bund, cheered deliriously. In his autobiography, Schmeling writes,

> Despite the weeks of training, I decisively lost the fight against Max Baer. I can't say why. Maybe it was the brutal heat that day in New York. Even before the fight sweat was pouring down my body. During the whole fight I felt paralyzed.
>
> "Move, for God's sake, move!" Max Machon [Schmeling's trainer] had yelled between rounds. "Move away from him, get him missing." But my legs were like lead and only rarely did I manage to avoid or neutralize Baer's punches. Standing still, I offered the Californian an easy target. By the time Baer's corner told him to finish it in the eighth round I could barely hold up my arms. After several knockdowns, referee Arthur Donovan finally stopped it in the 10th round. In the dressing room Max Machon said, "That wasn't a defeat, that was a disaster."[6]

While there are many photos of Schmeling and various opponents in his autobiography, there is none of Baer. It is no wonder, for there is a famous photograph of the two fighters immediately after the fight. In it, the referee is holding up Baer's triumphant right hand as Schmeling, still looking dazed, stares bewilderingly at the camera as if he isn't sure where he is and what he is looking at. There is another famous photograph taken after the fight, where Baer and Dempsey are sitting side by side. Baer's nose is bruised, his collar undone, and he presents his clenched right fist for Dempsey's inspection. Dempsey, as if not to injure Baer's right fist, gently holds the dangerous weapon as he looks at it with apparent admiration, a slight smile curving his lips. That fist had delivered the punches that Dempsey knew it could, once the tiger in Baer had been awakened and offered red meat.

The crowd continued to cheer as Baer left the ring. An infectious, gregarious grin pushed up his cheeks. He waved to the onlookers, many of whom waved back. As he walked past fans, they attempted to reach out to him, pat his back, or touch one of his gloved fists. Baer had done what they had hoped he would do. He was their champion, and they loved him. But there was only one fan who Baer had his eyes on when the fight was over, a blonde showgirl named June Knight, who sang and danced in many a Broadway show and had just been hired to appear in the *Ziegfeld Follies*. Between rounds, Baer could see her, suggestively licking her lips. When he had been declared the winner, she waved and threw him a kiss. For her, the night was still young and full of erotic promise. And Baer was intent on enjoying himself.

His divorce from Dorothy Dunbar was incomplete, and he was looking to forget her and the pain of divorce. He hoped to find such relief in the arms of June, his new lover; he also wanted to forget the two lawsuits he was enduring from two women who alleged breaches of promise in their legal actions. The glamour boy of the ring was also an athlete of the boudoir, a man who allegedly and frequently promised marital bliss but had no intention of keeping those promises. Or perhaps he had made those utterances during passionate embraces, when he was carried away by the opportunities of the moment.

While Baer could escape the claws of disappointed lovers with symbolic payments, it would not be so easy to dispense with the claims of his former manager. Lorimer had attached a portion of Baer's winnings. Since the days of Lorimer's management, Baer had sold more than 100 percent of himself to eager investors. Extricating himself from such a mess required years of negotiated compromises.

A trumpet blast from Hollywood would offer a new opportunity. Impressed by Baer's outsized Jewish identity, many Jewish studio owners wanted him to sign contracts to star in movies for their establishments. They admired Baer and thought that his good looks and cocky, good-humored personality would play out well on the silver screen. A starring role in a major film would make Baer an even bigger celebrity. In Hollywood, Baer became the toast of the town, and he was feted by producers and directors alike. Stars and starlets freely offered themselves to him, and Baer, living out his dream as a playboy of the western world, never turned them down. Greta Garbo, for one, was so impressed by Baer's demolition of Schmeling and so happy to see a Nazi crushed and humiliated that she engaged Baer in a brief affair. She invited him into her home, and he only left after the affair had run its course. She had been Baer's reward for defeating the Nazi puppet.

For Max Schmeling, life offered a different scenario: He had lost a fight to Steve Hamas in 1934, the same year he fought to a draw with Spanish boxer Paulino Uzcudun. Fans and promoters thought that Schmeling's career was sadly running out of steam. Then he beat Walter Neusel and both Hamas and Uzcudun in successive rematches. Interest in Schmeling flared again. The following year, 1936, he had his most celebrated victory over Joe Louis and became, once again, the hero of the Third Reich. A film of his win over Louis was incorporated into a documentary and shown in theaters throughout Germany. Schmeling was the ideal of the German athlete: strong, impervious, and relentless in his pursuit of supremacy. It was not until 1938, when he unexpectedly lost to Louis in a rematch, that Schmeling's flaming star turned into a burnt-out meteor and vanished from the Nazi firmament. He was now persona non grata at high-level Nazi functions. He would no longer be invited to supper with Hitler and Goebbels. He was not anonymous, but he was no longer the ideal to which athletes should aspire. A fallen hero is more of a disgrace than a man who was never a hero.

But Schmeling was more than just a boxer. He was a man of character and had a well-developed conscience. While Hitler had removed his favor from Schmeling, he still hated the Jews and initiated the "Night of Broken Glass," aka "Kristallnacht." Appalled by what was happening to his Jewish friends, Schmeling found the Nazi purges detestable. As Jews were being beaten in the streets of Berlin, their store windows smashed and their merchandise looted, their synagogues torched, Schmeling saved the lives of two Jewish children by hiding them in his apartment. Once again, Schmeling showed that he was no friend of Nazism and that he was willing to place his conscience above the prejudices of the masses.

In 1939, Schmeling made his fistic comeback, winning the European heavyweight championship by knocking out Adolf Heuser; following that fight, the local newspapers mistakenly printed the following headline: "MAX SCHMELING KO'S ADOLF HITLER IN ADOLF HEUSER STADIUM." To say that the headline put Hitler's teeth on edge would be an understatement: He flew into a rage, not only at Schmeling, who had nothing to do with the headline, but also at subversive pressmen and typesetters, who—he thought—were out to embarrass the leader of the Third Reich. The typesetters, fearing imprisonment, quickly corrected their error, and their revised headlines appeared within hours of the one that had set off conspiracy theories among the Gestapo. Poor Schmeling. He was definitely persona non grata with the Nazi hierarchy. He had first lost to a Jew and then a Negro, and then he had beaten Hitler in a heavyweight bout. The losses had profoundly disappointed Goebbels, who had wanted to use Schmeling for propaganda purposes. The Schmeling documentary that Goebbels had ordered had been shelved after his loss to Louis, and his heroic fistic accomplishments would never see the darkness of a theater for as long as the little propaganda minister with the crippled foot was in power.

When the Nazis initiated war by invading Poland in September 1939, Schmeling was appalled. The last thing he wanted was to join the military. He was by no means a pacifist, but he saw no purpose to war. Prominent men of the arts, as well as celebrated athletes, were exempted from the military draft, which targeted ordinary German citizens in their late teens and 20s. Schmeling was in his 30s. He never thought he would be called up. The Nazis, however, wanted to dispose of their apolitical, unreliable pugilist. He was drafted into the paratroopers and told he would be an instructor. "Don't worry, you won't see combat," he was told. That turned out to be a lie. He would be a frontline soldier, ripe for death. In his autobiography, Schmeling says, "My enlistment was a personal vendetta; I kept looking for a way out."[7] To no avail.

During that time, Schmeling received news that his longtime friend and manager, Joe Jacobs, had died in New York of a heart attack. Jacobs was only 41 years old. His sadness was replaced by relentless basic training to become an elite paratrooper. His training completed, he was parachuted into the Battle of Crete. Once on the ground, during the first day of the conflict, Schmeling was hit by enemy fire and badly wounded in his right knee. He was evacuated and sent to the hospital; after that, the Nazis, particularly Joseph Goebbels, thought Schmeling was a broken man who would be left and forgotten on the dust heap of history, while their great and glorious empire would continue on for the next thousand years.

However, Schmeling further antagonized the Nazi hierarchy. It was as if Goebbels had become a victim of his own blunders. An American journalist named Bill Flannery, of the International News Service, visited Schmeling while he was recuperating in a Greek hospital. Flannery had been offered this opportunity by Goebbels, prior to the U.S. entry into the war, so that a prominent German athlete could attest to the cruelty of British soldiers. Schmeling denied that British soldiers had indulged in cruelty; in fact, he said that Greek villagers may have attacked German soldiers in acts of reprisal for destroying their homes. When asked if he thought that the United States and Germany would go to war against one another, Schmeling replied, "For me, that would be a tragedy. I have always seen America as my second home."[8]

Goebbels again flew into a rage; the skinny little worshipper of Hitler screamed that Schmeling should be imprisoned as a traitor, if not shot by a firing squad. He attempted to have Schmeling stand trial in the National Socialist People's Court, but that was only for civilians, not soldiers. When Schmeling was finally brought to trial in a military court, he was acquitted, for Germany and the United States had not yet come to military blows and so there was no harm in Schmeling's comments; furthermore, much to Goebbels's chagrin, no witnesses could be found to attest to British cruelty. With no further legal remedies, Goebbels demanded that Schmeling's name never again appear in a German newspaper, that his image never be seen in a newsreel, and that his name be stricken from any listings of German athletes. He was now a nonperson. When Schmeling was finally discharged from the military in 1943, no one took notice of the nonevent. He had been a soldier for three years and spent a mere two days as a frontline soldier.

Schmeling had yet another opportunity to disappoint the Nazis. This time, much to his surprise, he was asked to go on a diplomatic mission. One would have thought that the Nazis would have washed their hands of their disappointing former heavyweight champ, but they were like a dog with a bone. They could not let go, it seemed. They asked Schmeling to visit the pope at his residence inside the Vatican to try and repair relations between Germany and the Vatican, which had been fractured by the SS.

Schmeling was brought to the Papal Palace and ushered past the Swiss Guards and into the pope's private chambers, where, after a brief waiting period, he was received by the pope. Pope Pius XII entered the room and heartily greeted Schmeling, whom he had admired from afar. He thought that Schmeling was a marvelous athlete and had watched films of his fights. The pope, according to Schmeling's autobiography, expressed his sadness about the immense destruction of Europe and the death and wounding of people throughout the world during the war. He said that he would pray for peace. Schmeling thanked the pope for his time and departed.

When Schmeling returned from Rome, he was ordered to report to the foreign office. He promptly did so. After Schmeling recounted what the pope had said, he was asked if the pope had said he would pray for a German victory. Schmeling said the pope never said such a thing; he said he prayed for peace. Newspapers in Rome and throughout the world reprinted what Schmeling had told the German foreign office. The German newspapers, however, did not print a word about the meeting. Goebbels once again was furious. That he permitted such a visit to occur may be indicative of a blind and misplaced optimism. After this last misadventure, Goebbels probably wished that Schmeling had never existed. Was there ever such a great German athlete who turned out to be such a propaganda disaster?

By war's end, a defeated Germany was a collection of rubble and broken dreams, and the hated perpetrator of heinous war crimes. Schmeling, however, was finding a place for himself in a new Germany, and his rise from the ashes of defeat would make him a different kind of role model than he had been in the 1930s. He started out by giving exhibition bouts to support himself and his wife. He then embarked on a comeback tour, training rigorously, determined to earn back the love and admiration of the German public. He would give them hope for a better future.

Train as he did, he was no longer the lion of the ring. He won three bouts against less-than-challenging opponents and lost two. By October 1948, he knew he was finished as a boxer. He was well beyond his prime and would never be able to recover his old stamina, flexibility, and skills. Still, he was beginning to assume the role of an elder statesman of boxing, not only in Germany, but also (surprisingly) in the United States, where his principled defense of Jews and defiance of Hitler's anti-Jewish laws became increasingly well-known and appreciated. He eventually owned a Coca-Cola bottling company in Germany and became a multimillionaire, beloved by many Germans.

In 1954, Schmeling returned to the United States. His first stop, on his way to Chicago, was at a Jewish cemetery to visit the grave of his friend, mentor, and manager, the once-irrepressible Joe Jacobs. He was greeted by an ancient caretaker, shriveled and bent over, who wore a black yarmulke. When he learned that Schmeling was there to visit Jacobs, the caretaker guided him as if he were a maître 'd directing an honored guest to the best table in the joint. Upon reaching the grave, the caretaker introduced Schmeling to his dead friend. He said, "It's Max Schmeling. He didn't forget you. His first stop, Joe, was to visit you."[9] Schmeling believed that if it had not been for Joe Jacobs, he never would have had a successful career in the United States. There were tears in his eyes as he touched Jacobs's tombstone. He paused there for a few moments, then departed, never to return.

After the war, Schmeling and Joe Louis became friends, and Schmeling paid for Louis's funeral in 1981, for Louis's wealth had been wiped out by the IRS. Louis had donated many of his purses to help the war effort, and the IRS claimed he hadn't paid the taxes on those winnings. The unpaid taxes, penalties, and interest combined to leave Louis dependent on earning a meager living from friends and associates who employed him. In 1992, Schmeling was inducted into the International Boxing Hall of Fame. He remained an avid boxing fan and died on February 2, 2005, at the age of 99. Although he and Max Baer became friends, exchanging annual Christmas cards, their paths did not cross again after that fateful and savage bout in New York, a presage of the world at war.

8

THE MAN IN THE MOVIES

Having defeated Max Schmeling, the symbol of Nazi superiority, Max Baer became a celebrated hero to not only ordinary Jews and boxing fans throughout the United States, but also to the Jewish moguls who had built the great Hollywood studios: Paramount, Warner Brothers, MGM, Columbia Pictures, 20th Century Fox, Loews Pictures, Universal Studios, and others. They all wanted Max Baer; for them, he was the Jewish hero exemplified: a Maccabee warrior personified. And from a cinematic point of interest, he had the necessary ingredients for stardom: He was handsome, athletic, highly publicizable, and a marketable commodity, and he could deliver a comedic line with the best of them. (In fact, after his boxing career was over, Baer appeared as a stand-up comedian with Slapsie Maxie Rosenbloom, a Jewish light heavyweight champion. In addition to their nightclub appearances, they made a series of two-reel Columbia shorts from 1950 to 1952. The titles include *The Champs Step Out*; *Two Roaming Champs*; *Wine, Women, and Bong*; and *Rootin' Tootin' Tenderfeet*, which was a remake of Laurel and Hardy's *Way Out West* [1937].) There would be one big-money movie that could have led to many others, but for a variety of reasons it did not. The starring vehicle was *The Prizefighter and the Lady*. For Louis B. Mayer, Max Baer would be a surefire winner at the box office.

In 1933, the name Max Baer was marquee gold. His personality was gold, his physique was gold, his looks were gold—at least that was the estimation in Hollywood. Baer was a hot-blooded commodity that could be redeemed at the box office. He was the champion of the free world. He could have written his own ticket and cashed it in, no questions asked.

Had royal personages arrived on Sunset Boulevard, they would not have gotten a more enthusiastic welcome than the Big Bad Baer. He was invited to all the A-list parties. He was wined and dined at the best restaurants. Major stars wanted to share their beds with him. While the accuracy of reports in the gossip columns that he had affairs with numerous Hollywood beauties remains in question, there is no denying that some of the flashiest stars of Hollywood—Jean Harlow, for example— could not get enough of their love object. For Baer, the availability of women proved to be an overabundance of delight, a playboy's dreams turned into one reality after another.

When it was announced that he would be starring in *The Prizefighter and the Lady*, in which he would dance and sing a song that was being specifically written for him, the spotlight never dimmed. Everyone knew that Baer was a great fighter and an irrepressible jokester, but they had no idea the man could sing and dance. Some were doubtful, while others marveled at the possibility of his formerly undisclosed talents. Whether doubters or believers, they all wanted to see the final result.

Max Baer became a headline name, and not just in *Ring Magazine*; he was also regularly featured in the pages of the *Hollywood Reporter* and the *Los Angeles Times*. The PR team at the studio went into overdrive. Baer had been minted and polished for maximum gossip-column value. He was the gladiator as movie star. As the publicity mounted, he increasingly had his pick of ever-more delicious starlets. Some studio wit commented that Max spent more time being bare than being Baer. Having sampled the best of Hollywood's ambitious young starlets, Baer moved on to those who didn't need his reflected glory; they just wanted his body. He chose many of the most glittering stars in the heavenly expanse of Hollywood; in addition to Jean Harlow, who pursued Baer with a sexual hunger that surprised and eventually repelled the great Lothario, there was also the great beauty of the age, the enigmatic and otherwise elusive Greta Garbo, who was thrilled that Baer had beaten a symbol of Nazi bigotry, barbarity, and bestiality. In her deep, throaty, accented purr, she let him know how much she appreciated all of him. While Garbo's affair with Baer supposedly lasted for only six months, it was longer than most of her other reported relationships.

Before filming could begin on *The Prizefighter and the Lady*, there was confusion and discord that had to be settled. Initially, one of Hollywood's greatest and most influential directors, Howard Hawks, was supposed to direct the film. His resume includes such masterpieces of the silver screen as *His Gal Friday*, *Twentieth Century*, *Bringing Up Baby*, *Only Angels Have Wings*, *Ball of Fire*, *To Have and Have Not*, *The Big Sleep*, *Red River*, *Monkey Business*, *Gentlemen Prefer Blondes*, and *Rio Bravo*, to name just a few. Hawks signed on thinking that the movie would star his friend, Clark Gable. Gable, the studio agreed, was a fine actor, a box-office draw, handsome, charming, and a great leading man, but he was not as appropriate for the movie as Max Baer, the genuine fistic article. Sure, Baer was a great fighter, but Hawks did not think that Baer was sufficiently an actor and felt he was not suitable for the picture. He decided to withdraw from directing him. Hawks did not think that an untested boxer could carry an entire movie; however, the studio declared that Baer would be the star, also insisting that Hawks stay long enough to give him some important acting lessons. Hawks finally and reluctantly agreed. After all, he wanted to continue working, and the studio system in those days could make or break a director. He was fortunate not to have been fired.

For Hawks, it was bad enough that Gable did not get the part he had wanted him to play, but it was even more galling that Norma Shearer, whom he thought would be ideal for the female lead, was replaced by brassy blonde bombshell Jean Harlow. Harlow was all right in her way, perfect for some parts, but she was no Norma Shearer. In the swirl and tumult of casting decisions that the studio had created for Hawks, he was further perplexed when told that Harlow was out and would be replaced by the lovely, young, effervescent Myrna Loy. At that point, the merry-go-round seemed to be spinning out of control, throwing off potential stars as if by centrifugal force. Would it stop spinning long enough that production could begin?

Although no longer signed on to direct the final version of the movie, Hawks was still on the studio's short leash and generous payroll, and was becoming increasingly angry; nevertheless, he stayed on, intently directing the film's early scenes. He really had no choice. Directors in those days were hired hands. While he had no choice but to direct the film in its infancy, he didn't have to keep his opinions to himself. Hawks still believed that Baer was no actor, that he did not have the makings for stardom, and that he shouldn't be starring in the movie, which, in its early stages, was running behind schedule. Running behind schedule meant running over budget, and that was not something that brought a smile to the face of Louis B. Mayer, founder of MGM, a movie colony mogul, the studio's five-star general, the film's producer, and a Baer enthusiast. In other words, he was the boss of all bosses, capo di tutt'i capi. To note that Mayer was becoming increasingly irritated with Hawks is an understatement.

The boss finally fired Hawks and installed the proficient, skillful, and generally compliant W. S. Van Dyke as the new director. Although Hawks had efficiently directed the early scenes of the movie, he is uncredited in the final cut. Van Dyke, the credited director of the movie, was known as a solid, reliable craftsman who made his films on schedule and under budget; he was appreciated and applauded by the studio heads, who gave him the nickname "One Take Woody" for his quick and efficient style of filming. With "One Take Woody" at the controls, a movie was not only sure to come in under budget, but also destined to make money at the box office. In addition, he knew how to direct actors and actresses so that they earned critical and popular encomiums on their way to stardom. Among those he directed were four notable thespians who received Oscar nominations: William Powell, Spencer Tracy, Norma Shearer, and Robert Morley. Van Dyke's movies invariably were profitable, which ensured ongoing employment. Yet, of his many successful movies, he is probably best known for directing *The Thin Man* series, starring Powell and Myrna Loy. For Mayer, a consummate budget-cutter and lord and ruler of his company's finances, Van Dyke was the perfect director.

Spending most of his time romancing and seducing Hollywood beauties, Baer hardly had time to learn his lines, his dance numbers, and a song before filming began on *The Prizefighter and the Lady*. Although a notorious seducer of glamorous women, he was in awe of Myrna Loy and nervous about appearing on the screen with her. He had seen her on the silver screen many times and admired her beauty and sexual appeal; while he would have been perfectly confident to attempt an off-screen seduction of her, he found the camera intrusive and inhibiting. How could moviegoers possibly perceive him as being on par with Myrna Loy?

Loy quickly estimated Baer's insecurity and commented that he was as "unprotected as a white rabbit." The assistant director, Early Haley, told Loy that Baer was terrified of coming near her. She reached out to her reluctant costar, reassuring him that he would do just fine. His shyness vanished, and they quickly became friends. In fact, Loy was so sympathetic that she even became his confidant. They were often seen together, conferring like conspirators. He confessed to her the guilt he felt about the deaths of Frankie Campbell and Ernie Schaaf, and that he would rather spend the rest of his life acting in movies than battering opponents in a boxing ring. She told him that he had natural ability and that there was no reason why he couldn't have a career in show business. He further confessed to her that he worried that the brutal power of his right fist, his best weapon in the ring, was so devastating that it could easily kill another man. To give it up would make him virtually defenseless; therefore, if he continued fighting, he had no choice but to rely on the power of that right fist. Boxing wasn't the only subject that Baer discussed with Loy: He even revealed that he didn't know what to do about Jean Harlow, who was pursuing him relentlessly and who he was trying to avoid.

To observers, Baer seemed to regard Loy almost as a kindly sister: He treated her with a tender affection that she found touching. Loy is quoted by Emily Leider in her book *Myrna Loy: The Only Good Girl in Hollywood* as saying that when they had to do a kissing scene, Baer's kissing was "simply delicious . . . it was like the first kiss of a boy who had never kissed a girl before he kissed me."[1] That the great Lothario acted like a love-smitten teenage boy amused those who knew of his reputation as a great womanizer, but it absolutely charmed Loy.

Although Loy helped reduce Baer's nervousness, she didn't entirely succeed. To minimize some of the jittery tension that Baer felt, members of the cast and crew played a number of practical jokes on him. For example, Jack Dempsey wired Baer's chair with live electricity, causing Baer to yelp and leap out of his seat; during the filming of a fight scene with Primo Carnera, Loy released a mouse into the boxing ring because she knew that Baer had a mouse phobia. The entire crew erupted in laughter as Baer, a big bruiser of a man, rushed away from the mouse. One of Baer's endearing qualities throughout his time in Hollywood was his ability to laugh at himself and tell self-deprecating jokes, a characteristic he had maintained since his teenage years.

While doubtful of his thespian abilities, the longer Baer rehearsed and felt comfortable in the presence of the other actors and actresses, the more he began to gain confidence in himself. In fact, once the nervousness and jitters evaporated, Baer quickly found his niche as an actor. His comfort level increased to the point that his natural abilities were soon apparent to everyone on the set. He even got to sing an original song, "Lucky Fella," written for him and the movie by Jimmy McHugh and Dorothy Fields. To entice audiences to see the movie, the studio produced an artful poster that showed Baer with his gloved fists raised above his handsome head, cocky grin on his face, as a bevy of beauties adoringly looked up at him. *The Prizefighter and the Lady* was meant to attract crowds of men and women: It has romance, boxing, and a rags-to-riches story in which love is the guiding force that makes the marriage of the stars so durable and captivating.

While most boxers were peripheral characters in movies, Baer was the star. The peripheral characters in *The Prizefighter and the Lady*, cast for the sake of pugilistic verisimilitude, included Jack Dempsey, Jess Willard, and James J. Jeffries, each of whom preceded Baer as world heavyweight champion. The most interesting boxer to appear in the movie, however, was 6-foot-6 Primo Carnera, the largest-ever heavyweight champion of the world. As mentioned earlier, Carnera, prior to becoming a boxer, had been a circus strongman in Europe, where he was much beloved by children, who regarded him as a fairy-tale figure who had become a real person. As a circus strongman, Carnera was also lovable. As a boxer, however, he was seen as a fool by sports reporters and was treated as a gullible one by his dishonest handlers. His was a story of a decent man being handled indecently.

Following the completion of filming, Baer would challenge Carnera for the heavyweight title. One would have thought that Carnera's managers, prior to a championship bout, would have promoted their fighter as indestructible in the media and to the public. One also would have thought that they would have enhanced Carnera's self-confidence, keeping him from being humiliated, belittled, and cast as a loser in the movie. But his managers and owners were not only an unsavory assortment of gangster gamblers, but also apparently short-sighted and greedy, willing to use Carnera to make a quick buck, regardless of the effect their actions had on the psyche, bank account, and image of their golden goose. They thought little of letting Carnera's character (who was named Carnera in the movie) fight to a draw with Baer's cinematic character, Steve Morgan. No sensible manager would let their world heavyweight champion fight to a draw in a movie with a highly publicized contender, nor would they permit him to be knocked down twice, which he was. What's even more appalling is that the original script called for Carnera to lose the fight; however, his managers, although myopic and greedy, at least had enough sense to object to that. But their greed would overcome what little sense they had, for they finally agreed to accept a draw in the movie's fight scene for an additional $20,000. It has been speculated that little, if any, of that money went to Carnera. He not only fought to a fictionalized draw, which demeaned him and his image, but he also was fleeced by the people who should have been protecting his image, as well as his financial well-being.

Baer was a different story. He was no puppet being manipulated by the wrangling of deceitful and greedy managers. He had his eyes on the main chance, the main event, the prize of the heavyweight championship of the world. He wanted that heavyweight title more than anything else. He had been working toward that goal since 1929. It had been his dream, and now it was within his gloved grasp. He was determined to send Carnera to the canvas and have his own arms raised in a decisive win. The heavyweight championship of the world would be his. His dream come true.

To help him reach that goal, Baer took full advantage of his fight scenes with Carnera. He studied Carnera's moves and learned Carnera's technique so well that he could not only imitate each of Carnera's moves, but also replay the entire repertoire in his mind. But that was just the physical aspect of Carnera; it was not enough for Baer: He also wanted to defeat Carnera psychologically. He had nothing against Carnera the man. In truth, he liked the fighter and admired his courage and willingness to get in a ring and expose himself to pain and suffering. He also admired Carnera's ability to take a punch and still come back for more. He was not a great fighter, but he had heart. Those feelings of admiration and appreciation, however, were not enough to prevent Baer from insensitively teasing Carnera, imitating his broken English accent, and playing practical jokes on him so that the stagehands, lighting technicians, grips, and others would laugh derisively at the foolish, gullible giant. Carnera, at one point, became so frustrated and angry with Baer that he charged bullishly at him with clenched fists outstretched. He was like a bull charging at a provocative matador. A fight was avoided by the quick intercession of the crew, who, moments earlier, had been an audience amused by Baer's gags. By the time of their actual fight, Baer believed that he had set Carnera up to lose. Nonetheless, during the fight, Baer would be surprised at the beating Carnera was willing to take to defend his championship. Baer would wind up asking the referee to end it. He didn't want to kill another man.

While the future heavyweight fight with Carnera was prominently foreshadowed in the movie, its story line revolved around the love interests of the Baer character and his lack of fidelity in his marriage. The plot fit Baer like a well-made autobiographical boxing glove. To wit: A washed-up, alcoholic manager sees Morgan knock out an obnoxious drunk in a bar. The manager, known as the Professor (played by wonderful character actor Walter Huston), is impressed by Morgan's ability to land a devastating right punch, but he wants to see how Morgan will perform against an experienced opponent. Morgan knocks out the boxer in the first round, and the Professor, deeply impressed, now knows that he is handling a potential champion.

While doing road work one morning, Morgan witnesses an automobile accident. He rushes over to an overturned car, in which a dazed woman is sighing. She's beautiful, and Morgan, galvanized by her beauty, rapidly rescues her. The woman is named Belle Mercer (portrayed by the lovely Myrna Loy). Morgan is smitten by her beauty and devotes himself to nursing her back to health. Once her health has been restored, Mercer thanks Morgan for his beneficent ministrations and departs. Morgan learns that she works as a singer in a nightclub owned by a notorious professional gambler, Willie Ryan, with whom she is having an affair. Morgan becomes increasingly obsessed with Mercer, and Ryan becomes jealous and angry. Morgan follows Mercer to her apartment; he declares his love for her, and, this time, she reciprocates his feelings.

The Morgan–Mercer romance proceeds, and they soon marry. Mercer returns to the nightclub and tells Ryan that she has married Morgan. Although angry, Ryan unhappily accepts the fait accompli. Morgan, however, being tough, strong, handsome, and virile, attracts a number of beautiful young women and finds himself being irresistibly drawn to them. Just before Morgan is to fight for the heavyweight championship, he is discovered in his dressing room by Mercer in the arms of a chorus girl. Disillusioned and frustrated, Mercer angrily departs and returns to the nightclub. She vows to Ryan that she is through with Morgan. Yet, Mercer has second thoughts and decides to attend Morgan's championship bout with Carnera.

During the fight with Carnera (who is both the real and fictional heavyweight champion in the movie), Morgan is so depressed that he loses round after round. Mercer enters the arena and takes a seat near the ring, urging her husband to win. Now that Morgan realizes Mercer still loves him, he fights on like a tiger. It's too late for a dramatic win, but Baer succeeds in fighting Carnera to a draw. While there is no victory in the ring, love wins out, the boxer is redeemed, the screen darkens, the lights in the theater come on, and the audience departs, assured that all is right in the world. According to studio surveys, the audience loved the movie. *The Prizefighter and the Lady* was a critical success, although it lost money. Critics throughout the country put it on their top-10 lists of must-see movies.

After seeing the movie, Nat Fleischer, eminent boxing writer and editor of *Ring Magazine*, wrote in his book *Max Baer: The Glamour Boy of the Ring*, "[Baer] was a real camera-find, photographed splendidly, possessed natural comedy talents, and when it came to love-making on the screen, stood out in bold relief as a natural-born Romeo."[2] Of course, Romeo and Juliet's love affair ended tragically, and Romeo was never a philanderer.

In a review of the movie entitled "Ace of Aces" in the *New York Times*, a critic with the unlikely name of Mordaunt Hall (no Mordant wit he) writes,

> Max Baer may have astonished many pugilistic enthusiasts by his defeat of Max Schmeling last June, but the chances are that many more persons will be surprised by his extraordinarily capable portrayal in the picture *The Prize Fighter and the Lady*. This California giant has such an ingratiating personality and an easy way of talking one forgets signs of fistic encounters on his physiognomy.[3]

The film was praised by not only movie critics coast to coast, but also by sports columnists. They were delighted that one of the greatest fistic champions in the United States was also a talented thespian. What would he do next? And although many forecast that he would go on to become a bright Hollywood star in the firmament of studio-controlled galaxies, the prediction was in neither the astrological nor the astronomical charts. Baer did not star in another movie, for he had alienated the studio by being more devoted to seducing stars than polishing his own.

Baer had to settle for making a series of comedic two-reelers with Slapsie Maxie Rosenbloom that were shown as filler between double-billed features or just before the coming attractions and newsreels. When television came along, Baer was often a guest on weekly sitcoms, where he invariably played himself. His opportunity to be a major movie star had arrived suddenly and ended abruptly. He was in the Hollywood tradition of the shooting star, briefly lighting up the heavens of celebrity and quickly fading to a glimmer.

Although Baer was not destined to be a star, *The Prizefighter and the Lady* was rated one of the 10 best movies of 1933. When it came time for the Academy Awards ceremony, Frances Marion, who wrote the original story on which the movie was based, was nominated for an Oscar for Best Writing of an Original Story.

In Germany, the movie did not fare as well as it did in the United States. Because Baer had beaten Schmeling and because he was considered a Jew by the Nazis, the German-dubbed version of the film was banned. While the English-language version of *The Prizefighter and the Lady* premiered at the Capitol Theater in Berlin on March 16, 1934, the Reich minister of propaganda, Joseph Goebbels, denied permission for the German-dubbed version to be shown in any German town or city. He stated to his underlings that the "chief character is a Jewish boxer."[4] During his fight with Schmeling, Baer had said that each of his punches was symbolically aimed at the head of Hitler. When told of Goebbels's orders banning his movie, Baer contended that "[t]hey didn't ban the picture because I have Jewish blood. They banned it because I knocked out Max Schmeling."[5]

In the years since its release, *The Prizefighter and the Lady* has been the subject of many trivia quizzes. The following are some of the more interesting tidbits about the movie:

- Myrna Loy, in an interview, said that Baer told her that he had observed Primo Carnera so closely that he knew his every move; he was able to use that knowledge to defeat Carnera for the championship in 1934. Well before the fight, she sensed that Baer would win. "He was a real student of Primo," she said.
- Baer wore the robe with the name Steve Morgan embroidered on the back when entering the ring for his real-life title fight with Carnera. He pummeled and defeated Carnera on June 14, 1934,

after knocking him down a record 11 times in as many rounds. For many fans, it was sad to see the heavyweight champion so badly humiliated by a smaller, tougher, faster, and more skillful and determined boxer.

- Production photography and Movietone newsreels show that the Three Stooges had cameo appearances in the film; however, they are nowhere to be seen in the final version. One may wonder if being on Hitler's death list for their satirical song "I'll Never Heil Again" has anything to do with their absence.

The Prizefighter and the Lady was Baer's last major movie role. Nevertheless, the entertainment industry had entered his blood and would be an integral part of his life for the next 25 years.

9

AFTER THE LAST BELL

As a boxer, actor, comedian, referee, and even wrestler, Max Baer was much sought-after for the value and allure of his personality. He had charm, good looks, and charisma. Men and women were drawn to him, vicariously experiencing the excitement that surrounded a beloved champ. He was offered boxing contracts, movie contracts, and guest shots on comedy radio programs. After winning the heavyweight championship from the towering 6-foot-6 Primo Carnera, whom he had knocked down 11 times in their title fight and whom he had jokingly taunted by saying—loud enough for reporters to hear him—"last one up is a sissy," Baer was fodder for gossip columnists and sports reporters. The media loved him. He was a walking, talking reality show unto himself.

Primo Carnera, however, was a ridiculed victim of manipulation and swindle by the gangsters and gamblers who controlled his career. The most notorious of the gangsters who owned a piece of Carnera was Owney Madden, who, as a young man, had committed several murders for his New York City gang, the Gophers. Madden profited handsomely from prohibition and owned numerous nightclubs in New York City, including two legendary watering holes, the Cotton Club and the Stork Club, both of which have been subjects in movies and novels, and both of which were gathering places for celebrities, socialites, politicians, and gangsters.

After prohibition ended and the flow of illegal cash went from a gushing river with waterfalls to a gently moving creek, Madden was looking for new sources of illegal income and ventured into boxing, where he figured he could earn huge sums by fixing fights and betting on the outcomes. Unlike Arnold Rothstein, who fixed the 1919 World Series, Madden realized it would be comparatively easier to fix boxing matches, where you only had to pay off one participant, not four, five, or nine. Madden and a group of nefarious and notorious characters were able to buy a substantial piece of Carnera by forcing his manager, Leon See, to sell a major share. It was a deal See couldn't refuse, not if he wanted to live long enough to return to his home in Europe. To paraphrase Michael Corleone in *The Godfather*, See could either put his signature on a contract resigning his interest in Carnera or his blood would be on the table, and his heirs would have to deal with Madden and his associates.

Carnera was nearly a stereotype of the good-natured giant of a man who never used his considerable strength to hurt anyone. Children loved him, women approved of his gentle nature, and men admired his strength without ever feeling that he posed a threat to them. As previously mentioned, Carnera, before coming to the United States, had been a circus strongman, moving from his native Italy to France. He seemed to have been born with enormous, melon-sized muscles and fists that looked like blocks of cement. The towering muscle man looked like he could defeat anyone who had the egotistic gall and deluded machismo to challenge him. His very size would dissuade potential bullies from challenging him. Facing Carnera in a fight would be like looking into the barrel of a gun.

See, envisioning dollars dancing arm in arm like chorus girls in the nightclub of his mind, thought Carnera could be trained as a fighter and become a huge success in the United States, the land of golden opportunity. Madden and his pals agreed that Carnera could be trained like a circus animal to do their bidding and be a cash cow, a golden goose, a fistic entertainer from whom they could wring every last dollar. To say that they were greedy, unfeeling, coarse human beings would be an understatement. And like any aggressive merger and acquisition specialists, they weren't about to let a former employee of the old company stay on board. Lean, mean money machines was their modus operandi. They did permit See to occupy a purely ceremonial role until they were able to wean the giant away from his trusted handler. Then it was good-bye, Mr. See.

The innocent giant, now a mob-controlled puppet, was nicknamed the "Ambling Alp" by sportswriters and promoters. They claimed he was as tall as the Alps and just as immovable. To ensure that his Alpine image remained solid as ice, his early fights were against pushovers and has-beens or fighters who were paid to take dives that looked like genuine losses. If they resisted, a gun was used to make them understand the necessity of their cooperation. Each man chose to take the money and live to enjoy it. Of the mismanagement of Carnera's career, Paul Gallico writes,

> This was a shameless swindle from start to finish. His managers found out they could get away with anything. And so they proceeded to do just that. . . . I often wonder what that hulk of a man thinks today as he looks back over the manner in which he was swindled, tricked, and cheated at every turn, as he recalls the great sums of money he earned, all of it gone beyond recall. [1]

While he was being propped up in mob-promoted fights in Los Angeles, a local reporter asked him what he thought of the city. Carnera, with all the confidence of an eager boy scout, misunderstood the question and replied in broken English that he would knock out Los Angeles. Reporters were amazed, amused, touched, and, in some cases, saddened by the giant's naïveté. The poor guy was not only barely conversant in English, but he had also been systematically deluded by his managers into believing that he was really a first-rate pugilist. He was an actor who didn't know he was acting, and so he believed in the reality of the part he was given to play. As Budd Schulberg relates, "The hapless Primo Carnera, all 6-feet-6, 256 pounds of him, couldn't beat a third rater without considerable help from his owners. With fights 'arranged' all the way to the title, he was finally led to slaughter by Joe Louis and Max Baer." [2]

He was the least arrogant of men; he simply believed that he had genuinely defeated all of his opponents. In his mind, they had been tough guys who put up a good fight. But he had put up a better one. "Just look at all the bouts I won," he was reported to have said when questioned about his abilities.

Schulberg sympathetically portrays this sad, vulnerable man in his boxing novel *The Harder They Fall*, which was also made into an award-winning movie of the same title. That title, incidentally, comes from the old boxing adage, "The bigger they come, the harder they fall," and Carnera proved to be the perfect fit. Joseph Page, in his insightful and empathetic biography *Primo Carnera: The Life and Career of the Heavyweight Boxing Champion*, writes,

Most of Carnera's handlers were greedy cheats at best and organized crime thugs at worst. Men such as Owney Madden, Billy Duffy, and Luigi Soresi leeched off Primo during his rise as a professional fighter and were nowhere to be found after he was broken down—they had bled him dry, and he was no longer of any value to them.[3]

While the generally accepted opinion of Carnera is that he had insufficient skill to be a successful fighter and that he was not a powerful puncher, Page comes to the rescue of Carnera's reputation and presents a case for his subject's fistic abilities, which, at the very least, causes one to reconsider Carnera as a better-than-competent, although not great, fighter. Peter Wood, former Golden Gloves boxer and author, comments that, "Carnera, at the start of his career, wasn't much of a boxer; however, as he trained more and more, he became better. He was never a good fighter, never a hard puncher, but he could sometimes protect himself against those who were not much better than he was."[4]

Carnera's reputation as a sham was furthered by the fact that his handlers had hired Abe Attell, the former featherweight champ, to train the heavyweight. While Attell had been a skillful and indomitable fighter in his prime, he was later known as a corrupt gambler (he was accused of helping Arnold Rothstein fix the 1919 World Series) who had many friends in organized crime. Sportswriters and promoters assumed that Attell was just there to teach Carnera the fundamentals of boxing and give him a veneer of professional skill, to make him look good, but not too good. Others thought that Attell's training regimen had actually resulted in Carnera having some formidable skills that he had previously lacked. Regardless of one's opinion, the skills that Attell imparted to Carnera became essential in his defensive arsenal of punches and so could not be seen as simply window dressing. Although a corrupt gambler and an associate of organized crime, Attell did not want to be seen as a patsy. He wanted the boxing world to know that had done his best to train Carnera. He certainly taught Carnera more than the mere fundamentals of the sport. While Carnera had improved his jabs, he was still not a powerful puncher. Nothing and no one could change that. And it was understood that truly proficient fighters who had assembled records of major wins would probably defeat the Ambling Alp.

Carnera's championship bout with Max Baer was an obvious demonstration of a powerful, skillful boxer overwhelming a less skillful, less powerful one. Although Baer liked to clown around in the ring and often refused to lend himself to vigorous training, he was able to belt Carnera around as if he were a slapstick comic version of a boxer. Carnera's handlers had attempted to threaten Baer into throwing the fight, but Ancil Hoffman, Baer's manager and friend, told the gangsters to take a hike. And, surprisingly, they did. The brutal defeat of Carnera was a pathetic spectacle that led his handlers to think that the gravy train had left its last stop on the tracks to easy money and the journey would soon be over.

Shortly after Carnera lost the heavyweight title, he was deserted by the gamblers and gangsters who had made millions of dollars from his efforts. Owney Madden reportedly sold his interest in Carnera and took off for Hot Springs, Arkansas, a noted hangout in the 1930s for underworld figures, many of whom were on the lam from the law back east. Madden lived there undisturbed for the rest of his life, periodically returning to Hell's Kitchen in New York, where he would hustle some cash from his associates before returning to the sunny pleasures and implied safety of Hot Springs. His old gang, the Gophers, was no longer dominant in the neighborhood. They were either being replaced by younger thugs or recruited into a new gang headed by Mickey Spillane.

Following his brutal defeat by Baer, Carnera was laid up in a hospital with a broken jaw, a fractured rib, and a broken nose. The men who had made millions off of him refused to spend one dime on Carnera's medical care. Instead, it was Max Baer, who had asked the referee to stop the fight because he saw no point in the man being repeatedly pummeled, who stepped forward to pay his opponent's hospital expenses. During the remaining years of Baer's life, he and Carnera became good friends, as Max did with all his former opponents, with the exception of the foul-mouthed, street-style brawler "Two Ton" Tony Galento. When Baer died, Carnera couldn't attend the funeral, for he was in Europe; however, shortly thereafter, Carnera flew to California to pay his respects to his fallen pal. A driver took him to the cemetery where Baer was buried. It was nighttime, and the gates of the cemetery had been locked. Carnera and his driver climbed over the gates and found Baer's tomb. Carnera knelt on the ground, crossed himself, and said a prayer for the man who had admired the giant's courage and paid for his recovery. He knelt there for several minutes, stood, bowed his head, whispered something, and turned and left.

Following his humiliating defeat by Baer, Carnera had a few more fights, but they were of little interest to the public. He was of little interest even to boxing fans. Scammed out of his boxing earnings, Carnera turned to another form of entertainment that promised to be more remunerative than boxing had been. He was offered a career as a wrestler. He looked the part and was widely known. He proved to be a huge success. Audiences loved him and applauded his every win. Even better for the veteran fighter, he was no longer being managed by scoundrels and so was not being cheated. He was finally being paid his fair share of the gate and was on his way to being able to support his family, which consisted of a wife and two children.

Although there is a sad, pathetic figure of a ridiculed wrestler based on Carnera in Rod Serling's play *Requiem for a Heavyweight*, in reality, Carnera ended up in the ideal venue for his talents and physique. No one could point an accusing finger at him and say he was involved in fixed fights, for everyone assumed that wrestling was a scripted sport with prearranged outcomes. It didn't matter. It was entertainment, and the public paid to be entertained. Sportswriters could no longer complain about the level of opponents Carnera was facing. He no longer had to explain himself. Wrestling was a popular spectator sport, one with its own repertory company of favored heroes and villains.

A kind and generous man, devoted to his family, Carnera was happy to please the public and earn money while doing it. He bought a beautiful villa in his native Italy and opened a liquor and grocery store in Los Angeles. He did not redeem his reputation as a boxer in the minds of boxing fans, but he had earned the public's affection as an entertainer. Wrestling should have been his career from the start. It would have been a natural progression from circus strongman to popular wrestler. Paul Gallico, who was sports editor of the *New York Daily News* and founder of the Golden Gloves amateur boxing competitions, summarizes the professional life of Prima Carnera as follows:

> Poor Primo! A giant in stature and strength, a terrible figure of a man, with the might of 10 men, he was a helpless lamb among wolves who used him until there was nothing more left to use, until the last possible penny had been squeezed from his big carcass, and then abandoned him. His last days in the United States spent alone in a hospital. One leg was paralyzed, the result of beatings taken around the head. None of the carrion birds who had picked him clean ever came back to see him or to help him.[5]

In 1998, Carnera's children, devoted to the memory of their father, established the Primo Carnera Foundation, which provides financial and emotional support to neglected and abused children, helping them complete their educations and lead productive lives. It is a legacy that Carnera would have been proud to endorse. He was a good-hearted giant who empathized with those whom he felt had been given little. He was a man who realized that there is always someone who is worse off: You may not have shoes, but what of the person who has no feet? Carnera deserved better than what he got, but his is the story of many boxers.

Max Baer fared much better than the man he knocked out for the heavyweight championship. To many of his Depression-era fans, Baer was the man they wanted to be. He was known as a ladies' man, a glad-hander, a kidder, a clown, a tummler, a Jewish avenger (especially after his victory over Max Schmeling), as someone who was generous in distributing his largess. He had not only paid Carnera's hospital bills, but also fought bouts to benefit the wife and children of Frankie Campbell. He gave Mrs. Campbell a check for $15,000. He had given a former sparring partner a brand new sports car. For Baer, money was a gift to be used for creating happiness, to make the lives of friends easier. The garment worker, the civil servant, the store clerk, the stock boy, the messenger, the newsstand operator, the waiter, the bartender, the shipping clerk, the janitor, and those on relief admired Baer for his beneficence. He was a sport in a world that was not very sporting. He was what, in different circumstances, they would have liked to be.

While Baer was a devotee of the fun life, of Broadway chorus girls and sporting men, of good times in nightclubs, he was a comparative stranger to the country's boxing gyms. In fact, when it came to boxing, Baer's often lazy and neglectful attitude toward training caused many of his boxing colleagues to wonder if he could retain his title against an opponent more skillful and determined than the awkward giant Primo Carnera. Barney Ross stated that Baer was a great fighter with a powerful right hand, but he just wouldn't commit himself to a rigorous training regimen. Those sentiments were echoed by Jack Dempsey, who otherwise seemed to regard Baer as his protégé.

The fact that Dempsey and Baer each had one Jewish grandparent, that they had similar appearances, and that at his best Baer fought with the ferocity once associated with Dempsey, made the two heavyweights natural allies and friends. Dempsey said that Baer's powerful right hand could have made him the dominant heavyweight of his generation and the heavyweight champion for a decade, if only he would have devoted himself to rigorous training. Ross and Dempsey, along with many others, thought that Baer's easy defeat of Carnera had given him a false sense of his superiority over other boxers. Indeed, Baer thought of himself as the best fighter in the world. He had not only taken the title from the hapless Carnera, but also brutally defeated Max Schmeling, who was considered the best heavyweight in Europe.

Baer's next opponent, James J. Braddock, had something to prove to himself, his wife, his manager, and the world. He needed to be the champ. He had lived too long as a failure, a boxer who could not live up to his promise, a man dependent on poorly paid hard-labor jobs or welfare, then known as relief. He needed to be the champ to keep food on his family's table, keep a roof over their heads, and create a financial security blanket that would sustain them in the years to come. Baer had no such motivations. He felt, to use a song lyric, that he had the world on a string. Whenever he jerked that string, the world happily responded. While he was popular with fans, he was not one of them; he had not been driven into poverty by the Depression. Rather than being an everyman, he was everyman's fantasy.

Braddock, however, was the real thing, an everyman for nearly every working man or out-of-work man; he elicited sympathy and empathy. He was the reverse of Max Baer, the Broadway bon vivant. The men of the Depression, the forgotten men, the men in shantytowns, the men selling apples on Wall Street, the men living on charity or wages fit for an indentured servant, dockworkers, and the men who could never seem to catch a break could identify with Braddock's history. If he won, he would cheer the hearts of poor men throughout the country. If he could do it, maybe they too could reach for the gold ring in the merry-go-round of life, for the golden key that opens a door to a better life. He would become their Cinderella Man.

Rigorous training was for other boxers, journeymen needing to make a name for themselves, not for the great Max Baer, who perceived himself as boxing's conquering hero. He could be a clown in the ring, getting laughs from the spectators, and still knock out his opponents. He was a much better entertainer than a boxer. And he thrived on the laughter he inspired. He wasn't even sure he wanted to keep fighting. It was a brutal game. He no longer wanted to wake up in a sweat in the middle of the night feeling guilty for killing a man. He didn't have a killer instinct; maybe he had it at one time, but those days had passed. He often refrained from delivering devastating blows for fear that he might kill another Frankie Campbell. Look at what had happened to poor Ernie Schaaf.

In his book *Cinderella Man*, Jeremy Schaap writes, "An effective fighter can't have a conscience—at least not when he's in the ring."[6] Boxing was now for the money, for the pleasure of hearing the crowd's cheers, and just for the fun of it. Such an attitude was not the one required by an aspiring champ. It was not the attitude that would lead to rigorous training. Baer was a 26-year-old bon vivant, riding high on his vainglorious opinion of himself. As the world's heavyweight champion, he assumed he was unbeatable.

Unlike Baer, Braddock, age 29, trained for his fight with Baer as if his life depended on it, and maybe it did. There were certainly bookmakers and their minions who wanted him to win. After all, he was a 10–1 underdog: The payout on a Braddock win would be substantial. Baer seemed oblivious. He was prepared to defeat Braddock as if the effort would be no more than a lark; he would rely on his powerful right fist to do to Braddock what it had done to Schmeling and Carnera. He was so nonchalant about the bout that he accepted the sexual favors of a pretty young woman in his dressing room just prior to the fight. When Ancil Hoffman walked into the dressing room as a smiling Max was pulling up his shorts, Hoffman yelled at his fighter. He was furious. The woman, with an embarrassed smile on her face, dashed out. The prefight sexual pleasures Baer had enjoyed presaged his lack of seriousness during the opening rounds, when he would be startled by Braddock's intense aggressiveness.

The fight was held on June 13, 1935, in the Madison Square Garden Bowl in Long Island City, New York. The referee was the respected and capable Johnny McAvoy. George Kelly and Charley Lynch were the judges. Braddock had one of the best trainers and cutmen in his corner, the inimitable Whitey Bimstein, who trained or seconded more than 60 fighters, including Jack Dempsey, Gene Tunney, Benny Leonard, and Rocky Graziano, to name four of the most illustrious. Baer wore trunks with a large Star of David on the left leg. He seemed lethargic and bored. The fighters were introduced to the fans; Baer's most enthusiastic ones were women and Jews. Everyone else seemed to be rooting for "Plain Jim," the common man with uncommon courage.

When the bell rang for round one, Braddock rushed from his corner like a snarling, angry tiger. He took Baer by surprise, much as Baer had done with Schmeling. He landed punch after punch as Baer attempted to hold him off with an extended stiff left arm. Braddock knew his man, knew that Baer could quickly end the fight with a devastating knockout using his right fist. He circled Baer so that he would not be a target of that right fist. He did so throughout the fight, frustrating Baer, who easily lost the first five rounds. By the seventh round, Baer seemed to realize that he was about to lose the title, and he began fighting like his old self, delivering powerful punches that seemed to take a toll on Braddock, if only temporarily. Baer had apparently lost his lethargy and was able to dance away from many of Braddock's punches. At other times, the two men fought head-to-head, delivering a series of short body blows and occasional chops to the head. They frequently had to be separated by the referee.

It was clear that Braddock was outboxing Baer and had the determination and relentlessness of an indomitable bull. He lowered his head as if he had horns and pushed himself against Baer, and the two would exchange blow after blow. Baer seemed to have brief adrenaline rushes but would quickly tire. He was unable to do the kind of damage with his right fist that he had been known for. After the fight, it was reported that he had injured his right hand in one of the early rounds and that it was broken.

In the ninth round, Baer seemed to regain his strength, if not his stamina, and he became the aggressor. Yet, he was unable to finish off Braddock, who seemed determined to stay on his feet regardless of his tentative hold on consciousness. In the 10th round, Baer rushed from his corner and landed a flurry of punches—hooks, uppercuts, and quick rights. The latter, however, were short punches that relied solely on the strength of his arms, not his powerful shoulders. In the 11th round, he managed to stagger Braddock, but the advantage only lasted for a moment.

Throughout the fight, Baer was unable to connect with that long right-hand punch that could have helped him keep the title. Braddock was cleverly evasive. Baer's attempts to defeat Braddock were too little, too late, and he knew it. When the final bell announced the end of round 15, Baer and Braddock briefly hugged, each man knowing what the decision would be. When Al Frazin, the ring announcer, spoke into the dangling overhead microphone, he began by saying, "The winner and new world champion . . ." He was quickly drowned out by the roar of approval from the crowd.

Baer had been told for weeks before the fight that he would lose unless he engaged in a rigorous training program. He laughed off the advice. Of course, in retrospect, his loss to Braddock was a foregone conclusion. The easygoing entertainer had been matched against a hungry, determined, perhaps even desperate man who needed to redeem himself. Even Jack Dempsey relates,

> Max Baer's dilly-dallying and clowning caught up with him in the ring. There was not a dissenting voice raised when the long shot was declared the winner. Braddock won cleanly on aggressiveness and clean hitting. I do not wish to take anything away from Braddock. He fought the best, and his best was better than Baer's miserable defense of his title. [7]

Baer had held the title for less than a year and thought it was his to enjoy for years to come. He hadn't imagined losing it, and he had never thought he would need to regain it. During the fight, when Hoffman told him he was losing on points to Braddock, Baer had tried to even the score. It was not only too late for Baer to make a change in the ring, but also for him to change his lifestyle; his devotion to clowning around rather than fighting had cost him dearly. When the fight was over and the referee and judges had awarded the title to Braddock, there was dismay among Baer's fans. His Jewish fans, in particular, felt let down and saddened by the man who should have held the title for many years. Baer had defeated the great symbol of Nazism, the best fighter that Europe had to offer. And he took it all for granted. Indeed, in his case, pride went before the fall. Baer would be the only Jewish heavyweight champion other than Daniel Mendoza, who had preceded him by more than 100 years, during the age of bare-knuckled bruisers.

Baer made another mistake when he agreed to fight Joe Louis, the "Brown Bomber," one of the greatest heavyweight champions of the 20th century. For months, Baer's hands were constantly in pain, and his right hand had been broken during his fight with Braddock. All four knuckles were broken, and there was a fracture in a bone that went from the wrist to his knuckles. Of less importance, but still a pugilistic liability, was a bone chip in his left wrist. Why would a fighter suffering from such injuries agree to a fight? Baer had already signed a contract to do so. In addition, if he didn't fight Louis, he would forfeit an opportunity for a rematch with Braddock. Hoffman pleaded with his fighter to cancel the bout. Baer refused. He did, however, agree to visit an orthopedic surgeon at Johns Hopkins Hospital.

The visit was conducted sub rosa, for neither Baer nor Hoffman wanted the media and the boxing commissioners to learn of it. Baer was fearful that his injury would result in the postponement of the fight, and the passage of time would make a comeback unlikely. When the surgeon said that it would take nine months, following surgery, for Baer to use his right fist in a fight, Baer thanked him and decided against the operation. Nine months was too long for a man impatient to regain the admiration of his fans. Baer was undoubtedly a proud man, and pride led him to believe that he could again become the world champion. He needed to win, to prove to himself and his new wife, Mary Sullivan, as well as to his fans, that he was still a powerful knockout artist. All he had to do was defeat Louis and then Braddock. It was not to be.

Baer signed on for a fight that was scheduled for September 24, 1935, at Yankee Stadium. He believed he would be ready and make the most of the opportunity. Yet, Louis was a 2–1 favorite. The ring community had been watching and evaluating the Brown Bomber, and they had never seen anyone quite like him. He had the speed and skills of a champion. More than 84,000 excited fans paid to view the fight. Those with the right connections were just as enthusiastic, and so 11,000 free passes were issued. The gate was a little less than $1 million. Each fighter would get approximately $200,000.

As the date of the fight got closer, Baer began to have second thoughts. His right fist was not healing. Hoffman asked Baer to cancel the fight, but Baer refused. This was a once-in-a-lifetime opportunity; he could not afford to throw it away. But without the use of his right fist, he would be powerless to defend himself, powerless to deliver a knockout blow. Prior to the fight, while sitting in his dressing room, Baer permitted a doctor to inject his hands with Novocain. No matter how hard he would punch Louis, he would not feel any pain. Sure, he would do more damage to the hand, but he could undergo surgery after the fight.

Unfortunately, the weather intervened to wither Hoffman and Baer's plan. A heavy, steady rain was washing away the time before the fight. The minutes passed in the downpour, and the fight was temporarily post-poned; the longer the postponement, the less effective the Novocain.

After a drenching 45 minutes, feeling was beginning to return to Baer's hands—an unwelcome reminder of his vulnerability. The rain ceased, and the fight was on. If the rain had been a reliable friend and continued for another 15 minutes, the fight would have been cancelled that night. But it wasn't, and Baer would have to face a humiliating loss—and he knew it. He told Jack Dempsey, sitting beside him in the dressing room, that he didn't want to do it. Dempsey responded that if Baer didn't get into the ring with Louis, he would have to fight Dempsey in the dressing room. Baer was like one of those bulls that had been tormented and softened up for a matador who was ready to inflict the coup de grace.

Unbeknownst to Baer and Hoffman, one of Baer's former trainers, who had been fired, sent information to Louis's trainer about Baer's weaknesses and the best way to defeat the former champ; however, Baer didn't need to be betrayed to lose the fight; he knew that was inevitable, but he was determined to put up enough of a defense so as not to embarrass himself.

At the beginning of the first round, both fighters came out of their corners and traded tentative jabs, sizing one another up. Baer surprisingly launched a flurry of punches, but none seemed to deter Louis. He kept coming at Baer, boxing with the skill he was known to possess. Baer attempted to hold Louis off with a stiff, extended left arm. It was a paper-thin defense that Louis got around with ease. It was like holding off a tiger with a broomstick.

Round two was much like round one. Round three was the prelude to the end. Baer was knocked down, not once, but twice. It was the first time the former champion had been floored. There was little reason to go on, but Baer would not humiliate himself. He was lucky that the bell saved him from the referee's 10 count. Or was he?

In round four, the matador was ready to drive the bull to his knees. This time the full count of 10 was not impeded by the bell. It happened quickly, but not quickly enough for those looking at the timer's clock: the three-minute round had lasted three minutes, nine and a half seconds. It didn't matter; the end had come. There was no point in disputation. Why delay the inevitable? Why subject a once-proud champion to further injury? For those who were fans of Baer, it was an ending that brought sadness, if not tears. At the time, no one knew that Baer had put up a noble fight with a broken right hand, the weapon that had caused many fighters, if not completely fearful, to at least stay out of range of the notorious right hand that had killed a man. The bloodlust of the crowd had raged and went unsatisfied. They had paid for a full bout. For those who lived vicariously through the lives of brave men, the denouement was a frustrating disappointment. As Baer left the ring, the crowd booed and jeered. They didn't know that Baer had offered himself to them and then sacrificed himself.

Baer would survive with his brain and sense of humor intact. He said that being beaten to a pulp was not worth the money and was certainly not what the crowed had paid to see. No man should feel that he can pay $25 to see another man have his brains beaten out and then go home and sleep soundly.

Baer was no coward, and he thought that once his right hand had healed, he would fight Louis again. Hoffman attempted to convince boxing promoter Mike Jacobs that a second fight would have a million-dollar gate, but Jacobs refused. Baer's right fist, when healed, could deliver just the kind of punch that could knock out the formidable Louis. It was, after all, as Dempsey himself had said, the hardest-hitting, most powerful right punch in all of boxing. Jacobs did not want to take a chance on Baer's fist connecting with Louis's chin. It was an opportunity aggressively sought by Hoffman but protectively rejected by Jacobs. For many years to come, Jacobs would get a percentage of Louis's winnings, until the IRS went after Louis for unpaid taxes, reducing him to near poverty. For Jacobs, one potential million-dollar gate was less than what the future offered. Yet, it could have been one of the greatest comebacks in boxing history.

"Could have, would have" are the maybes of any sport, and a Baer–Louis rematch was one of those. And so Baer's career in the ring was nearing its end. He had made a lot of money, but he had spent it as quickly as a playboy could. Hoffman worried about Baer's future, so he took Baer's earnings from the Louis fight and bought his fighter an annuity. For the rest of his life, Baer had a financial cushion. Hoffman had given Baer a mere $100 from the Louis fight and then told him what he had done. Baer remained eternally grateful.

Baer no longer loved the sport that had elevated him to the status of national celebrity. He was tired of hitting opponents and tired of being hit, and he certainly found it difficult to use his amazing right fist to a deadly advantage. He fought a few more times, winning and losing. There were flashes of the old, bad Baer, but there was also a more reluctant combatant, someone who did not want to deliver the kind of blows that had frightened so many of his earlier opponents. When he had another fighter on the ropes and easily could have won, he backed off, for fear of the damage he could cause. The conscience of Max Baer the man had overtaken and conquered Max Baer the boxer.

The world of professional entertainers was metaphorically cutthroat. There were no real bruises, just symbolic ones that disappointed egos. Competitive entertainers may have been backstabbers, but they didn't use real knives. For successful entertainers, those who worked regularly and made good money, it was a more fun-loving world than the world of damaged boxers; it was a world into which Baer was drawn and one that enthusiastically welcomed him. With his good looks, muscular physique, and quick wit, he was a natural on the entertainment circuit.

Baer teamed up with former light heavyweight champion Slapsie Maxie Rosenbloom, who was just beginning his career in the movies and in nightclubs as a hapless, lovable goon with a soft heart, if not a soft head. In fact, poor Slapsie died at age 71, of dementia pugilistica, following years of blows to his head. He had been given his nickname by the popular journalist and creator of the characters in *Guys and Dolls*, Damon Runyon, who had belittled Maxie for slapping his opponents with an opened glove, not a clenched one, which he did because he didn't have a powerful punch. It's amazing what he was able to become without having a hard punch.

Like Baer, there was something clownish about Rosenbloom. The fans adored him because he was fun to watch and because he overcame his limitations to defeat other fighters. As a natural entertainer, it's no wonder he was cast as Big Julie in the 1961 stage revival of *Guy and Dolls*, a role that won the praise of critics. Rosenbloom proved ideal for playing a pug and a thug; however, he failed to win the same role in the movie starring Frank Sinatra and Marlon Brando. In that rendition, the part of Big Julie is played by a second-rate comedian named B. S. Pully.

Before venturing into show business, Rosenbloom had an illustrious career as a light heavyweight, winning the title in 1932. He was 5-foot-11, and his weight fluctuated between 160 and 198 pounds, depending on who he was scheduled to fight. Because he did not have a powerful punch, he compensated by being fast on his feet, attempting to stay out of range of more powerful opponents. He could move fast and slap even faster, like a kangaroo on methamphetamines. Since opponents often had difficulty tagging him with knockout punches, his fights usually went the full number of rounds and ended with a decision, mostly in Rosenbloom's favor. He fought in more than 300 bouts and won 208, although only 19 by knockout. Even that small number is impressive considering his inability to deliver a powerful punch.

By the time he retired from the ring, Rosenbloom was well known in Hollywood, not only as a boxing celebrity, but also for his obsessive gambling and womanizing. As if in an attempt to understand himself, he married a psychotherapist, but the marriage lasted only eight years. Rosenbloom may have learned little about himself, but one thing he did learn was that he didn't want to get married again, especially to another psychotherapist. Venturesome and with the backing of the right kinds of friends, he looked for opportunities to put his comedic talents on display. He opened two Slapsy Maxie's comedy clubs, one in Los Angeles and the other in San Francisco. It has been speculated that the real owner of the clubs was Mickey Cohen, the notorious mobster and pal of Bugsy Siegel. The spelling of Rosebloom's nickname as Slapsy rather than Slapsie was also a decision made by Cohen. The "y" on the end appeared to be more masculine than the "ie." A gangster and former boxer as tough as Cohen would not have signed his name Mickie, so why should Slapsy be Slapsie? Maxie, however, remained Maxie.

Because his comedy clubs attracted major stars, directors, and producers, Rosenbloom got steady work in films, appearing in more than 100 movies during the course of his career. In addition, he was a regular on the *Fred Allen Show* with Marlene Dietrich and appeared in the Playhouse 90 drama *Requiem for a Heavyweight*, written by Rod Serling and starring Jack Palance. The production also included Max Baer in the cast.

Like many Jewish boxers of his era, Rosenbloom was dedicated to the founding and support of a Jewish state. He had read about what had happened to the Jews of Nazi-controlled Europe. No one had lifted a finger to help them. Maybe if they would have had their own country, history would have been different. He wanted to avoid another Holocaust. Thus, Rosenbloom fought in numerous benefit fights to raise money for the founding of Israel. At the Slapsy Maxie comedy club, Mickey Cohen hosted an evening of thugs and pugs, stars and starlets, guys and dolls, and gunmen and gun molls, and insisted that they generously support Israel. He passed around several large hats and instructed everyone to be as generous as they could be. When calculating the contents of the hats, Cohen was pleased to count $200,000 in contributions. He thanked those in attendance and said how pleased he was. And those in attendance knew it was far better to win Cohen's approval than his disapproval. It had been said that Rosenbloom provided the comedic chatter and that Cohen was the implicit menace. It was good cop/bad cop routine.

Baer and Rosenbloom were a different kind of duo; they were almost as ideally suited to be a comedy team as Abbott and Costello or Laurel and Hardy, although not as popular. Baer and Rosenbloom were teamed for a series of comedic movie shorts in the early 1950s. The series was known as the Columbia shorts. In addition, the two did a stand-up comedy routine billed as "The Two Maxies." Not satisfied with his cinematic pursuits, Rosenbloom contributed his writing talents to a movie entitled *Skipalong Rosenbloom*, starring the two Maxies. It is a corny but somewhat humorous parody of a western about the town of Buttonhole Bend, which is ruled by the notorious bandit Butcher Baer (played by Max Baer), whose gang has murdered every sheriff who has tried to bring law and order to the decent, law-abiding folks of Buttonhole Bend.

When the bank opens, the Baer gang steals the deposits. Skipalong Rosenbloom, played by (who else?) Slapsie Maxie Rosenbloom, comes to town and is tricked into becoming the sheriff. He falls in love with Miss Caroline Witherspoon, played by Jacqueline Fontaine, the town's admired schoolmarm. Inspired by his love for justice and Witherspoon, as well as the kind folks of Buttonhole Bend, Skipalong finally corners Butcher in Square Deal Sal's saloon, beats him up, and corrals the rest of the gang. He is a hero to the town and the love of his life, the lovely schoolmarm.

Baer was in great demand for his comedic talents, but his life was short and so he had fewer acting opportunities than Rosenbloom, acting in only 20 films, including *Africa Screams* with Abbott and Costello and the critically acclaimed *The Harder They Fall*, Humphrey Bogart's final movie. Based on the novel of the same title by Budd Schulberg, *The Harder They Fall* is a classic film noir, relating a story that is a striking echo of reality. In fact, it is an obvious roman à clef of the career of Baer's opponent Primo Carnera, who sued Columbia Pictures for $1.5 million shortly after the movie's release.

The Harder They Fall tells the story of a contender named Toro Moreno, a character based on Carnera, and his upcoming title fight with the champ, Buddy Brannen, based on and played by Max Baer. It is ironic that Baer and Carnera had appeared in the *Prizefighter and the Lady* prior to Baer defeating Carnera and being crowned world heavyweight champion. Bogart's character, Eddie Willis, is based on another real-life boxing figure, Harold Conrad, who was a well-known boxing promoter and boxing writer. In the movie, Willis is out of work and needs money, and he agrees to use his publicity skills to build the reputation of Moreno and publicize the fight between Brannen and Moreno, for a share of the profits.

Moreno is unaware that the mobsters who own his contract have fixed his fights to harvest a small fortune from their bets. While making money for themselves, they have merely paid for Moreno's living expenses but promised him a big payday. Prior to fighting for the title, Moreno wins another fixed fight against a character named Gus Dundee, played by heavyweight fighter Pat Comiskey, the "Idol of New Jersey," whom Baer had knocked out in a 1940 bout.

Baer had so badly beaten Comiskey that he had asked referee Jack Dempsey to end the fight, for Baer thought that if the fight continued he might kill Comiskey. He did not want another such incident on his conscience. After Dempsey declared Baer the winner, Baer rushed to Comiskey to make sure that he was okay. It's no wonder that a documentary about Baer's life is entitled *Tenderhearted Tiger*.

In *Requiem for a Heavyweight*, there is no tenderhearted opponent for the Comiskey character, Dundee. Before the fight, he had complained of headaches and neck pains from a previous fight. This is reminiscent of Ernie Schaaf, following his fight with Baer. He, too, had complained of head and neck pains, and then died in a later fight with Carnera. In Dundee's fight with Moreno, he had agreed to lose. He steps into the ring, lets Moreno batter him, and then collapses onto the canvas. He is rushed to a hospital, where he later dies of a brain hemorrhage.

Before his fight with the Baer character, Moreno is told by Eddie Willis that his fights have been fixed and that he will lose to Brannen. Moreno doesn't believe him until a character played by former heavyweight Jersey Joe Walcott knocks him out in his dressing room. The mobsters, knowing that their fighter will lose, bet large sums on Brannen to win. Moreno suffers a grievous loss; his jaw is broken, and he feels completely humiliated. His earnings are stolen by his managers, who want to sell his contract to other unscrupulous promoters. Willis, however, angry at his own complicity in promoting Moreno as an unbeatable heavyweight, turns over his share of earnings to the defeated fighter and helps him flee the country before the mobsters can further destroy him while continuing to earn large sums from their hapless and ignorant chattel. The movie received rave reviews, and the name Max Baer was on the lips of producers and directors, who wanted him for upcoming projects. In addition to his movie roles and comedy routines, Baer worked as a disc jockey for a Sacramento radio station, a PR official for an automobile dealership, and, on occasion, a wrestler.

Following years of enjoying the favors and charms of models, chorus girls, and movie stars, Baer chose as his lifetime partner a former waitress named Mary Ellen Sullivan, a down-to-earth woman who was charming, beautiful, warm, funny, and devoted to her husband. They married in June 1935, and had three children, two boys and one girl. Their oldest son, Max Jr., born in 1937, grew up to become a successful actor, playing the role of Jethro Bodine in the popular television series *The Beverly Hillbillies*. He is also a writer, producer, and director, as well as a casino owner and developer.

Max Baer Jr. recalled that his father was fun, loving, and affectionate. When the elder Baer drove his son to school, he would give him a hug and a kiss. Baer Jr. was about 11 or 12 years old at the time, and he was embarrassed to be seen getting such affectionate treatment from his father. Thus, when father and son were several blocks from the school, young Baer would give his father a hug and kiss, and then leap from the car and run to school. Max Baer Jr. loved and admired his father. Indeed, his father was his hero. Baer Sr. never wanted his son to become a boxer, a desire common among boxers. It was a brutal sport that no loving father wished his son to take up. Instead, young Baer followed in his father's show business footsteps, becoming a beloved character in a highly successful sitcom.

In 1959, Max Baer refereed a televised 10-round boxing match in Phoenix, Arizona. As soon as the bout was over, he bounded out of the ring and joined a happy, boisterous group of fight fans at a local bar. He would often become the center of attention at such gatherings but was never much of a drinker. He would nurse one drink the entire evening and rarely finish it. A drink was a prop to be held at a bar or cocktail party.

The next day, Baer left for Hollywood, where he was scheduled to appear in several television commercials. He checked into the Hollywood Roosevelt Hotel, where he was greeted by a staff glad to have him as a guest. Baer was always a generous tipper, and hotel employees were always pleased to take care of him. While shaving the next morning, Baer experienced a sharp pain in his chest. He put his razor down on the bathroom sink and walked into the living room of his suite. He sat down and took a deep breath, but the pain persisted. He picked up the phone and called the hotel's front desk. The pain was now so intense that he rubbed his chest as if he could massage it away. As he did so, he asked the desk clerk to send a doctor right away. The clerk said he would immediately send the house doctor. Ever the jokester, even while in pain, Baer replied, "A house doctor? No dummy, a people doctor."[8] He laughed.

There was a rapid series of knocks on his door, and Baer opened it to an anxious-looking doctor. Baer said he thought he was having a heart attack and told the doctor that he had experienced two such attacks earlier in Sacramento. The doctor quickly gave him medicine. The fire department had been called, and a few minutes later a fireman entered the room. He quickly proceeded to administer oxygen to Baer. He seemed to have recovered, nodding in gratitude at the fireman, and suddenly began rubbing his chest again. The second attack was more intense than the first. Baer clutched at his chest and, gasping, said, "Oh God, here I go."[9] His eyes closed, and he stopped breathing. The doctor checked for a pulse and shook his head. He confirmed that Max Baer, former world heavyweight boxing champion, was dead. He was only 50 years old.

News of Baer's death quickly spread throughout Hollywood and Sacramento. The next day, there were front-page stories announcing the death of a great champion, the fiercely powerful boxer who had once seemed indestructible. It was also noted that he had been the clown prince of the ring.

His funeral was attended by more than 1,500 mourners. Sacramento residents had never seen such a tribute to a dead hero. The ceremony was attended by movie stars, former boxing champions, a sprinkling of gamblers, trainers, cornermen, hundreds of fans, and some curious folks who wanted to know what all the fuss was about. Joe Louis and Jack Dempsey, two of the most feared and successful heavyweight champions of the 20th century, served as pallbearers, as did many of Baer's former opponents.

To conclude the service, the American Legion firing squad gave Baer a 21-gun salute, honoring his military service as a boxing instructor during World War II. His funeral also received front-page news coverage in the *New York Times* and other big-city newspapers. As Mary Ellen Sullivan Baer had wished, the Jewish gladiatorial boxing hero was laid to rest in a garden crypt in St. Mary's Catholic Cemetery. To honor Baer's memory, civic leaders petitioned to have parks in Livermore and Sacramento named for him. In addition, the Max Bear Heart Fund was established in 1959, to support heart research and education at universities, medical centers, and hospitals throughout the United States and Canada. Baer has since been inducted into the Boxing Hall of Fame, the World Boxing Hall of Fame, the International Boxing Hall of Fame, and the International Jewish Sports Hall of Fame. Members will never forget Baer's stunning defeat of the symbol of Nazi racial superiority.

CONCLUSION
The Empty Ring

For many contemporary boxing fans, the sport has hit the skids. While some heavily promoted fights on pay-per-view attract large audiences willing to pay to see a championship bout, there are few stars of the sweet science. Instead, there are a number of heavy(over)weight pugs who will try to slug it out, thinking that they may one day become title contenders. It's also unlikely that we will see such contemporary champions as Max Baer and Ken Norton appearing in movies. The sports pages of major newspapers predominate with coverage of baseball, football, basketball, and sometimes soccer, rarely focusing attention on boxing. If there was a golden age of boxing, it has surely passed, as have the intense ethnic rivalries that existed among immigrant groups in the first half of the 20th century, which were the basis for matches between boxers of different religions.

One of the most respected newspapers in the country, the *New York Times*, rarely covers boxing matches now, except as human interest or business stories. It recently did a story about the dangers of boxing and the permanent brain injuries suffered by boxers. Thomas Hauser, in his book *Boxing Is . . .: Reflections on the Sweet Science*, writes, "There was a time when big fights were chronicled in the *New York Times* with banner headlines in large type that stretched across the front page."[1] No more. The editorial bias against boxing at the *Times*, as well as other newspapers, reflects the significantly diminished popularity of boxing.

The masculine role models, the flamboyant Don Juans, and the swaggering tough guys have long since left the scene. The attitude of Max Baer that boxing is not worth the price of being severely hurt has flowed down the inclines of history, so that even contemporary boxers view the sport as an opportunity to make some quick money and then retire before their brains are turned to mush. Max Baer Jr. (aka Jethro Bodine) told me that his father did not like boxing: He did it for the money and because he wanted to be famous. Said Baer Jr.,

> My father was making 35 cents a day slopping pigs, and boxing offered $35 per fight in 1929. The stock market had crashed, he was poor, and boxing was a road out of poverty. Later in his career, he would often pull his punches because he didn't want to inflict permanent damage on his opponents. [2]

Howard Davis, whom I publicized in the 1980s, is quoted as saying in his *New York Times* obituary, "I see boxers get knocked out and lie there four or five minutes. It's frightening. Even if you get paid a million and a half dollars, it's not enough. It's a very dangerous sport."[3] And that's probably why the *Times* prefers not to cover it. Like many of the great Jewish fighters, Davis (who was African American) regarded boxing as a means to an end: financial independence. It was all about the money. "I hope to make enough money so that I can retire early and buy a business," Davis had once told me.

For the poor children of immigrants and ghettoized minorities, boxing was a means of escape into a world of affluence and glamour. If they were smart, and many of them were, they boxed for five, six, or seven years and then retired and invested their money in restaurants, hardware stores, dry-cleaning stores, car dealerships, fast-food franchises, and even boxing gyms, whatever would give them a livable return on their investments. They considered themselves fortunate if their injuries had only been temporary and they could guide themselves unhindered through life without intellectual or health obstacles. In his book *When Boxing Was a Jewish Sport*, Allen Bodner relates,

> The fear of death in the ring was not a major concern to the boxers, but the fear of brain injury, or punch-drunkenness, was. It was never very far from their minds. A number of boxers expressed gratitude that they

had quit in time. Broken limbs heal, but damage to the brain, dementia pugilistica, is permanent.[4]

In the 1990s, when I taught a marketing and PR course at the New School University in New York City, I learned from one of my students, a middle-aged woman, that her father had been a professional boxer for nearly seven years, from 1934 to 1941, before joining the U.S. Navy at the outbreak of World War II. Her grandparents were Russian Jewish immigrants who first lived on New York's Lower East Side and then in Chicago's Maxwell Street ghetto, making the same journey taken by Barney Ross's parents. Her grandfather had a series of menial jobs, while his wife, who could barely speak English, took in laundry and was a seamstress. The woman's father, who hated being poor and being taunted and periodically attacked by young anti-Semites, had started fighting Irish and Italian kids on the streets. If you didn't fight to defend yourself, you were considered a coward or a sissy. My student reflected,

> He used to tell me that when he wanted to go swimming or play baseball or basketball, he and other Jewish kids would have to run a gauntlet of Irish and Italian kids. If you didn't know the skills necessary for defending yourself, you got beaten up. The Jewish kids became quite tough, and a number of them, like my dad, became professional fighters in their late teens. The money wasn't great, but often it was more than their parents were earning. My dad had a number of professional fights, but he never became a champion, or even a contender, but for those seven years, he made more money than his mother and father's combined incomes. He made enough to dress smartly, take a vacation in the summer, rent a room away from his parents, and still contribute to his parents' household expenses.
>
> When the war started in December 1941, he enlisted in the Navy. It was the end of his days and nights as a boxer. He felt that he had a better chance of surviving in the Navy than he did in the ring: Every time he fought, he got belted on the head. He tried to avoid getting hit on the head, but you can only avoid it so much without having to run around the ring like a scared chicken. But he had the nose of a fighter, you know, where the bridge has been pushed in, and one his ear lobes looked like melted wax that had hardened.
>
> After the war, my dad went into the real estate business. He would borrow money and buy buildings. He had a real knack for picking up undervalued properties and turning his investments into very profitable

commodities, though he rarely sold anything. He went on to develop some suburban shopping centers and buy a few small office buildings. Before he died he said to me that boxing had taught him to be tough. To be a dealmaker. "You know," he said, "a lot of people are frightened of being successful, frightened of taking chances, frightened of failure, frightened of getting in over their heads, and losing everything. Boxing taught me not to be afraid; if you're smart you can often turn fighting to your advantage. You not only have to outbox the other guy, you have to outthink and outstrategize him. I learned to be successful from that, and boxing turned out to be a pathway for my success." My dad died a rich man without any traces of dementia.

The story of this woman's father is also the story of many Jewish boxers in the 1920s and 1930s. Many of them fought because it was their only opportunity to break free from the social and economic restrictions that hampered minorities from achieving the American dream.

Certainly, my father's friend, Abe Simon, exemplified the journey of the Jewish boxer. His was a story I first heard when I was about 10 years old. Simon had been a football player for Richmond Hill High School in Richmond Hill, Queens, New York. One day, there was a group of boxing promoters in the stands watching the Richmond Hill team play the Jamaica High School team. The Jamaica team had a terrific running back. He was as swift and elusive as a jaguar, and Richmond Hill did not have a player of such speed and cunning. Simon's coach told him that when he had an opportunity to tackle the running back, "Don't just tackle the son of a bitch, break his damn leg." The coach then offered Simon a reward if he succeeded. He did, and Richmond Hill won the game.

In the locker room, Simon was told by the team's assistant manager, my Uncle Joe, that there were some men outside who wanted to speak with him. Simon met the men in a hallway and they invited him to a local ice cream parlor, where they sat in the last booth, away from kids who might overhear their conversation. The men had learned that Simon's parents were poor and that Simon had few good economic prospects following his high school graduation. "How would you like to earn big bucks as a prizefighter?" they asked. "You're big, strong, and powerful. You can give and take punishment. You'll make the kind of money that you can't make anyplace else." Simon agreed and went on to have a moderately successful career. He had one of boxing's most legendary trainers, Freddie Brown, a partner of Ray Arcel and Whitey Bimstein.

Simon became a contender for the heavyweight championship after knocking out Jersey Joe Walcott with a powerful right fist to the chin in the sixth round of an eight-round fight. That led to his being a contender for the heavyweight title. But, unfortunately for Simon, he lost two attempts at that title, being beaten twice by Joe Louis. Simon had acted in movies (*On the Waterfront*, *Requiem for a Heavyweight*, etc.) and worked in various other areas following his retirement from boxing. He may have boxed too long, for in later years, he often complained of headaches that resulted from his years as a boxer.

After years of offering up their heads as punching bags, many boxers end up suffering from Parkinson's disease, Alzheimer's disease, or pugilistica dementia, better known as punch-drunkenness. Unlike football players, who wear protective helmets and still suffer concussions, boxers are even more vulnerable. And it's not only their bruised craniums and battered brains that suffer. Their eyes, as soft as jellyfish, are pounded and jabbed, causing detached retinas and the development of scar tissue. Their eardrums are also pounded, and the resulting tintinnabulation is not the pleasant sound of Sunday morning church bells. In old age, without pensions and unions, most fighters (the journeymen, the palookas, the noncontenders) are unable to pay their medical bills. Medicaid may be their only option. The few who do reach championship status may be able to fund their medical bills following retirement, but they are the fortunate exceptions.

Beau Jack's trajectory is an example of the unfortunate downward spiral of so many boxing careers once the last bell has sounded. Jack was a two-time lightweight champion who was the main attraction at Madison Square Garden 21 times; he sold more tickets and filled more seats than any other boxer at the Garden. He fought from 1939 to 1955, and was particularly popular during World War II. Mike Tyson's trainer, Cus D'Amato, named Jack the "greatest lightweight ever." While that claim can be disputed, Jack's skill certainly placed him in the top tier of great lightweights. After his earnings were depleted, Jack earned a meager living by shining shoes at the Fontainebleau Hotel in Miami Beach. He picked up a little extra cash by training boxers at the famous Fifth Street Gym, also in Miami. It is understandable why none of Jack's seven children chose to be boxers.

Another sad case was Jerry Quarry, a poster figure for the destructive power of boxing. During the latter part of his career, Quarry took a cognitive performance test, and the results revealed that his brain had suffered severe damage. He was well on his way to developing pugilistica dementia. His brain was in the process of atrophying. Nevertheless, he continued fighting. By 1990, his boxing earnings had vanished like a mirage in the heat of reality. He had no other option but to apply for Social Security payments; he was only 45 years old. At age 47, he managed to sign for another fight, during which he served as a human punching bag, a sacrificial lamb. Anyone who witnessed it was appalled at the beating Quarry received. A fan had said he thought that cruel and unusual punishment had been declared unlawful. A few years later, Quarry's mental abilities were so depleted, he could not feed himself. His was a pitiful end to a once-successful boxing career, for out of 66 bouts, he had 53 wins.

As sad as his case was, it was not unique. Boxing breeds an epidemic of brain injuries, as well as deaths. Among the more notorious boxing deaths have been Doo Koo Kim, Ernie Schaaf, Davey Moore, Benny Paret, Jimmy Doyle, and dozens of lesser-known boxers. Disregarding the potential injuries, men continue to enter the ring, modern-day gladiators hoping to cash in on years of rigorous physical training. One need only look at the massively hyped match between Manny Pacquiao and Floyd Mayweather, which generated more money than any other fight in boxing history and a huge pay-per-view television audience. Promoters and fans hoped that this bout would reestablish boxing as one of the most popular American sports. Since then, however, the sports pages have remained generally void of information on boxing matches. Nevertheless, prior to and immediately following the much-hyped match, such major newspapers as the *New York Times*, while still refraining from covering the sport, could not resist writing about the amount of money the two fighters would earn. It became more of a compelling business story than a sports story. Any other match would have failed to arouse an editor to donate even a single column inch to a boxing match.

The editorial neglect of boxing was given prosecutorial zeal by an indictment from the American Medical Association's vote in 1984, urging that boxing be banned. The AMA issued the following statement:

> The continued existence of boxing as an accepted sport in civilized
> society has been long debated. The position of the American Medical
> Association (AMA) has evolved from promoting increased safety and
> medical reform to recommending total abolition of both amateur and

professional boxing. In response to the AMA opposition to boxing, the boxing community has attempted to increase the safeguards in amateur and professional boxing. The United States of America Amateur Boxing Federation, which is the national regulatory agency for all amateur boxing in the United States, has taken several actions to prevent the occurrence of acute brain injury and is currently conducting epidemiologic studies to assess the long-term neuropsychological consequences of amateur boxing. In professional boxing, state regulatory agencies such as the New York State Athletic Commission have introduced several medical interventions to prevent and reduce neurologic injury. The lack of a national regulatory agency to govern professional boxing has stimulated the formation of the Association of Boxing Commissions and potential legislation for the federal regulation of professional boxing by a federally chartered organization called the United States Boxing Commission.

The AMA's imprimatur was all that was needed for many who had been decrying boxing's brutality. Yet, promoters, gamblers, and boxers shrugged off the indictment; the charges would never stick in the minds of fans, certainly not in the minds of those who spent tens of millions of dollars to witness the Pacquiao–Mayweather match.

If a poor young man can ascend out of poverty into a world of wealth and privilege, he will usually be willing to risk his heath and even his life. When a sport can generate millions of dollars, it can be like honey to flies. One need only look at a sport far more brutal than boxing, caged mixed martial arts, to see how individuals can be drawn into the promise of cash and fame. At least in boxing there are rules and regulations: no kicking, biting, jabbing an opponent in the eye, hitting below the belt, hitting with the back of the hand, head butting, and so forth. Desperate men will take desperate actions to erase their desperation.

Sports have always been a pathway to wealth for those with superior athletic skills. And while many may not be good enough to become professional baseball, football, or basketball players, they may have sufficient punching prowess to floor a series of less-powerful opponents. Today, poor young African Americans, Latinos, and other minorities, not unlike the Jewish boxers of the 1920s and 1930s, are still willing to put their lives at risk for a big payday. And while many are sodden, uninteresting pugilistic specimens who sluggishly move about the ring, the opportunity to possibly see another Henry Armstrong, Joe Louis, Sugar

Ray Robinson, or Muhammad Ali keeps fans lining up at the ticket windows. Those great champions were fleet of foot, had the instincts of a cheetah, and had the fistic ability to aim their punches where they would inflict the most damage. One can look at films of their fights and marvel at their fistic marksmanship and strategic brilliance, for example, Joe Louis's amazing disabling shot to Max Schmeling, which ended their second, highly touted bout. That single blow for democracy and against Nazism inspired books, articles, and movies.

Many of the great ones, however, stayed in the game too long. Their brains had suffered and begun to atrophy, and their speech was often a series of slurs and mumbles. The smartest and most skillful ones had been able to use their defensive skills to avoid being permanently damaged by opponents. But if a fighter didn't get out of the game in five to seven years, he ran a significant risk of being a pugilistic casualty. Max Baer, in his bruising fight with Joe Louis, said that he was not willing to be a human punching bag just to satisfy the expectations of fans. He had no intention of ending up like Frankie Campbell or Ernie Schaaf. Baer was one of the smart ones. He left the ring with money in the bank, his face unscarred, and his brain operating at boffo comedic speed.

The expectations of fans can drive a boxer to seek admiration and applause, no different from an actor on a stage. The audience for a boxing match, however, is far more intense than one for a Broadway play. Unless one has attended such a match, it is impossible to imagine the intensity, excitement, or speculation on the outcome. Spectators are not blood thirsty, but they are riveted, enthralled, and fascinated. Boxing gives boys and men the opportunity to identify with a gladiator and vicariously imagine that they are as tough as their heroes. They cheer when their favorite lands a devastating punch, and some leap from their seats, as if they had landed the punch themselves. And this does not only occur at actual boxing matches.

Last year, I attended a promotional book event at the main branch of the New York Public Library on Fifth Avenue. The building is one of the great architectural landmarks of the city. And there, in a cavernous basement auditorium, hundreds of people, myself included, cheered for Mike Tyson as he entered to promote his autobiography. When films were shown of his devastating knockouts, the audience erupted in cheers similar to those that were probably heard during gladiatorial combats in the

Roman Coliseum. As long as that visceral, almost atavistic enthusiasm exists, boxing will survive.

The Jewish boxers of the 1920s and 1930s often entered the profession against the wishes of their parents. Some changed their names so their parents wouldn't recognize them in newspaper stories; others brought home so much money that their parents reluctantly or happily accepted the career choice. Many of those Jewish boxers, having earned their way out of the lower classes, would not permit their own sons to follow in their rope-skipping footsteps. They had the same values as their parents. Instead of letting their sons assert their macho pride in the ring, they encouraged them to attend college and become well-paid professionals, their brains fully operational. Max Baer Jr. stated that his father never wanted his two sons to take up boxing. Max Jr. attended college, majoring in business and philosophy, and today he is a wealthy entrepreneur. In *When Boxing Was a Jewish Sport*, Bodner states, "Of the [Jewish] boxers interviewed, nearly 90 percent of their children are college graduates, and many earned advanced degrees."[5]

In addition to not wanting to suffer brain damage, many fighters wanted to escape the clutches and hooks of the Mafia; for organized crime, boxing proved a wonderfully remunerative world following the end of Prohibition. Bootlegging was so profitable during Prohibition that boxing was of relatively minor interest to the mob. Sure, Al Capone championed Barney Ross, but the money he bet on Ross was small potatoes compared to the millions that he had made from importing, manufacturing, and distributing alcoholic beverages. The end of Prohibition, however, caused opportunistic and entrepreneurial gangsters to turn to boxing and other activities. Unlike team sports, where one had to pay off numerous members of a team to affect a desired outcome, boxing required no such multifaceted maneuvers. One could either pay off a fighter to take a dive or pay the judges and referees to produce a profitable outcome; furthermore, while team sports like baseball, football, and basketball derived their players from high school and college graduates and then sent them to farm teams in the minor leagues, hungry boxers came from the mean streets of their neighborhoods and into sweat-laden boxing gyms, which offered them the opportunity to turn dreams into reality, ambitions into rewards.

These boys and men were ready to punch their way to success. They were hungry for money and recognition. They wanted the respect and admiration that would come from being champs. There were no farm teams for aspiring young boxers. They often learned their craft in grubby ghetto gyms and were usually trained by former fighters, who could introduce them to unscrupulous promoters, matchmakers, and bookmakers. Boxing gyms were the sport's chapels, where boxers and promoters married their talents. Those marriages, however, were not between equals. The promoters and managers often led their fighters around like lambs on leashes.

My stepfather witnessed Sonny Liston being told what to do by a little tough guy half Liston's size. The boxer, known for inspiring fear in his opponents, responded like a well-trained circus animal. My stepfather was surprised and appalled. He thought that Liston should have socked the guy or simply told him to fuck off. But had he done so, Liston might have been visited by more thugs, men who could have broken his knuckles and put him out of commission and out of the money for months. As it so happened, he died a mysterious death that was rumored to be the result of his threatening some mobsters with exposure for fixing the Ali–Liston fight unless he was paid the money he had been promised. Or he may have been paid back with a hotshot of heroin for not taking a dive when ordered to do so by the mob. Poor Sonny probably had his fill of taking dives for the short end of a payday.

The ugly underside of boxing and fixed fights, and the control being exerted by the mob, did not come out of the shadows and into public view until Jake LaMotta testified before a Senate investigations committee. It began in 1947, when LaMotta, boxing's "Raging Bull," was knocked out in four rounds by a mob-controlled fighter named Billy Fox. Even earlier than that, LaMotta had been approached by his brother, who told him that mob guys would pay him $100,000 to take a dive in a fight with Tony Janiro. LaMotta said he would only agree if his next fight would be for the championship. His brother went back to the mob and was told no. He was told that his brother was not a contender and that he should be smart, take the money, and take the dive. LaMotta refused and angrily beat Janiro, pummeling him into a humiliating defeat.

It is extraordinary that after the first rejection, the mob would not approach LaMotta again, but one of their emissaries did. This time he was told that if he took a dive against Billy Fox, his next fight would be for the world middleweight championship. LaMotta agreed. He figured that Fox, like Primo Carnera, who was a mob-controlled fighter, would never again be a competitor, just a brief obstacle. He also figured that Fox's principal owner, Blinky Palermo, would deliver on the promised opportunity for a title bout.

LaMotta fought so badly that it was obvious to onlookers that the loss had been preordained. The New York State Athletic Commission (NYSAC) called LaMotta into its offices for questioning. LaMotta claimed that he had suffered an internal lower back injury prior to the fight but that he had kept the information to himself so that the fight would take place. Even the doctor who had examined him before the fight was unaware of the injury. It was an unbelievable story. It left the NYSAC, as well as sportswriters and fans, incredulous; LaMotta was fined $1,000 and suspended from boxing, indefinitely.

That the mobsters who controlled the fight walked off with their huge gambling winnings seemed to go unnoticed. The NYSAC never called the promoters, trainers, or owners in for questioning. Yet, it was obvious that the fix could not have been LaMotta's idea alone; he could not have engineered it by himself, certainly not without the connivance of the mob. None of that seemed to trouble the commission. That no one but LaMotta was sanctioned generated a stink of hypocrisy about the commission. It was apparent that the NYSAC was a paper tiger.

It wasn't until 1960, in front of a Senate investigations committee hearing on mob control of boxing, that LaMotta revealed what had actually happened; he explained that Palermo and a Carbo associate had offered him money to lose the fight. LaMotta wasn't interested in the money. He wanted a shot at the championship. The mob agreed, and so the fixed fight took place. LaMotta wrote the following:

> The first round, a couple of belts to his head, and I see a glassy look coming over his eyes. Jesus Christ, a couple of jabs and he's going to fall down? I began to panic a little. I was supposed to be throwing the fight to this guy, and it looked like I was going to end up holding him on his feet . . . by [the fourth round], if there was anybody in the Garden who didn't know what was happening, he must have been dead drunk.[6]

Poor Billy Fox. It was suspected that most of his previous fights had been fixed: He was a puppet of the mob. And once his earning potential had been significantly diminished, the mob cut the puppet's strings and tossed him onto the ash heap of pugilistic history.

For LaMotta, many new and exciting bouts lay ahead. He would finally have the opportunity to contend for the title, to fight Marcel Cerdan for the middleweight world championship. But it came with a price tag. Cerdan's managers wanted $20,000 from LaMotta for the privilege of fighting their man. LaMotta was only expected to get $19,000 for the fight; however, with the confidence befitting a "Raging Bull," he paid the admission fee and bet $10,000 on himself to win. It was a gutsy move, and it paid off handsomely. The Raging Bull was not only fierce and fearless, but he also had mountainous self-confidence. He knew he was going to win. No doubt about it.

Prior to LaMotta's testimony, the public did not have a window into the behind-the-scenes manipulations of boxing. There were stories, rumors, and opinions about fixed fights but little, if any, substantiated knowledge about its nefarious machinations. Some of it was carried out in mob-run social clubs or the backrooms of certain bars and restaurants. And while there were plenty of Jewish gamblers and mobsters who had their hooks in naïve young boxers, the Mafia became a predominant force. The most notorious of these promoter-managers was the infamous Frankie Carbo. He inherited his control from promoters of the 1930s. It has been reported that Carbo had his hooks into Mike Jacobs long before Jacobs retired to his Fair Haven, New Jersey, mansion.

Carbo worked with his henchmen, Blinky Palermo and sometime associate Hymie "the Mink" Wallman. In addition to that triumvirate, the gang included Ettore Coco, James Plumeri, Harry Segal, and Felix Bocchicchio. They became known as the "Combination," and their amalgamation of chicanery and skullduggery were hard to beat. Of that group, Carbo was the most prominent and so became known as the "Czar of Boxing." To the outside world, Carbo was Mr. Grey, a smooth-talking, affable gentleman who looked like a typical businessman. Cross him, however, and the least you could expect was two broken kneecaps. One member of the combination reportedly said that a pair of kneecaps does not beat a full house, meaning—of course—the Combination. The house always wins.

The Combination had the keys that opened the doors to profitable boxing matches. If you wanted to gain entrance, you had to pay the exorbitant price for a ticket, which entitled you to have partners. If you did not cooperate with the Combination, you could kiss your opportunities good-bye.

Who was Frankie Carbo? Where did he come from, and how did he get his start? His story is similar to that of many 20th-century hoods. He was born as Paolo Giovanni Carbo on the Lower East Side of Manhattan in the neighborhood that produced Lucky Luciano, Meyer Lansky, and Bugsy Siegel. By the age of 11, he was serving a stretch for juvenile delinquency in an upstate reformatory. A number of years after his release, he attempted to force a taxi driver to pay him protection money. The driver refused, and Frankie killed him. With the help of a clever lawyer, Carbo pleaded guilty to manslaughter and was sentenced to four years in prison. He served less than two years.

During Prohibition, Carbo worked for bootleggers in Philadelphia, where he murdered bootlegger Mickey Murphy. He beat that rap and went to work in Brooklyn for Louis "Lepke" Buchalter, the CEO of Murder Incorporated, the mob's murder squad for hire. For Lepke, Carbo committed two more murders and again walked out of a brief internment a free man. Nonetheless, his murderous career nearly came to an end when Abe "Kid Twist" Reles, the most feared hitman of Murder Inc., who regularly used an ice pick to dispose of his victims, was going to testify against him and other members of Murder Inc., as well as Albert Anastasia, a high-ranking member of La Cosa Nostra known as the "Lord High Executioner."

Carbo and his associates were, of course, nervous. Reles could send them all to the electric chair, euphemistically known—with some understatement—as the "hot seat." There would also be testimony against Bugsy Siegel, a West Coast associate of Carbo's. In Los Angeles, the two gangsters had conspired, with Lepke, to kill Harry Greenberg, also known as "Big Greenie," who—like Reles—was about to testify against the mob. According to testimony given at trial by Al "Tick Tock" Tannenbaum, Siegel drove the getaway car and Carbo fired five shots into Greenie; it is possible that Tannenbaum's testimony may have been his attempt to minimize his own culpability in the murder of Big Greenie, for Tick Tock had been the one originally assigned by Lekpe to kill Greenie. So much for the Machiavellian, tortuous, and serpentine arrangements and betrayals of the mob's murderous tactics.

The conspirators were indicted and tried, but the jury was deadlocked. A mistrial was declared, and some observers naturally suspected that a few jurors had been bribed. If cops and politicians can be bribed, then why not jurors? A second trial was scheduled, with Reles expected to testify. It couldn't happen. It wouldn't happen. Not if the mob could control events.

Reles was being kept under the supposedly watchful eyes of six sharp-eyed cops in a sixth-floor room at the Half Moon Hotel in Coney Island. Even the president of the United States did not have such an army of bodyguards. Yet, Reles, in a failed imitation of Houdini and without the knowledge of his bodyguards, allegedly fell to his death while climbing out of his hotel window and rappelling downward on two sheets tied together; the sheets only reached to the fifth floor. How would Reles navigate the final four floors? The cops said they did not see the attempted escape. They were as surprised and disappointed as the prosecutor. They were supposedly out in the hallway, smoking and kibitzing, even though Reles was panicky about being left alone. Reles's body had slammed into an abutment, his body fluids draining out of him. He lay bleeding and broken until an ambulance carted him away. According to a biography of Frank Costello by his former attorney, the cops had been paid $100,000 to toss Reles out of the window of his room. The wits of the mob never failed to repeat their most popular epigram: "The canary could sing, but he couldn't fly." And so, yet again, Frankie Carbo walked the streets of New York a free man.

By the time Mike Jacobs retired, the Carbo-controlled Combination was well ensconced in the world of professional boxing. When the NYSAC learned that Carbo's organization had taken control of Jacob's Beach, Carbo and his organization were fined $2,500. Carbo regularly paid much higher amounts in bribes, so one can imagine him smiling as he wrote the check, thinking he had gotten off cheaply.

In a 2002 interview in the *Observer*, Budd Schulberg stated,

Frankie Carbo, the mob's unofficial commissioner for boxing, controlled a lot of the welters and middles. . . . Not every fight was fixed, of course, but from time to time Carbo and his lieutenants, like Blinky Palermo in Philadelphia, would put the fix in. When the Kid Gavilan–Johnny Saxton fight was won by Saxton on a decision in Philadelphia in 1954, I was covering it for *Sports Illustrated* and wrote a piece at that time saying boxing was a dirty business and must be cleaned up now. It was an open secret. All the press knew that one—and other fights—were fixed. Gavilan was a mob-controlled fighter, too, and when he fought Billy Graham it was clear Graham had been robbed of the title. The decision would be bought. If it was close, the judges would shade it the way they had been told. [7]

Carbo was like a consul general: If you wanted a visa to fight in the ring at Madison Square Garden, Carbo was the man to see. While he and his cohorts were known as the Combination, they formally operated through an organization known as the International Boxing Club, which was really a bookie operation that set odds on bouts by fixing the outcomes.

Politicians and police did not interfere with Carbo. After all, boxers came from the lower classes, which had no juice with politicians. The lower classes had given up their sons to be fighters and then bet on their favorite sons to win, just as they bet on the numbers, another lower-class business run by the mob. Politicians did not feel it was in their interest to oversee (even if they could) what happened in the smoke-filled rooms where the outcomes of boxing bouts were decided. In many cases, the mob paid tribute to the politicians, offering to help finance their elections and use their soldiers for get-out-the-vote operations on election days. They could provide plenty of "walking around money" to ensure the proper outcomes. Why would the politicians want to turn off the faucets from which their campaign contributions flowed?

If a boxer complained to his local congressman, city councilman, or local party boss, his complaints were never acted on. "I'll look into it and get back to you," he was told. If a boxer complained to members of the Combination and refused to accept his destiny, he was quietly banned from the game. If he complained repeatedly to the authorities, his banishment could be accompanied by a beating. Blackjacks could be more lethal than fists.

Sportswriters and those connected to the world of boxing knew that the mob controlled much of what went on, and they accepted it as part of the culture. Some of them also profited from tips and earned more than their salaries from the bookies. There was a terrific amount of money to be made from promotions, bets, the sale of tickets, and tangential items. A boxer might be induced to invest his money in a bar and restaurant, and then find that the mob was a silent partner. The opportunities were manifold, and the mob took advantage of each one of those; they were some of the country's most rapacious capitalists.

It was not until 1960, when the Senate began investigating mob involvement in boxing, that the public learned what others had known for a long time. The public not only learned about Jake LaMotta's fixed fight with Billy Fox, but also that two of the mob's most misused and maltreated boxers were Primo Carnera and Sonny Liston, generations apart but similarly sacrificed by the greed of professional gamblers. Carbo and Palermo were convicted of racketeering by Attorney General Robert Kennedy. The best that prosecutors could do was have Carbo charged for managing boxers without a license. Carbo was sentenced to a two-year term in a bleak cell at Rikers Island prison in the East River. He was released in 1960 and subpoenaed to appear before a Senate committee that was investigating mob control of boxing. Carbo was asked a number of pointed questions, to which he responded 25 times by declaring, "I cannot be compelled to be a witness against myself." The Fifth Amendment to the Constitution was an effective defensive shield behind which many mobsters protected themselves from being convicted for their crimes.

In his book *Beyond the Ring*, Jeffrey Sammons says, "Jimmy Plumeri, alias Jimmy Doyle, appeared before [New York district attorney Frank] Hogan's 'boxing grand jury' and boasted that his record of one conviction out of nine arrests attested to his 'political influence.'" There was little that Hogan could do, although he tried mightily. Hogan was known as "Mr. Integrity" and served from 1942 to 1974, without a blemish on his outstanding career. Yet, the political firewall that he faced was virtually impenetrable. Jimmy Cannon, the wonderfully evocative boxing columnist, commented that because of people like Carbo and Palermo, "boxing was the red-light district of sports" and had further descended to become the "swill barrel of sports."

Leaving behind the world of mobsters and brain injuries, many Jewish boxers were happy to embark on less stressful lives. They had immigrated to lands of plenty. For those who had carefully invested their money and been able to steer clear of many of the mob's machinations, as did Max Baer, life was good. Their promised land consisted of affluence, comfort, and assimilation into a larger society. As the years passed, they were considered a dying breed, a species on the verge of extinction. It didn't matter. Most of them were satisfied to have money in the bank and functioning brains. They had come a long way from the 1920s and 1930s, when Jews were the most predominant group in professional boxing and anti-Semitism was rife throughout the country.

By 1928, the ranks of boxers could have been a Hebrew-language association of tough guys. There had been more Jewish boxers than Irish, Italian, African American, or Latino ones. Since 1900, the ethnic pattern of boxers has gone from Irish to Jewish to Italian to African-American and Latino. Each group has been a reflection of the economic and social positions of its members and its members' parents. As generations became more assimilated and achieved economic prosperity, boxing was no longer needed as a means for ascending the ladder of success. A boxing fan who had gone to sleep at the end of the 1930s and awoke at the end of the 1940s would have been surprised and confused by the absence of Jewish boxers. They vanished, as if by magic. No other group had left the sport so quickly, and few of today's boxing fans even know that boxing was once a Jewish sport. It's no wonder that Bodner's *When Boxing Was a Jewish Sport* arrived to the astonishment of those who knew little, if anything, about boxing's Jewish golden age.

The era of Jewish boxing had been on the verge of falling into the dustbin of history. Not only had Jewish poverty been largely eliminated, but also the kind of pervasive anti-Semitism that existed in the 1920s and 1930s. Following the end of World War II, a new golden age of acceptance and success began and continues to this day. Jews populate all walks of life and no longer have to fight with their fists to achieve their goals. Few of today's Jews have experienced the anti-Semitism endured and fought against by their grandparents and great-grandparents. It's no wonder that Joseph Heller was able to write the following in his novel *Good as Gold*: "How can I write about the Jewish experience . . . when I don't even know what it is? I haven't the faintest idea what to write. . . . I don't think I've ever run into an effective anti-Semite."[8] His narrator used to feel that everyone in the world was Jewish. One can hardly imagine him or his children feeling compelled to put on a pair of boxing gloves to overcome the bullying and abuse caused by anti-Semitism. The Tenement Museum in New York documents and celebrates that history. The ghetto is no more, and the figure of the Jewish boxer is a heroic image in history.

APPENDIX A

Barney Ross's Boxing Record

Wins: 72 (22 by knockout)
Losses: 4 (none by knockout)
Draws: 3
Bouts fought: 79
Rounds fought: 607

The result of each bout is noted as a knockout (KO), technical knockout (TKO), loss (L), draw (D), or win by points alone (W). Each is followed by the round of the decision and/or the number of rounds fought.

Date	Opponent	City	Result/Round
September 1, 1929	Ramon Lugo	Los Angeles	W/6
September 14, 1929	Joe Borola	Los Angeles	W/6
October 12, 1929	Joe Borola	Los Angeles	W/6
October 21, 1929	Virgil Tobin	San Francisco	KO/2
November 19, 1929	Joey Barth	Chicago	W/5
December 5, 1929	Al DeRose	Chicago	W 6
January 10, 1930	Louis New	Chicago	W/6
January 24, 1930	Johnny Andrews	Chicago	W/4
February 22, 1930	Jiro Kumagai	San Francisco	W/4
April 8, 1930	Eddie Bojack	Cleveland	KO/2
April 21, 1930	Carlos Garcia	Chicago	L/6
April 25, 1930	Mickey Genaro	Chicago	W/6
July 1, 1930	Eddie Koppy	Detroit	W/8
August 7, 1930	Louis Navaro Perez	Chicago	KO/1
September 19, 1930	Young Terry	Chicago	D/8
October 14, 1930	Sammy Binder	Chicago	KO/2
November 6, 1930	Petey Mack	Chicago	KO/1
November 21, 1930	Harry Dublinsky	none listed	D/8
January 14, 1931	Harry Falegano	Chicago	W/8
February 20, 1931	Young Terry	Chicago	W/10
March 20, 1931	Jackie Davis	Chicago	W/6
March 27, 1931	Roger Bernard	Chicago	W/6
April 8, 1931	Mike O'Dowd	Moline, IL	W/8
April 24, 1931	Lud Abella	Chicago	TKO/2
May 1, 1931	Jackie Dugan	Moline, IL	KO/8
May 13, 1931	Billy Shaw	Cicero, IL	W/8
July 15, 1931	Babe Ruth	Benton Harbor, MI	KO/4
July 30, 1931	Jimmy Alvarado	Detroit	W/8
October 2, 1931	Glen Camp	Chicago	W/10
November 4, 1931	Lou Jallos	Chicago	W/8
November 13, 1931	Young Terry	Moline, IL	W/8
November 18, 1931	Jimmy Lundy	Kansas City	W/8
February 8, 1932	Mickey O'Neill	Milwaukee, WI	W/6
February 18, 1932	Billy Gladstone	Chicago	W/6

March 2, 1932	Nick Ellenwood	Muncie, IN	W/10
April 5, 1932	Frankie Hughes	Indianapolis	W/10
May 20, 1932	Dick Sisk	Chicago	TKO/6
July 28, 1932	Henry Perlick	Chicago	TKO/3
August 26, 1932	Ray Miller	Chicago	W/10
September 15, 1932	Frankie Petrolle	Chicago	KO/2
October 21, 1932	Battling Battalino	Chicago	W/10
November 11, 1932	Goldie Hess	Chicago	W/10
November 22, 1932	Johnny Farr	Milwaukee, WI	W/10
January 30, 1933	Johnny Datto	Pittsburgh, PA	KO/2
February 22, 1933	Tommy Grogan	Chicago	W/10
March 22, 1933	Billy Petrolle	Chicago	W/10
May 3, 1933	Joe Ghnouly	St. Louis	W/10
June 23, 1933	Tony Canzoneri	Chicago	W/10
July 26, 1933	Johnny Farr	Kansas City	TKO/6
September 12, 1933	Tony Canzoneri	New York City	W/15
November 17, 1933	Sammy Fuller	Chicago	W/10
January 24, 1934	Billy Petrolle	Bronx, NY	W/10
February 7, 1934	Peter Nebo	Kansas City	W/12
March 5, 1934	Frankie Klick	San Francisco	D/10
March 14, 1934	Kid Moro	Oakland, CA	W/10
March 27, 1934	Bobby Pacho	Los Angeles	W/10
May 28, 1934	Jimmy McLarnin	Long Island City, NY	W/15
September 17, 1934	Jimmy McLarnin	Long Island City, NY	L/15
December 10, 1934	Bobby Pacho	Cleveland, OH	W/12
January 28, 1935	Frankie Klick	Miami, FL	W/10
April 9, 1935	Henry Woods	Seattle, WA	W/12
May 28, 1935	Jimmy McLarnin	New York City	W/15
September 6, 1935	Baby Joe Gans	Portland, OR	KO/2
September 13, 1935	Ceferino Garcia	San Francisco	W/10
November 29, 1935	Ceferino Garcia	Chicago	W/10
January 27, 1936	Lou Halper	Philadelphia	TKO/8
March 11, 1936	Gordon Wallace	Vancouver, BC	W/10
May 1, 1936	Chuck Woods	Louisville, KY	TKO/5
June 10, 1936	Laddie Tonielli	Milwaukee, WI	TKO/5
June 22, 1936	Morrie Sherman	Omaha, NE	KO/2

July 22, 1936	Phil Furr	District of Columbia	W/10
November 27, 1936	Izzy Jannazzo	New York City	W/15
January 29, 1937	Al Manfredo	Detroit, MI	W/10
June 17, 1937	Chuck Woods	Indianapolis	KO/5
June 27, 1937	Jackie Burke	New Orleans, LA	KO/5
August 19, 1937	Al Manfredo	Des Moines, IA	W/10
September 23, 1937	Ceferino Garcia	New York City	W/15
April 4, 1938	Henry Schaft	Minneapolis	TKO/4
April 25, 1938	Bobby Venner	Des Moines, IA	TKO/7
May 31, 1938	Henry Armstrong	Long Island City, NY	L/15

Statistics were compiled from BoxRec, http://boxrec.com/boxer/8996.

APPENDIX B

Max Baer's Boxing Record

Wins: 71 (53 by knockout)
Losses: 13
Draws: 0
Bouts fought: 84
Rounds fought: 422

The result of each bout is noted as a knockout (KO), a technical knockout (TKO), a loss (L), a win by points alone (W), a loss by foul (LF), a loss by decision (LD), a loss by technical knockout (LTKO), or an exhibition (EX). Each is followed by the round of the decision and/or the number of rounds fought.

Date	Opponent	City	Result/Round
May 16, 1929	Chief Caribou	Stockton, CA	KO/2
June 6, 1929	Sailor Leeds	Stockton, CA ·	KO/1
July 4, 1929	Tillie Taverna	Stockton, CA	KO/1
July 18, 1929	Al Ledford	Stockton, CA	KO/1
July 24, 1929	Benny Hill	Oakland, CA	W/4
July 31, 1929	Benny Hill	Oakland, CA	W/4
August 28, 1929	Al Ledford	Oakland, CA	KO/2
September 4, 1929	Jack McCarthy	Oakland, CA	LF
September 25, 1929	Frank Rujenski	Oakland, CA	KO/3
October 2, 1929	George Carroll	Oakland, CA	KO/1
October 16, 1929	Chief Caribou	Oakland, CA	KO/1
October 30, 1929	Alex Rowe	Oakland, CA	KO/1
November 6, 1929	Natie Brown	Oakland, CA	W/6
November 20, 1929	Tillie Taverna	Oakland, CA	KO/2
December 4, 1929	Chet Shandel	Oakland, CA	KO/2
December 30, 1929	Tony Fuente	Oakland, CA	KO/1
January 15, 1930	Tiny Abbott	Oakland, CA	LF/3
January 29, 1930	Tiny Abbott	Oakland, CA	KO/6
April 9, 1930	Jack Stewart	Oakland, CA	KO/2
April 22, 1930	Ernie Owens	Los Angeles	KO/2
May 7, 1930	Tom Toner	Oakland, CA	KO/6
May 28, 1930	Jack Linkhorn	Oakland, CA	KO/1
June 11, 1930	Ora Buck Weaver	Oakland, CA	KO/1
June 25, 1930	Ernie Owens	Oakland, CA	TKO/5
July 15, 1930	Les Kennedy	Los Angeles	L/10
August 11, 1930	Meyer "KO" Christner	Oakland, CA	KO/2
August 25, 1930	Frankie Campbell	San Francisco	KO/5
December 19, 1930	Ernie Schaaf	New York City	L/10
January 16, 1931	Tom Heeney	New York City	KO/3
February 6, 1931	Tommy Loughran	New York City	L/10
April 7, 1931	Ernie Owens	Portland, OR	KO/2
May 5, 1931	Johnny Risko	Cleveland, OH	LO/10
November 23, 1931	Les Kennedy	Oakland, CA	KO/3

December 30, 1931	Arthur DeKuh	Oakland, CA	W/10
January 29, 1932	King Levinsky	New York City	W/10
February 22, 1932	Tom Heeney	San Francisco	W/10
April 26, 1932	Paul Swiderski	Los Angeles	KO/7
May 11, 1932	Walter Cobb	Oakland, CA	TKO/4
July 4, 1932	King Levinsky	Reno, NV	W/20
August 31, 1932	Ernie Schaaf	Chicago	W/10
September 26, 1932	Gerald "Tuffy" Griffith	Chicago	TKO/7
April 4, 1933	Sam Greer	Denver	EX KO/2
May 1933	Wee Willie Medivitch	Denver	EX KO/1
May 1933	Harold "Millionaire" Murphy	Kansas City, MO	EX/3
May 1933	Buddy Baer	Kansas City, MO	EX/3
May 1933	Alvin "Babe" Hunt	Kansas City, MO	EX/3
June 8, 1933	Max Schmeling	New York City	TKO/10
June 9, 1933	Pete Wistort	Buffalo, NY	EX/4
June 15, 1933	Cecil "Seal" Harris	Pittsburgh, PA	EX/3
June 22, 1933	Cecil "Seal" Harris	St Paul, MN	EX/3
July 10, 1933	Alvin "Babe" Hunt	Oklahoma City, OK	EX
July 14, 1933	Billy Murdock	Salt Lake City	EX/2
July 14, 1933	Ed Sheppard	Salt Lake City	EX/2
July 14, 1933	Jack Dempsey	Salt Lake City	EX/1
July 1933	Jack Dempsey	Salt Lake City	EX/1
July 1933	Jack Dempsey	Louisville, KY	EX/3
June 14, 1934	Primo Carnera	Long Island City, NY	TKO/11
December 6, 1934	Johnny Miler	Des Moines, IA	EX/4
December 14, 1934	Les Kennedy	Kansas City, MO	EX/4
December 28, 1934	King Levinsky	Chicago	EX KO/2
January 4, 1935	Alvin "Babe" Hunt	Detroit	EX/4
January 7, 1935	Ernie Anderson	Flint, MI	EX/4
January 9, 1935	Dick Madden	Boston	EX/4
January 21, 1935	Tony Cancela	Tampa, FL	EX/4
January 28, 1935	Jim Maloney	Miami Beach	EX/4
February 15, 1935	Stanley Poreda	San Francisco	EX/4
April 10, 1935	Ed Wills	Grand Rapids, MI	EX/4

April 17, 1935	Harold Anderson	Flint, MI	EX/4
April 18, 1935	Hobo Little	Kalamazoo, MI	EX/4
April 23, 1935	Eddie Simms	Cleveland, OH	EX/4
June 13, 1935	James Braddock	Long Island City, NY	LD
September 24, 1935	Joe Louis	New York City	LKO/4
June 15, 1936	Tony Souza	Salt Lake City	W/6
June 17, 1936	Bob Frazier	Boise, ID	TKO/2
June 19, 1936	Harold "Millionaire" Murphy	Pocatello, ID	W/6
June 23, 1936	George Brown	Tyler, TX	KO/3
June 24, 1936	Wilson Dunn	San Antonio	KO/3
July 2, 1936	Alfred "Butch" Rogers	Dallas	KO/3
July 13, 1936	Jim Merriott	Oklahoma City, OK	KO/2
July 16, 1936	Junior Munsell	Tulsa, OK	KO/5
July 18, 1936	Cecil Smith	Ada, OK	W/4
July 24, 1936	Bob Williams	Ogden, UT	KO/1
August 19, 1936	James J. Walsh	Vancouver, BC	KO/1
August 20, 1936	Nails Gorman	Marshfield, OR	TKO/2
August 25, 1936	Cecil Myart	Portland, OR	W/6
August 29, 1936	Al Frankco	Lewiston, ID	KO/2
August 31, 1936	Don Baxter	Coeur d'Alene, ID	KO/1
September 1936	Sep Cyclone	Bench Rock Springs, WY	KO
September 2, 1936	Al Gaynor	Twin Falls, ID	KO/1
September 3, 1936	Eddie Franks	Provo, UT	KO/3
September 8, 1936	Sammy Evans	Casper, WY	KO/4
September 14, 1936	Ed "Bearcat" Wright	Des Moines, IA	W/6
September 21, 1936	Andy "Kid" Miller	Sheldon, IA	W/6
September 30, 1936	Babe Davis	Keokuk, IA	W/6
October 6, 1936	Tim Charles	Evansville, IL	KO/4
October 8, 1936	Art Oliver	Platteville, WI	L/6
October 19, 1936	Dutch Weimer	Toronto, ON	KO/2
April 15, 1937	Tommy Farr	London, England	L/12
May 27, 1937	Ben Foord	London, England	TKO/9
July 30, 1937	Al Rovay	San Jose, CA	EX/4
October 6, 1937	Nash Garrison	Oakland, CA	EX/4

March 11, 1938	Tommy Farr	New York City	W/15
October 27, 1938	Ellsworth "Hank" Hankinson	Honolulu, HI	KO/1
April 6, 1939	Nash Garrison	Oklahoma City, OK	EX/4
June 1, 1939	Lou Nova	New York City	LTKO/11
September 4, 1939	Ed Murphy	Silver Peak, NV	KO/1
September 18, 1939	Babe Ritchie	Lubbock, TX	KO/2
July 2, 1940	"Two Ton" Tony Galento	Jersey City, NJ	TKO/8
September 26, 1940	Pat Comiskey	Jersey City, NJ	TKO/1
April 4, 1941	Lou Nova	New York City	LTKO/8

Statistics were compiled from http://www.maxbaerboxer.com/Max_Baer_Fight_Record.html.

NOTES

INTRODUCTION

1. Steven Watts, *The People's Tycoon: Henry Ford and the American Century* (New York: Alfred A. Knopf, 2005), 381.
2. Charles Lindbergh, "Who Are the War Agitators?" (speech), Des Moines, IA, September 11, 1941. Also Anne Morrow Lindbergh, *War Within and Without: Diaries and Letters of Anne Morrow Lindbergh, 1939–1944* (New York: Harcourt Brace Jovanovich, 1980), 221.
3. Lindbergh, *War Within and Without*, 222.
4. Lindbergh, *War Within and Without*, 221.
5. Lindbergh, *War Within and Without*, 224.
6. Lindbergh, *War Within and Without*, 239.
7. James P. Duffy, *Lindbergh vs. Roosevelt: The Rivalry That Divided America* (Washington, DC: Regnery, 2010), 181.
8. Joseph S. Page, *Primo Carnera: The Life and Career of the Heavyweight Boxing Champion* (Jefferson, NC: McFarland, 2011), 31.

I. THE PROTOTYPES

1. Monte D. Cox, "Benny Leonard, the Ghetto Wizard . . . 'The Brainiest of All Boxers,'" *Cox's Corner*, http://coxscorner.tripod.com/bleonard.html (accessed 14 March 2016).
2. Arthur Brisbane, "In This Corner: Benny Leonard," *ESPN Classic*, https://www/youtube.com/watch?v=NSxreC59N9c (accessed 14 March 2016).

3. Monte D. Cox, "Interviews with Legends of Boxing," *Cox's Corner*, http://coxscorner.tripod.com/interview2.html (accessed 14 March 2016).
4. Interview with the author.

2. THE GREAT DEPRESSION, BOXING, AND MIKE JACOBS

1. Kevin Mitchell, *Jacobs Beach: The Mob, the Fights, the Fifties* (New York: Pegasus Books, 2010), 224.
2. Budd Schulberg, *Ringside: A Treasury of Boxing Reportage* (Chicago: Ivan R. Dee, 2006), 266.
3. Schulberg, *Ringside*, 267.
4. Mitchell, *Jacobs Beach*, 144.

4. FISTS OF FURY

1. "Tony Canzoneri vs. Barney Ross," *Boxing Rec*, http://boxrec.com/bout/16821 (accessed 14 March 2016).
2. Mike Casey, "Unforgettable Greatness: Tony Canzoneri," *Boxing.com*, January 19, 2012, http://www.boxing.com/unforgettable_greatness_tony_canzoneri.html (accessed 14 March 2016).
3. Barney Ross and Martin Abramson, *No Man Stands Alone: The True Story of Barney Ross* (Philadelphia: J. B. Lippincott, 1957), 155.
4. Andrew Gallimore, *Baby Face Goes to Hollywood: Fighters, Mobsters, and Film Stars* (Dublin: O'Brien Press, 2009), 281.
5. Gallimore, *Baby Face Goes to Hollywood*, 281.
6. Ross and Abramson, *No Man Stands Alone*, 167.

5. HERO AND DRUG ADDICT

1. Barney Ross and Martin Abramson, *No Man Stands Alone: The True Story of Barney Ross* (Philadelphia: J. B. Lippincott, 1957), 172.
2. Ross and Abramson, *No Man Stands Alone*, 179.
3. Ross and Abramson, *No Man Stands Alone*, 178.
4. "*Monkey on My Back* (1957): Notes," *Turner Classic Movies*, http://www.tcm.com/tcmdb/title/5506/Monkey-on-My-Back/notes.html (accessed 10 May 2016).
5. "*Monkey on My Back* (1957)."

6. *"Monkey on My Back* (1957)."

7. Douglas Century, *Barney Ross* (New York: Schocken, 2006), 146.

6. FROM RANCH HAND TO POWERFUL RIGHT HAND

1. Nat Fleischer, *Max Baer: The Glamour Boy of the Ring* (New York: C. J. O'Brien, 1942), 2.

2. Jeremy Schaap, *Cinderella Man: James J. Braddock, Max Baer, and the Greatest Upset in Boxing History* (Boston: Houghton Mifflin, 2005), photo caption.

3. Fleischer, *Max Baer*, 6.

4. Fleischer, *Max Baer*, 9.

5. Interview with the author.

6. Fleischer, *Max Baer*, 12–13.

7. Schaap, *Cinderella Man*, 97–98.

8. Schaap, *Cinderella Man*, 102.

7. JEW VERSUS NAZI

1. Amos Oz, "Behind the Sound and the Fury, " *Tikkun,* March 1998, 1–5.

2. Jeremy Schaap, *Cinderella Man: James J. Braddock, Max Baer, and the Greatest Upset in Boxing History* (Boston: Houghton Mifflin, 2005), 145.

3. George B. von der Lippe, trans. and ed., *Max Schmeling: An Autobiography* (Chicago: Bonus Books, 1998), 44.

4. Cited in "Joe Jacobs (1898–1939)," *PBS,* www.PBS.org/wgbh/amex/fight/peopleevents/p_jacobs.html (accessed 20 June 2016).

5. Nat Fleischer, *Max Baer: The Glamour Boy of the Ring* (New York: C. J. O'Brien, 1942), 25.

6. Von der Lippe, *Max Schmeling*, 89.

7. Von der Lippe, *Max Schmeling*, 162.

8. Von der Lippe, *Max Schmeling*, 168.

9. Von der Lippe, *Max Schmeling*, 191.

8. THE MAN IN THE MOVIES

1. Emily W. Leider, *Myrna Loy: The Only Good Girl in Hollywood* (Berkeley: University of California Press, 2011), 106.
2. Nat Fleischer, *Max Baer: The Glamour Boy of the Ring* (New York: C. J. O'Brien, 1942), 27.
3. Mordaunt Hall, "Ace of Aces," *New York Times*, 11 November 1933, 10.
4. Jeremy Schaap, *Cinderella Man : James J. Braddock, Max Baer, and the Greatest Upset in Boxing History* (Boston: Houghton Mifflin, 2005), 157.
5. Schaap, *Cinderella Man*, 157.

9. AFTER THE LAST BELL

1. Paul Gallico, *Farewell to Sport* (Washington, DC: Library of America, 2011), 52, 57, 63.
2. Budd Schulberg, *Ringside: A Treasury of Boxing Reportage* (Chicago: Ivan R. Dee, 2006), 17.
3. Joseph S. Page, *Primo Carnera: The Life and Career of the Heavyweight Boxing Champion* (Jefferson, NC: McFarland, 2011), 2.
4. Interview with the author.
5. Paul Gallico, *Farewell to Sport*, 53.
6. Jeremy Schaap, *Cinderella Man: James J. Braddock, Max Baer, and the Greatest Upset in Boxing History* (Boston: Houghton Mifflin, 2005), 269.
7. Schaap, *Cinderella Man*, 264.
8. Schaap, *Cinderella Man*, 275.
9. "Famous Last Words: Max Baer (1909–1959)," *Famouslastwords.com*, http://www.powerfulwords.info/famous-last-words/7-famous%20last%20words.htm (accessed 19 May 2016).

CONCLUSION

1. Thomas Hauser, *Boxing Is . . . .: Reflections on the Sweet Science* (Fayetteville: University of Arkansas Press, 2010), 206.
2. Interview with the author.
3. Daniel E. Slotnick, "Howard Davis Jr., Who Beat Grief to Win Boxing Gold, Dies at 59," *New York Times*, http://www.nytimes.com/2016/01/01/sports/howard-davis-jr-who-beat-grief-to-win-boxing-gold-dies-at-59.html?_r=0 (accessed 19 May 2016).

4. Allen Bodner, *When Boxing Was a Jewish Sport* (Albany: State University of New York Press, 2011), 137.

5. Bodner, *When Boxing Was a Jewish Sport*, 161.

6. Jake LaMotta, with Joseph Carter and Peter Savage, *Raging Bull: My Story* (New York: Da Capo Press, 1997), 161.

7. Cited in "Frankie Carbo," *Wikipedia*, www.digplanet.com/wiki/Frankie_Carbo (accessed 20 June 2016).

8. Joseph Heller, *Good as Gold* (New York: Simon & Schuster, 1979), 11.

BIBLIOGRAPHY

BOOKS

Arnold, Peter. *History of Boxing*. London: Chartwell, 1985.

Berkow, Ira. *Counterpunch: Ali, Tyson, the Brown Bomber, and Other Stories of the Boxing Ring*. Chicago: Triumph, 2014.

Bodner, Allen. *When Boxing Was a Jewish Sport*. Westport, CT: Prager, 1997.

Brady, Jim. *Boxing Confidential: Power, Corruption, and the Richest Prize in Sport*. Preston, UK: Milo Books, 2002.

Century, Douglas. *Barney Ross*. New York: Schocken, 2006.

Corry, Des. *Fighters Should Be Gentlemen: The Story of Jimmy McLarnin, Canada's Greatest Boxer*. Victoria, British Columbia: Friesen Press, 2014.

Daniel, Daniel M. *The Mike Jacobs Story*. New York: Ring Book Shop, 1950.

Duffy, James P. *Lindbergh vs. Roosevelt: The Rivalry That Divided America*. Washington, DC: Regnery, 2010.

Fleischer, Nat. *Max Baer: The Glamour Boy of the Ring*. New York: C. J. O'Brien, 1942.

Fried, Ronald K. *Corner Men: The Greatest Boxing Trainers*. New York: Four Walls Eight Windows, 1991.

Gallico, Paul. *Farewell to Sport*. Lincoln: University of Nebraska Press, 2008.

Gallimore, Andrew. *Baby Face Goes to Hollywood: Fighters, Mobsters, and Film Stars*. Dublin: O'Brien Press, 2009.

Gems, Gerald R. *Boxing: A Concise History of the Sweet Science*. Lanham, MD: Rowman & Littlefield, 2014.

Hauser, Thomas. *Boxing Is . . . : Reflections on the Sweet Science*. Fayetteville: University of Arkansas Press, 2010.

Heinz, W. C., and Nathan Ward, eds. *The Total Sports Illustrated Book of Boxing*. New York: Total Sports, 1999.

Heller, Joseph. *Good as Gold*. New York: Simon & Schuster, 1979.

Hemingway, Ernest. *The Sun Also Rises*. New York: Charles Scribner's Sons, 1926.

Kahn, Roger. *A Flame of Pure Fire: Jack Dempsey and the Roaring Twenties*. New York: Harcourt Brace & Co., 1999.

Kimball, George, and John Schulian, eds. *At the Fights: American Writers on Boxing*. New York: Literary Classics of the United States, 2012.

Leider, Emily W. *Myrna Loy: The Only Good Girl in Hollywood*. Berkeley: University of California Press, 2011.

Liebling, A. J. *A Neutral Corner: Boxing Essays*. San Francisco: North Point Press, 1990.

———. *The Sweet Science*. New York: Viking, 1956.

Lindbergh, Anne Morrow. *War Within and Without: Diaries and Letters of Anne Morrow Lindbergh, 1939–1944*. New York: Harcourt Brace Jovanovich, 1980.

Mitchell, Kevin. *Jacobs Beach: The Mob, the Fights, the Fifties*. New York: Pegasus, 2010.

Oates, Joyce Carol. *On Boxing*. New York: Dolphin/Doubleday, 1987.

Page, Joseph S. *Primo Carnera: The Life and Career of the Heavyweight Boxing Champion*. Jefferson, NC: McFarland, 2011.

Ross, Barney, and Martin Abramson. *No Man Stands Alone: The True Story of Barney Ross*. Philadelphia: J. B. Lippincott, 1957.

Roth, Philip. *The Facts: A Novelist's Autobiography*. New York: Penguin, 1988.

———. *Patrimony: A True Story*. New York: Simon & Schuster, 1991.

Sammons, Jeffrey T. *Beyond the Ring: The Role of Boxing in American Society*. Urbana: University of Illinois Press, 1988.

Schaap, Jeremy. *Cinderella Man: James J. Braddock, Max Baer, and the Greatest Upset in Boxing History*. Boston: Houghton Mifflin, 2005.

Schulberg, Budd. *The Harder They Fall: A Novel*. New York: Random House, 1947.

———. *Ringside: A Treasury of Boxing Reportage*. Chicago: Ivan R. Dee, 2006.

Sheed, Wilfrid. *Baseball and Lesser Sports*. New York: HarperCollins, 1991.

Sifakis, Carl. *The Mafia Encyclopedia*, 2nd ed. New York: Facts on File, 1999.

Sugden, John. *Boxing and Society: An International Analysis*. Manchester, UK: Manchester University Press, 1996.

von der Lippe, George B., trans. and ed. *Max Schmeling: An Autobiography*. Chicago: Bonus Books, 1998.

Watts, Steven. *The People's Tycoon: Henry Ford and the American Century*. New York: Alfred A. Knopf, 2005.

MOVIES

Body and Soul (1947)
Carnera (2008)
Champion (1949)
Cinderella Man (2005)
The Harder They Fall (1956)
Monkey on My Back (1957)
The Prizefighter and the Lady (1933)
Raging Bull (1980)
Requiem for a Heavyweight (1962)
The Set-Up (1949)
Somebody Up There Likes Me (1956)
The Sun Also Rises (1957)

NEWSPAPERS

Chicago Daily News
Chicago Tribune
Daily Mirror
Las Vegas Sun
Los Angeles Times
New York Daily News
New York Post
New York Times
Newark Star-Ledger

Sacramento Bee
San Francisco Chronicle

MAGAZINES

Tikkun

INDEX

ABOUT THE AUTHOR

Jeffrey Sussman is author of 10 nonfiction books. He has written many articles and stories about boxing for Boxing.com and contributes articles and stories to a wide range of publications. He is president of Jeffrey Sussman, Inc., a marketing and public relations firm based in New York City. As a teenager, Sussman was signed up by his father to receive 10 boxing lessons from a middleweight fighter at the famous Stillman's Gym, often referred to as the "University of Eighth Avenue" by boxing writer A. J. Liebling.